T0048613

MICHAEL SORKIN

TWENTY MINUTES IN MANHATTAN

Michael Sorkin is an architect and urban planner and the author and editor of many books, including *All Over the Map*, *Against the Wall*, *Variations on a Theme Park*, and *Exquisite Corpse*. He lives in New York City.

Also by Michael Sorkin

All Over the Map: Writing on Buildings and Cities

Indefensible Space:
The Architecture of the National Insecurity State (editor)

Against the Wall: Israel's Barrier to Peace (editor)

Analyzing Ambasz (editor)

Starting from Zero: Reconstructing Downtown New York

The Next Jerusalem: Sharing the Divided City (editor)

After the World Trade Center: Rethinking New York City (coeditor)

Pamphlet Architecture 22: Other Plans:
University of Chicago Studies, 1998–2000

Some Assembly Required

Giving Ground: The Politics of Propinquity (coeditor)

Wiggle

Local Code: The Constitution of a City at 42° N Latitude

Variations on a Theme Park: The New American City
and the End of Public Space (editor)

Hardy Holzman Pfeiffer Associates:
Buildings and Projects, 1967–1992

Exquisite Corpse: Writing on Buildings

TWENTY MINUTES IN MANHATTAN

MICHAEL SORKIN

NORTH POINT PRESS
A DIVISION OF FARRAR, STRAUS AND GIROUX
NEW YORK

the uses and abuses of preservation, the ambiguous legacy of modernism—ultimately, all the strands of urban life."

—John King, *San Francisco Chronicle*

"Sorkin's tone is conversational and intimate, which makes for an easy read and personalizes the book's big-picture issues . . . Lively and thought-provoking." —Julia Galef, *Metropolis*

"[Sorkin] is fascinated by the myriad ways architectural details foster or inhibit community, neighborliness, safety, diversity and intimacy. Sorkin has a light hand with history (he is never overbearing) and a worldly way with facts and anecdotes."

—Susan Salter Reynolds, *Los Angeles Times*

"If you want an introduction to what has been said and thought about the city around the world, and also what has been built and unbuilt as a result of all this theorising, this is probably as good a guide as can be had. Follow Sorkin on his walk, and you will certainly be better informed and perhaps a bit wiser as well."

—Joseph Rykwert, *The Architects' Journal*

"Delightful and informative, this romp will please anyone with affection for the big city." —*Publishers Weekly*

TWENTY MINUTES IN MANHATTAN

For our neighbors

North Point Press
A division of Farrar, Straus and Giroux
18 West 18th Street, New York 10011

Printed in the United States of America
Originally published, in slightly different form, in 2009 by Reaktion Books Ltd,
Great Britain
Published in the United States by North Point Press
First American edition, 2013

Library of Congress Cataloging-in-Publication Data
Sorkin, Michael, 1948–
   Twenty minutes in Manhattan / Michael Sorkin. — First American edition.
      pages   cm
   Originally published: London : Reaktion, 2009.
   ISBN 978-0-86547-757-5 (pbk.)
   1. Architecture—New York (State)—New York.   2. Architecture and
society—New York (State)—New York.   3. Sorkin, Michael, 1948– —Homes
and haunts—New York (State)—New York.   4. Manhattan (New York,
N.Y.)—Buildings, structures, etc.   5. New York (N.Y.)—Buildings, structures,
etc.   6. Manhattan (New York, N.Y.)—Description and travel.   7. New York
(N.Y.)—Description and travel.   I. Title.

NA735.N5 S68 2013
720.97474'1—dc23

                                                                2012028939

Designed by Jonathan D. Lippincott

www.fsgbooks.com
www.twitter.com/fsgbooks • www.facebook.com/fsgbooks

CONTENTS

THE
STAIRS

The walk from my apartment in Greenwich Village to my studio in Tribeca takes about twenty minutes, depending on the route and on whether I stop for a coffee and the *Times*. Invariably, though, it begins with a trip down the stairs. The building I live in is a so-called Old Law tenement and was built in 1892, a date inscribed on the metal cornice that also carries the building's name: Annabel Lee. Like most such tenements, ours is five stories high (a few are six, even seven), and I live with my wife, Joan, on the top floor.

The walk down is untaxing, but the walk back up the four and a half flights (including the stoop)—a total of seventy-two steps—can be enervating, especially when returning from the laundry with thirty-five pounds of newly washed clothes. (The ordeal of the upward schlep creates resistance, which tends to delays and larger loads—a vicious cycle.) On some evenings, following especially exhausting days, it seems that an extra flight has been inserted between the fourth floor and the fifth. There is something hypnotic about stair climbing, however, and as often as I find myself thinking I ought to be at the fourth floor when I am only at the third, I think I've only gotten to three when I'm actually arriving at four.

Stair climbing is excellent exercise if you do enough of it. I probably average twenty or so flights—around three hundred steps—a day. At .1 calorie per step (going down about .05), I am able to burn off a single chocolate bar a week. Where possible, I try to climb stairs but am often prevented not only by the height of buildings but by the fact that, in most of those with elevators, the stairs are treated as residual, there simply for emergencies. These enclosed stairwells are unpleasant places, frequently alarmed to prevent nonemergency use. By comparison, consider the fabulous stairwells of classic nineteenth-century Paris or Vienna apartments, whose broad flights wind around spacious interior courts. Although they sometimes hold tiny elevators, these open contraptions do not seal riders away but continuously include them in the life of the stairway.

These stairs do not simply add grandeur to apartment houses but serve as important social spaces, broad enough to allow stopping and conversing in mid-flight. Shared of necessity, they form a useful and gracious element of the collective environment. The generous dimensions of the stairs and courtyards (not to mention the open grillwork of the little elevators) mean that when one is on the stairs, the entire population of vertical travelers is visible or audible, promoting a sense of community within the building and giving a feeling of safety. Mysterious footfalls and unexpected meetings are easily modulated by the early sight of the approaching party. To get a sense of the character of such places, think of Ripley's attempt—in Patricia Highsmith's *Talented Mr. Ripley*—to carry Freddie Miles's carpet-wrapped body down the grand stair of a Roman apartment building (Matt Damon lugs Philip Seymour Hoffman in the movie version of a few years ago).

There are very few New York City apartment houses with the kinds of inviting stairways one might find in the elegant buildings of the nineteenth-century European bourgeoisie. One reason for this is that although the poor and single men had long been housed collectively in tenements and rooming houses, respectable apartment buildings came relatively late to New York, where the proliferation of large blocks of "French flats" (inspired by a typical conjunction of economics and cachet) only took off after 1870. Whether because of the primacy of the elevator (not usefully invented until 1852), meanness of construction, spatial parsimony, or the reduction (and resulting enclosure) of staircases to emergency means of egress, our stairways do not register many entries in New York's dictionary of urban glories. ("For two and a half months I did not see a stairway in America," wrote Le Corbusier in 1937.

"They are something that has been buried . . . hidden behind a door that you are not supposed to open.") Most of the city's great stairs—from the Metropolitan Museum to the New York Public Library to Federal Hall—are exterior, expressions of civic rather than domestic grandeur. In some buildings, the social celebration of the stair is displaced onto the elevator lobby: think of the Woolworth and the Chrysler Buildings and their rich ornamentation, something also found in many prewar apartment houses.

The stairs in Annabel Lee are a series of straight runs. That is, they go from floor to floor without doubling back every half flight. This is not necessarily the most compact layout for a staircase, as it often requires not just landings at each end but a corridor to walk back along to the beginning of the next flight. Efficiency depends on the number of entrances that are served on each floor: in Annabel Lee the layout is economical. To my eyes (and legs) the straight run is more elegant and enjoyable to ascend, especially when it is part of a single system of stair and corridor that brings people directly to their front doors. There's also less twisting and turning—fewer discrete flights—and from the bottom of each flight there's a clear view of the next objective.

For me, New York's best stairs are those in five- and six-story industrial loft buildings from the latter half of the nineteenth century, where the runs are not simply straight but continuous. There's a high concentration of these in SoHo, where many buildings have straight runs that rise, pausing only for landings, as far as they can before the depth of the building forces them to switch back. Although they answer to an original use logic—a broad, continuous stair is clearly an easier environment for carrying unwieldy objects—these wide stairways, ascending uninterrupted for four, even five stories, are among the most beautiful and dramatic architectural spaces the city has: an ambulatory signature. Along with cast-iron facades, skylit first-story extensions into rear yards, and metal sidewalks embedded with circular glass lenses to illuminate basements below, these stairs are part of a tectonic "loft" vocabulary that is both singular and crucial to New York's architectural memory chest.

These elements can be retrieved for contemporary use. A particularly beautiful example of a long straight-run stair is at Baker House, a dormitory at MIT designed by the great Finnish architect Alvar Aalto in the late 1940s. Glazed on one side and narrowing slightly as it climbs, the stair provides a wonderful space of circulation and sociability. The narrowing is both functional and artistic, acknowledging that a stair is likely to be used by a smaller number of people as it rises and forcing the perspective narrowing of the long view upward. A variation of this continuous run is the ramp of the Guggenheim Museum, New York's highest achievement in the interior rise, although some argue that the pleasures of circulation trump the logic of displaying works of art.

The possibility of including such stairways in buildings depends on their size. A standard formula for calculating the dimensions of interior stairs is riser plus tread equals seventeen or seventeen and a half inches. Assuming a tread of ten inches and a riser of seven and a half inches, sixteen stairs (exactly the number in my building) are required to ascend ten feet (a reasonable floor-to-floor dimension for an apartment), and the length of a flight is a little over thirteen feet (treads often extend slightly over risers), not including the landings at the top and the bottom, which bring the grand total to about twenty feet. A straight run of five stories would therefore need about ninety feet of building depth, longer for higher floor heights, like those found in most loft buildings.

Architecture is produced at the intersection of art and property, and this is one of the many reasons it so legibly records the history of communal life. The famous gridiron plan of Manhattan—laid out with sanguine optimism by city commissioners in 1811 and extended in 1835—divided the island from the then-existing settlement boundary in Greenwich Village all the way to its northern tip into blocks of two hundred by six to eight hundred feet. These blocks were in turn divided into lots of twenty-five by a hundred feet, which at a stroke became the basic increment of both ownership and construction, forcefully conducing the character of the city. The typical row house of the day occupied half its lot, yielding a building of twenty-five by fifty feet (typically with a side hall and stair and rooms facing either front or back) and a rear yard of more or less the same dimensions. This resulted in blocks with rows of twenty-four to twenty-eight houses.

The conceptual origins of the gridiron plan remain somewhat mysterious, although grids have a long history in urbanism, dating back to the Babylonians and Egyptians. Perhaps the first to identify the grid as an explicitly rational, socially organizing order was a Greek, Hippodamus of Miletus, a fifth-century B.C. planner, mathematician, and philosopher discussed by Aristotle. Hippodamus pioneered not simply geometrical urban organization but also ideas about neighborhood dimensions, zoning by use (sacred, public, private), the importance of central places (the agora), and the idea of a city's ideal scale and population. Plans attributed to him include Miletus, Piraeus, and Rhodes.

According to Frederick Law Olmsted, the origins of the New York grid were somewhat less conceptually ambitious: "There seems to be good authority for the story that the system . . . was hit upon by the chance occurrence of a mason's sieve near a map of the ground to be laid out. It was taken up and placed upon the map, and the question being asked 'what do you want better than that?' no one was able to answer." Criticism of the grid and its difficulties was voiced from the start. Olmsted himself noted several problems that arose from the fixed dimensions of the city's blocks: the impossibility of producing sites for very large buildings and campuses; issues of daylighting; the difficulty of creating systems of formal and symbolic hierarchy within the field of uniformity. This last reflects an earlier criticism by Pierre L'Enfant of a proposal by Thomas Jefferson (for whom the right angle was Enlightenment itself) for laying out the new city of Washington as a pure grid.

The 1811 plan for Manhattan created a number of problems that persist intractably to this day. For example, the lack of alleyways—like those found in Chicago or Los Angeles—has meant that waste collection and deliveries must all take place from the street. And the east-west orientation of the blocks, while logical for creating lower densities away from the more trafficked north-south avenues, means that direct sunlight can only come through the narrow southern side of each row house, although, since the grid is rotated 29 degrees to the northeast to align with the island's own lie parallel to the Hudson River, early morning sun can enter on the north (east). Finally, the long and narrow dimensions of the twenty-five-foot lots—logical for row houses—are deeply problematic for apartment buildings, which, in order to accommodate several units to the floor, must be considerably longer than a single-family house.

In the hundred years following the 1811 plan, New York's population (excluding Brooklyn, which did not become part of the city until 1898, when it was itself a city of a million) burgeoned by three million. Houses were transformed into tenements—multiple dwellings—which eventually came to occupy the entire depth of each lot, sometimes even backing directly onto adjoining buildings. The worst of these tenements were the so-called railroad type, in which rooms—as many as eighteen per floor—were simply strung together along a central stair. Because they were party-wall construction (row houses share a wall with their neighbors on either side), and because backyards were virtually eliminated, this meant that only two of the rooms—those facing the street—had direct access to light and air. Certain so-called improved tenements did feature tiny air shafts in the middle of the building, but their impact was negligible.

The effects of bad housing had been observed for some time by both private and public bodies: the state legislature produced a report decrying conditions as early as 1857, although with no immediate results. In 1865, the Citizens' Association of New York published an enormous study that reported that close to 500,000 of the 700,000 residents of New York were jammed into fifteen thousand substandard tenement houses. A mid-century spate of fires, epidemics, and riots underlined the physical and social risks of poorly built, unsanitary, and overcrowded housing, and in 1866 the legislature passed a comprehensive construction code. This was followed, in 1867, by the Tenement House Act, which, for the first time, set standards for multiple dwellings. These included better protection against fire (including fire escapes) and minimal sanitation: one water closet for every twenty tenants.

The 1867 law was revised in 1879 to require that a tenement cover no more than 65 percent of its lot, that any "back buildings"— buildings constructed in rear yards, sometimes inches away from adjacent structures—receive light and air, and that more WCs be provided. Lax enforcement of the law (yet another chapter in the long history of collusion of public and private interests that has so shaped the city) resulted in the proliferation of a formal compromise, the "dumbbell" or "Old Law" tenement, of which our Annabel Lee is a fine example. The dumbbell moniker reflects the plan of the building, pinched in the middle to allow an air shaft on each side.

When dumbbells are lined up on a block, the pairing of neighboring shafts yields a larger, shared shaft that brings some light and air into the middle rooms of the building. Over sixty thousand such buildings were constructed between 1880 and 1900, a year in which approximately 65 percent of the city's 3.4 million people lived in tenements, the vast majority in "Old Law" types.

The "Old Law" was itself supplanted by the state Tenement House Act of 1901, which remains the legal framework for low-rise housing construction in New York. Although it increased allowable lot coverage to 70 percent, the tenement act demanded strict enforcement to curb illegal excesses. Most important morphologically, it substantially enlarged the required dimensions of air shafts, transforming them into something closer to courtyards. The law also harmonized the height of buildings with both the width of the streets they faced and the dimensions of the courtyards they produced. It required every room to have a window and every apartment to have running water and a toilet, and it mandated construction and egress requirements to protect tenants from fire.

These provisions fixed the vocabulary for virtually all subsequent codes and zoning in the city, not simply by their focus on safety, hygiene, and "quality of life," but by their clear insistence on the reciprocity of public and private realms. The "New Law" described the simultaneous duties of a building both to the production of the space of the public street and to the space of its own private interiors. The definition of these spatial obligations was mediated through the management of the city's light and air, the conservation and deployment of the very matter out of which building was produced and which building, in turn, annihilated. As we shall see, this institutionalization of the idea of a trade-off negotiated between private and public benefit remains foundational for the way we plan.

Because Annabel Lee is now configured with two apartments per floor, there is no need for a fire escape on the front facade: the law requires two means of egress for each apartment, which is satisfied at our place by the stair and a fire escape in the back. The fire escape—a familiar element of New York's historic architectural prosody—is a kind of appliance, grafted to buildings as an afterthought and bemoaned by aesthetes from the get-go. Fire escapes, though, have saved thousands of lives and provided millions with balconies on the cheap. Despite the ubiquity of air-conditioning, heat waves still drive many to seek cooler air by using them as living or sleeping space. These metal balconies are joined vertically by metal stairs, which—because the descent must be close to straight down due to the small size of each balcony—are actually closer to ladders, minimally constructed and steeply pitched. In contrast to fire escapes, outdoor stairs—because they are less protected and more subject to the elements—are less steep than those inside: even Annabel Lee's stoop is more gently proportioned than its staircase.

A comfortable ratio of tread to riser is crucial to the comfort of the walk upstairs as well as to the ease with which one can enjoy alternative styles of climbing—taking two steps at a time, for example. Classical architecture (not to mention the compact but vertical traditional houses of the Dutch where the pitch can be even greater) generally had a steeper ratio than ours—1:1, yielding an angle of 45 degrees, a considerably harder climb and a sometimes frightening descent. Some years ago, Joan and I visited Chichén Itzá in the Yucatán. We climbed one of the pyramids on an external stair-case that was close to 60 degrees (taking its angle from that of the pyramid). Going up was strenuous but not that difficult. When we reached the top, however, the view back down was so precipitous that Joan was paralyzed with fear. We returned to earth only with much backward climbing, anxiety, and holding tight to a chain laid on the stairs for security.

Although this particular stairway did not frighten me, I did feel tremendous anxiety when I climbed the stairs of one of the towers of Antoni Gaudí's church of the Sagrada Família in Barce-lona, an experience never to be repeated. This is a very narrow spiral staircase, in stone, protected only by a very low baluster, lower than a typical handrail. The higher one ascends, the more dramatic—and scary—the view. My memories of my own terror are vivid, pressed against the inside wall, fearful that one of the crowd de-scending would slip or bump against me, causing a fatal tumble to the stone floor below.

Notwithstanding such terrors, the circular stair has both the elegance of a spiral and the compact form of a cylinder, and one might logically expect to see more of them. But a spiral stair is made up of a series of wedge-shaped treads (the circle is sliced like a pie) that—because of their irregularity—pose increased hazards to the climber. As a result, the spiral staircase (although some-times used internally in individual apartments) cannot be counted against the legal (hence economic) requirement for escape stairs and is thus a relative rarity in New York.

The symbolic weight of stairs is embodied in both their form and their magnitude. The grand stair has long been a marker of consequence and ceremony. The stair at the Paris Opéra (feebly imitated at the high-kitsch Met) is both grand and doubled, and one ascends either by the right side or by the left to arrive at the upper foyer. The astonishing interweaving double helix of the stair at the Château de Blois in the Loire valley—thought to be modeled on a sketch by Leonardo da Vinci—is surely top ten. Of course, the grandeur often diminishes as the height rises. In vertical circulation systems based on leg power, privilege resides at lower levels. In Renaissance palazzi the *piano nobile* (our second floor) was traditionally the most consequential level of a building, holding its most imposing rooms. Elevated from the ground to provide appropriate detachment and a view of life in the street, this floor was loftier in proportion than those below. The parlor floor is the bourgeois version, and New York brownstones are typical, with their impressive external stairs leading to the receiving rooms a level above the street.

This dialogue of desire and demand is a central generator of architectural form, and every legal formulation produces both its poets and its bandits. In general, the default is the economic max-out with a minimum level of compliance. The history of safety regulations can be easily read in shifting architectural forms. In New York one sometimes sees what appear to be small balconies that join adjacent apartments. These are an updated form of fire escape dating from a code revision in the 1960s, designed to allow tenants to pass from one side of a fireproof barrier to the other, thereby satisfying the two-means-of-egress requirement. A similar piece of economic and architectural ingenuity is found in the "scissor" stair. This invention places two straight-run flights within a single shaft in the form of a series of Xs. The two staircases are entered from opposite sides of the fireproof enclosure and separated by a vertical fireproof wall. People descend in opposing directions, crossing paths in the middle of each flight a few inches from each other behind the dividing wall. Since 9/11, this arrangement has been called into question. It is now generally agreed that had the staircases in the World Trade Center been more widely separated, many more would have survived, and the building code has been revised to reflect this thinking. The scissor stair will become obsolete.

Beyond matters of safety, the health benefits of stairs—and of walking in general—are no joke. The federal Centers for Disease Control now reports that the epidemics of obesity and diabetes that plague the United States are, in part, the direct consequence of a system of architecture and planning in which our every movement is via some mechanical conveyance—a car, a plane, a train, or an elevator. In the culture of sprawl—as well as in our contemporary formulation of historic links between status and indolence—walking is reduced to a leisure activity. Mechanical, cellular, non-bodily, nonsocial means of circulation reciprocally contribute to contemporary forms of alienation, to the "bowling alone" syndrome, the conduct of lives in quiet parallel. To the engineers who design these systems, though, the body is simply a somewhat sensitive device (to temperature, moisture, noise, acceleration and deceleration, decor) to be packed and moved as efficiently as possible by mechanical distribution engines.

Twenty-four years in Annabel Lee have offered me an abundant opportunity for precise empirical research into the physiological effects of stair climbing, and I have concluded that five stories is a genuinely reasonable limit for a walk-up apartment, certainly for those of us in middle age. Historically, this general limit has shaped the vertical dimension of most cities. There are many exceptions. Sana'a in Yemen and Genoa, Italy, for example, have historic cores that are measurably higher. Some of the Yemeni buildings—walk-up skyscrapers built of mud—have as many as ten stories. Despite such variations, cities have thrived for millennia within approximately the same range of heights—from about ten to eighty feet. This is as true of the *insulae* of ancient Rome as of the pueblos of the Southwest, or even the *longtangs* of Shanghai, all dense multiple dwellings. It is a mistake to reflexively identify height with density. The "small town" of Somerville, Massachusetts, has long been among the densest American municipalities, and Los

Angeles—the quintessential city of sprawl—now has a higher average density than New York.

The logic of this low scale is the product of the limits of comfortable vertical movement under human power, the desire for a proximate relation to the ground, and available construction technology. Trabeated systems—the post-and-beam method that still characterizes most building construction—are limited by the strength, availability, and wieldy-ness of the materials they employ. Wood, stone, and brick are all highly constrained in one way or another. Imagine trying to build a post-and-beam building out of stone, something like Stonehenge or Karnak. To produce such structures, enormous labor energy is required for quarrying, carving, transporting, and erecting. We still don't know how the Egyptians built the pyramids—not post-and-beam buildings, but huge piles of stone—although we do know that each took many decades, required thousands of slave laborers, and yielded almost no usable interior space.

Annabel Lee has a structure of brick and wood. Its four exterior walls are brick, solid where it abuts the neighboring party wall and with openings at front and back and down the air shaft for windows and doors. Brick is a material that works well vertically (it is strong in compression) but is more problematic horizontally. Bricks can be used for horizontal spans in the form of arches (or domes), but these are inefficient dimensionally. Adding the height of arches running from side to side in Annabel Lee—assuming they were to spring from above head height—would result in the building being at least 50 percent taller to yield the same number of stories and would require considerable additional time, resources, and skill to produce. The interior of the building—its walls and floors—is constructed of wood, which, while having the advantage of being light, easy to cut and join, and cheap, is, of course, not fireproof. The use of wood for structural purposes is now almost nil in Manhattan.

The relative homogeneity of building—and city making—in different cultures is the result of their social organization (large buildings and enclosures are the product of the need for large gatherings), their economic possibilities (only a very rich and powerful Church could produce the cathedrals), their available material and technological resources (very little timber construction is to be seen in desert cultures), and their styles of living (portable tepees and tents are logical if you're involved in seasonal migration). The same is true today. New York builds within an essentially narrow range of configurations, materials, and structural systems, its limits set by culture, technology, and economics: small apartments in high-rise buildings result from extremely high costs for land and construction, a growing predominance of non-nuclear-family living arrangements, and a legal framework that continuously negotiates the bar of bulk upward.

In the nineteenth century, industrialization and the social relations it produced rapidly transformed the urban pattern not simply upward but outward, and the dramatic horizontal expansion of cities was the outcome of a reciprocating meeting of technology, economic innovation, and reconfigured social life. The horizontal city would not be possible without the railroad (and the car), much as the vertical city would not be without the elevator and Bessemer steel. The modern bureaucracies that occupy our tall buildings would themselves be impossible without a new division of labor, without new forms of organizing capital, without easy means of mass communication, and without urbanisms of concentration (for their centralized operations) and division (to provide living places for their owners and managers at a distance from their workplaces and workers). Factories required huge sites, easy access to transportation and materials, abundant energy, and a nearby source of disciplined labor.

The "dark satanic mills" of the British Industrial Revolution radically remade urban forms and paradigms. They created the modern city's literal circumstances: giant factories; tangles of rail lines; miles of cramped, homogeneous worker housing; the noise, heat, and filth produced by massive amounts of coal burning to

drive their steam engines. These direct effects reproduced themselves across the whole landscape, driving mines, other factories,
railways, and downstream pollution as well as the demise of rural
economies, the growth of new habits of consumption, and the further reification of class. They also remade the idea of the city in two
ways that continue to dominate urban planning and its ideology.

.Until the nineteenth century, virtually all cities were "all use"
environments. Craft-scale production was typically carried out in
a workshop below the home of the craftsperson, which often also
served as the site of exchange. To be sure, there have always been
districts in cities—concentrations of the poor and minorities, of
particular trades, of large markets, sacred precincts, spaces of power.
The primary division was between the city and its hinterland,
between urban and rural or agricultural space. But industrialization produced a new working class always at risk of growing res-
tive and gave rise to the need to separate that class from the more
hospitable climes inhabited by the rich beneficiaries of their labor
as well as to locate it efficiently in areas where its relationship
to factories and to spaces of their potential expansion could be
exploited.

The simultaneous—and interconnected—rise of industrial-
ism, with its giant sites and increasingly specialized division of
labor, and of reformist regulatory legislation, with its public bureaucracies of enforcement, fundamentally redescribed the city.
Although the first truly comprehensive zoning law in the United
States was the 1916 New York City act, which harmonized restrictions on both use and form, the idea of official regulation of obnoxious or dangerous uses had been around for centuries. By the late
seventeenth century, Boston had laws requiring fireproof construction and governing the locations of slaughterhouses, tallow makers,
and stills. New York City had even earlier restrictions on pigpens
and privies, and similar statutory forms of spatial organization by
use were, by the nineteenth century, part of the legal order of virtually every American town and city. A casual glance at the current
New York City zoning law—which residually restricts abattoirs,

dye works, rope makers, and other anachronisms—offers both a history of the regulation of obnoxious uses and an archaeology of deindustrialization.

Since the consolidation of the five-borough city in 1898, New York has produced only one comprehensive plan, and it was never adopted. Zoning by use and density continues to be the primary default for the organization of the city and the main medium of urban planning. Although classic zoning retains relevance for the isolation of uses that are genuinely incompatible, for the management of densities, and for certain broad strokes of urban character, today's postindustrial economy (at least in the "developed" world) offers the opportunity to dramatically rethink the segregating basis for zoning. As production becomes increasingly clean and knowledge-based, as our urban economies tip dramatically to service industries, as racism and ethnic animosities ebb, and as the model of mixed use becomes more and more persuasive and visible, cities are in a position to dramatically rethink zoning as a medium for leveraging and usefully complicating difference, rather than simply isolating it.

The enormous transformations brought by the industrial city produced another by-product: the dramatic growth of the culture of reform and the consolidation of the discipline and instruments of modern planning. Critics ranged from revolutionaries like Friedrich Engels, whose description of the conditions of the Manchester working class remains unsurpassed, to sentimental architectural observers like A. W. N. Pugin, who lamented the disappearance of the traditional townscape and its stable (if hardly egalitarian) social relations. In the United States, urban reform flourished in a muckraking critical tradition that included Jacob Riis, author of *How the Other Half Lives*, Lincoln Steffens of *The Shame of the Cities*, and many others, like those in the settlement house movement pioneered by Jane Addams. Movements for improved public health, sanitation, asylums, prisons, poorhouses, working conditions, and wages, not to mention the struggles for the abolition of slavery, for universal suffrage, for immigrant rights, and for a more equitable distribution of wealth, arose. Much of what they campaigned for is now part of the mental furniture of New Yorkers.

All of this activity was motivated not simply by the desperate conditions of the city's tenements but by a deeper therapeutic impulse that is one of the hallmarks of the politics of modernity. In the wake of Enlightenment rationalism and its ideas of the perfectibility of human life—so important to the intellectual formation of America's founders—the country underwent a debate not simply about curing disease but about "curing" criminality, insanity, and a multitude of nonconforming behaviors through the creation of exemplary environments. The whole American experiment can be seen as a medium for erasing, or at least managing, deviancy, for subsuming difference under a new and tolerant—or homogenizing—norm.

One such deviation with special meaning in New York was—and is—the differing linguistic and social habits of the immigrants who came to dominate the city's population by the mid–nineteenth century. Among New York's elites, these immigrants were increasingly seen as the sources of crime, disease, disorder (especially after the great draft riot of 1863), and—as the century progressed—a radical politics that threatened the stability of traditional institutions and power. Housing reform, then, was the product of a genuine altruism combined with a scientific effort to control the spread of disease both among citizens and to the established body politic. Olmsted was a leader in this spatialized *mission civilisatrice* and argued for the potential of cities and their spaces of collective recreation to produce health, longevity, and *neighborliness*.

Jacob Riis, a Danish immigrant who rose to become a leading newspaper reporter and pioneer photographer and for whom his friend Theodore Roosevelt coined the term "muckraker," typified the ambiguous situation of reformism, its simultaneous compassion and contempt for those it sought to "elevate." *How the Other Half Lives* is both a withering indictment of the slums and a Cook's tour of racist attitudes directed against those living there. Here is the "Chinaman": "Ages of senseless idolatry, a mere grub-worship, have left

him without the essential qualities for appreciating the gentle
teachings of a faith whose motive and unselfish spirit are alike beyond his grasp . . . Stealth and secretiveness are as much part of
the Chinaman in New York as the catlike tread of his felt shoes . . .
He is by nature as clean as the cat, which he resembles in his traits
of cruel cunning, and savage fury when aroused. His business, as
his domestic life, shuns the light . . . The average Chinaman, the
police will tell you, would rather gamble than eat any day."

As to the Jews: "Money is their God. Life itself is of little value
compared with even the leanest bank account . . . It is surprising
to see how strong the instinct of dollars and cents is in [Jewish
children] . . . But abuse and ridicule are not weapons to fight the
Israelite with. He pockets them quietly with the rent and bides
his time. He knows from experience, both sweet and bitter, that all
things come to those who wait, including the houses and lands of
their persecutors." Riis applies this same fine sociology to Italians,
Irish, blacks, Bohemians, Germans, and the other objects of his
Christian charity. I wonder how much of my animus to my own
landlord (of whom, more later) is the self-hating residue of my own
encounter with such attitudes.

The huge critical reaction to urban slums was reflected not just in
muckraking but in the energetic creation of model alternative living
arrangements of the most visionary sort. In America, the nineteenth century was the great era of the "intentional community," a
profusion of such utopian settlements as Brook Farm, Oneida, and
Nauvoo. While many of these were religious in character, many
more were inspired by the secular radicalism espoused by Robert
Owen, Charles Fourier, and others—traditions that also became
the political substrate for much of architectural modernism, itself
attracted to the blend of egalitarian distributive ideas, quasi-religious
notions of righteous simplicity, and a preoccupation with health
and hygiene it shared with the more orthodox stream of urban reformism. Underlying these theories and initiatives was a faith and

a fallacy: the power of formal arrangements to transform social life. A darker version of this instrumental belief was found in societies of coercion. During the early nineteenth century, a vigorous debate raged between the prison societies of Boston and Philadelphia about the arrangement of cells and daily association most likely to remake the troubled souls of their involuntary inmates. Numerous prisons were divided along the lines of their alternative morphologies.

New York has a long relationship with such models, and the planning and growth of the city records an ongoing dialogue with shifting exemplars of the good at every scale, from buildings to parks and public spaces, to infrastructure, to totalizing visions for the city as a whole. The move from Old Law tenements to New, for example, was facilitated by a number of architectural competitions and studies sponsored by charitable organizations such as the Improved Housing Council of the Association for Improving the Condition of the Poor, the Society for Ethical Culture, and the Charity Organization Society. Their efforts—paralleled by similar work in other cities in the United States and Europe—attracted widespread participation by architects and greatly expanded the typological possibilities for housing, by making alternatives legible to a broad public. They were also able to re-situate the discourse of reform at appropriate scales, to recognize that housing improvement could be achieved only by looking at larger lots and at the configuration of entire city blocks. This readjustment of the relationship of morphology and density is a constant in the elaboration of the form of the city.

To accommodate exponential increases in density (the most crowded tenement blocks sometimes exceeded fifteen hundred people per acre, an appalling figure), the modern city grew in every direction. This all-axis growth of the metropolis (including the subterranean expansion of sewers, subways, and other literal infrastructure) has had, as it were, both an upside and a downside. It seems clear that for reasons of both sustainability and sociability, human power as a means of locomotion in the city should be optimized. Cities designed to facilitate walking will—because of their accessible dimensions—likely be more neighborhood-focused and compact as well as more mixed in use. To be reached by walking, a destination—whether a school, office, or shop—must be close at hand. A reasonable walking time (in this culture) for basic necessities is generally considered to be about ten minutes, which translates (at an average walking speed of three to four miles per hour) into six to eight short blocks (or three to four long ones). Using this dimension as a radius, we might begin to think of a comfortable scale for a neighborhood as ten to fifteen New York City blocks.

But not every block is created equal, and although the time constraint can be treated as a constant, fluctuations in density are enormous. The city has blocks that are filled by high-rise apartments and others that are essentially suburban, thousands of dwelling units versus tens. If an individual dwelling is understood as the center of a walking radius, each neighborhood resident will find a greater or lesser degree of her quotidian circle in adjacent neighborhoods, suggesting that the idea of neighborhood itself must be treated elastically. While convenience is a function of distance, numbers generate business and support the variety of shops and institutions that constitute some version of a complete set of services. Thus, the pattern of distribution of shops and businesses tends to reflect the residential densities in which they are embedded. The suburban shopping mall is a "natural" by-product of the low densities of the suburbs, themselves only made possible by the transportation monoculture of the car. An intermediate condition is the main or high street of a small town or village. In the densest part of the city, shops become a nearly ubiquitous presence at street level, and it is not unusual to find a dry cleaner, a greengrocer, a pharmacy, a liquor store, and a restaurant or two on virtually every block. The sense of neighborhood comfort and tractability—of familiarity—is, as Jane Jacobs has argued, also a by-product of the size of the blocks themselves, causing Jacobs to make an eloquent case for the superiority of smaller blocks in facilitating choice and variety.

Jane Jacobs, who died in 2006 at the age of eighty-nine, is the patron saint of Greenwich Village and a thinker and activist who did more than any other to advocate the ideas of good city form and behavior that broke the stranglehold of modernism on planning. With the publication of *The Death and Life of Great American Cities* in 1961, Jacobs did not simply expose the sinister, reactionary outcomes of urban renewal and its regimented, antisocial architectures but offered an alternative based on a close reading of the successful aspects of traditional cities. In particular, Jacobs's arguments were buttressed—like those in this book, inescapably in dialogue with hers—by the observation of the life in her own neighborhood, especially the area around her apartment on Hudson Street, about six blocks from Annabel Lee. Jacobs is particularly revered in these parts because she was not simply a profoundly acute observer and theorist but also an activist, a canny and indefatigable leader in the fight to defend the Village from the urban-renewal and highway schemes of her legendary nemesis, Robert Moses.

While no summary can do justice to the depth and richness of Jacobs's critiques or prescriptions, her basic argument concerned the need of urban neighborhoods for "a most intricate and close-grained diversity of uses that give each other constant mutual support, both economically and socially." To work on the city was to deal with an organization of great complexity, with the cultivation and conservation of an ecological richness that necessarily had a life of its own, one that thrived on both eccentricity and consent. For Jacobs, the forms of the good city were the outcome of their symbiosis with the practices of the good life, a life she identified with mutuality, self-government, neighborliness, diversity, intimacy, convenience, contentment, and safety.

The primal scene of the kind of public life that marked Jacobs's thinking was the street, a site and a medium that had become weirdly anathema to modernist planning. Le Corbusier famously remarked, "We must kill the street," and he and others sought to banish it in favor of a uniform matrix of greenery, on which buildings stood in detached "communities," each rigorously separated by use and statistics and diagrammatically joined by highways to the rest, a vast organizational diagram made concrete. Horrified by this paternalist nightmare, Jacobs saw in the liveliness, commerce, tight association, and choices offered by streets the agora of the everyday, the site of democratic exchange. Her prescriptions were all aimed at—and verified by—their success in producing the very particular social, economic, and architectural ecology that she found in places like the Village, the North End of Boston, and the Back of the Yards neighborhood in Chicago.

As a writer and thinker, Jacobs was careful and unabashed about her advocacy. Seeking change, she did not hesitate to engineer both physically and socially, and she suggested four particular conditions necessary (if not necessarily sufficient) to implement her vision: urban districts that had two or more primary functions that would, ideally, generate activity at different rhythms throughout the day and night; short blocks; buildings mingled in a loose grain that included numbers of old structures; and adequate residential density (at least a hundred units per acre, covering most buildable ground) to make the thing cook.

Like the architects and planners she so devastatingly criticized, Jacobs was not denying the instrumental power of building nor the need to be precise about its particulars. Despite frequent claims to the contrary (belied by a cursory reading of her work), she was not hostile to the artistic qualities of good modernist projects. The parting of the ways was in wildly divergent readings of the urban present, one of which—looking at the dense tenements of the south Village—saw shabby, aging buildings and, with a shudder of distaste, moved to wipe them out, while the other saw those same buildings as background, the containers for a rich and vigorous community, teeming with satisfaction and life. Moses and the geometers, seeing architecture they found unsightly and unrefreshed, reflexively devalued the lives led within it. Jacobs, connecting with the intricate, satisfying bonds of a flourishing community, assumed that there were qualities in the organization of its supporting spaces that were working very well and set out to discover what they were.

Most of Jacobs's subsequent writing was on economics, and she regarded her primary contribution as lying within that field. *Death and Life* is itself marked by a dogged, clear-eyed economism that underlies its originality. Because Jacobs was not an architect and lacked architecture's prejudice for authentication by form, she approached the city as a medium of exchange rather than a static artifact. She believed in what she called her "golden rule"—that the city works by intensifying reciprocity—and her theories grew from this identification of the health of the metropolis with commerce, in every sense of that word. Her contribution was in understanding the spaces and habits of the system as a permanent and evolving transaction and in seeing urban form as something to be judged for its effects on life.

Jacobs's message is widely misappropriated by many who peel off the physical skin of her argument to buttress their own visual concerns. This is to misread her fundamentally. Jacobs's case for the necessity of old buildings among the new, for example, was not motivated by a simple affinity with the picturesque. She saw those buildings as the conservators of uneven, variegated development and appreciated their funkiness not for its decomposing charm but as a source of lower rents, continuity of economically marginal uses, and the natural habitat of urban difference. Short blocks were the guarantors of choice and mixing. Density was the pressure cooker of commerce. Numbers were important not to abstract but to measure.

The idea of a mixed-use and self-sufficient neighborhood—a place in which all the necessities of daily life are close by—has fallen victim to both zoning's blunt instrument and the "rational" clarities of high modernism. As political and social units, neighborhoods are defined by both scale and population. Modernist planning took this basic understanding of urban order and reduced it close to degree zero. There were to be "neighborhood units" (a coinage from the late 1920s), an increment in the reductive hierarchy of superblocks, towers, highways, and open spaces that formed the modernist urban repertoire. The process was obsessed with absolute numbers, including the minimum dimensions of rooms, open space per capita, and the one-size-fits-all head counts of neighborhood units. This was often pegged at five to seven thousand and was used as a formula for determining the distribution of schools, shops, sports fields, and other facilities. The failure of such planning is not in its effort to be comprehensive or to equalize access to necessary facilities. It is, rather, the attempt to rationalize choice on the basis of a homogeneous set of subjects, a fixed grammar of opportunities, a remorseless segregation of uses, and a scientistic faith in technical analysis and organization that simply excludes diversity, eccentricity, nonconforming beauty, and choice. The utopian nightmare.

But the pursuit of masses of housing for masses of people who lacked it was inspirational. And the idea of a tractable social increment, whether an idealized polis or a neighborhood school population, is at the core of any idea of neighborhood. Jane Jacobs examined this relationship of population, dimension, sociability, and power. For her, the problem with modernism was always with the uniformity and bareness of the vision and—most fundamentally—with an autocratic worldview that thwarted rather than liberated participation. The inflexibly normative neighborhood unit comes apart with any shift in its hermetic terms, which is to say always. The real situation of many American neighborhoods was exposed by the 1954 desegregation ruling by the U.S. Supreme Court, the "separate is not equal" verdict. Segregated neighborhood schools are produced by segregated neighborhoods.

Back to the stairs. The five-story limit is reasonable only for the reasonably fit. Stairs can put a strain on the elderly, the handicapped, the encumbered, and the young. I have had several major experiences of this problematic aspect of stair climbing, all following surgeries. After the first of these, I was virtually immobilized and unable to leave the apartment for nearly a month. Had I lived alone, this might have been a serious problem, although my neighborhood abounds in establishments that deliver—one of the miracles of New York life being the phone call to a local Chinese (or virtually any other) restaurant (the collective kitchen for the city, a nicely displaced twist on communitarian desires to be free from the noisome chore) that propels a deliveryman upstairs in incredibly short order. Here, the problem is simply getting up and walking down the hallway to ring the buzzer. No need, even, for cash: credit cards are accepted and deliverymen know how to secure the imprint by vigorously rubbing the dull end of a pen over a hand-held, sandwiched card and receipt. Unfortunately, the regular failures of our decrepit bell/buzz-back system frequently queer this arrangement.

The second surgery was for the repair of a complex fracture and forced me to wear a giant fiberglass boot and to negotiate the world on crutches. Getting up and down the stairs became something to be avoided whenever possible, but since, after a week or so, I was ablaze with cabin fever and ready to go back to work, it was necessary to go down and up at least once a day. This was extremely slow going, and there were a number of near catastrophes when I missed the tread with a crutch and came close to tumbling down the rest of the flight. I became very sensitive to loose treads and railings, to pockets of bad lighting, to missing tiles and other cracks in the floor, to the force and speed of automatic door closers, and to a million other aspects of the city the healthy easily ignore.

The city is an obstacle course of almost pathological thoughtlessness for the handicapped. Even the office of my crack orthopedic surgeon was approached down a short flight of stairs. Its door required serious pulling to open, and the front desk and waiting room were difficult to maneuver around under the best of circumstances and so hard for those in wheelchairs that the receptionist actually had to shift furniture. Public transit held its special horrors, and such simple actions as mounting the curb became challenging. On the bright side, people were generally kind and helpful, although many cabs fled at the sight of my lumbering, wobbly approach.

Prompted by years of advocacy from handicapped rights groups, the situation slowly improves under the banner of a "barrier-free" environment, and the legal framework for construction has grown markedly more enlightened since the passage of the Americans with Disabilities Act in 1990. Curb cuts, entry ramps, subway elevators, and braille floor markers are all part of both an ongoing retrofit and the fundamental vocabulary for all future building. There is, however, an obvious conflict between the idea of a barrier-free city and one that is based in human locomotion. The latter—especially to the degree that it involves lots of stairs—makes the former impossible to fully realize. While work is rapidly advancing on prosthetic exoskeletons and other devices that would allow the halt to walk and offer superhuman capabilities for the rest of us, their promise is limited in the near term. They do, however, beg the increasingly relevant question of where the seam between ourselves and our environment will fall.

A city in which every point is equally accessible to every citizen is neither likely to result from such technologies nor necessarily desirable. Although the unfeeling, utilitarian rigors of cost-benefit analysis do not really address the ethical imperatives of "universal" access, the idea that difference demands difference rather than homogeneity must be recognized, even as we push the envelope of empowerment. While any building in New York City might be made fully accessible, this would often require extreme measures. If there's no room on the sidewalk for a ramp, it must be carved from the space of the building itself, perhaps substantially reducing the size of the apartment into which it is inserted and eliminating its view to the street. If there's no room within the stairwell to add an elevator, a hundred square feet must be removed from every space through which the shaft passes. Should a newly built row house for a fully mobile family be obliged to include an elevator for a hypothetical handicapped user?

While there is no excuse for an elevator building to be other than barrier-free, the issue presents problems for the walking city. One way of sorting out the issue is to admit that no city offers—for whatever reason, from the perquisites of private property to the restrictions imposed on dangerous places like subway tunnels or manholes—"universal" access. The question needs to be reframed. The accessibility of public space—beginning with the space of the sidewalk and street and continuing to all places that are intended for public use—is fundamental and must be defended and enlarged. Although the city should not be designed to exclude, equality does not imply sameness. This means that some people will have some difficulty in some places.

Theories of justice frequently focus on the distribution and logic of rights, expending much energy debating the difference between the individual and the collective varieties. A collective right to the city was seminally articulated by the French philosopher Henri Lefebvre (and continues to be elaborated by important successors like David Harvey), a right understood not simply as individual access to the goods, services, and spaces of the city but as the right to change the city in accordance with our deepest desires, to steer the very process of urbanization and the way in which the city nurtures the kinds of people we wish to become. But even (and perhaps especially) when couched in general terms, the realization of the good city must still offer morphological satisfaction to an ever-expanding group of individuals.

Movement toward universal access needs to progress in both the physical and the social realms and on both demand and supply sides, though I do not mean to suggest by this that a market model will produce the desired result. Medical advances will increasingly enable people to enjoy free mobility based on bodily autonomy. Technology will provide innovative and adaptable means of all-axis circulation. Justice will extend the "right of the city" to more and more people. Wise planning legislation will ensure the widespread and logical provision of housing units—and medical assistance—for people with demanding limitations. It is possible to extend the physical diversity, complexity, and difficulty of the evolving city without leveling the kinesthetic character of access into a uniformity of ramps, flatness, and wide openings. Access, moreover, is a matter of overcoming many barriers that are not physical, barriers of price and prejudice that are thick in the city.

Our neighbors on the fourth floor are three women (in two apartments), all closing in on seventy. One of them, Margot, was actually born in the building, to which she returned after very interesting seasoning in Paris and Cairo in the 1950s. She works for a progressive nonprofit, is active in local politics—is, indeed, someone living a life of citizenship, one of my best fantasies of what it means to be a "Villager." Because of her cheap rent-controlled apartment, Margot was able, years ago, to buy a place in the country to which she and her partner repair on weekends in their beat-up station wagon. Margot is our resident good citizen, the best and most active of us tenants on the front lines of daily life. She embodies the elective aspect of representative democracy, as well as the idea that contributions to the commonweal must be of many different sorts. She rises to defend and enlarge our right to the city.

The New York City rent laws are highly contested by landlords and vigorously defended by tenants, and Margot sometimes makes me fantasize about a meritocratic or public system for awarding these subsidies, not simply a tenure-based one. Margot would "earn" her low rent because she is, in return, doing civic duty for us all. This is not an argument likely to be embraced by our landlord nor to be recognized by the municipal and national subsidy apparatus, which tends to focus its benefits on owners rather than tenants (per the generous tax relief offered corporations that agree to remain in the city) and on buildings rather than people (per restrictions on the alteration or demolition of historic structures). As incomes grow tighter and tighter in relation to the costs of living here, civic activism becomes increasingly problematic for those whose leisure time is constrained, either by the need to make a living or by constant incitements to turn leisure time into a space of consumption. This tends to produce two "classes" of activists, those with the "free" time to work on matters of elective concern and those who are forced into combat by some imminent threat to their welfare. It takes a lot of time and money to be Brooke Astor.

Without people like Margot—long of tenure and committed to a broad idea of social equity—our neighborhood would not be what it is. We are lucky to be home to a wide range of local activists who people the barricades in defense of beleaguered shade trees, quiet streets, historic sites, public education, social diversity, reasonable rents, and a thousand other aspects of what makes ours a good neighborhood. It's a struggle that proceeds both by intervention and by example, and I never fail to be moved by the sight of a neighbor planting flowers in a tree pit or by a handmade sign enjoining dog walkers to prevent their pups from peeing on the petunias.

Neighborhoods, of course, change over time. But neighborhoods are not like generations, fixed cohorts that march through experience together: they house multiple synchronicities. Neighborhood continuity devolves on matters of individual tenure, on the character of the physical fabric, on the mix of people and activities, and on the various media by which these values are communicated. There is an elaborate reciprocity among these elements, and just as people produce neighborhoods, so neighborhoods produce people. The Village has been both a magnet for bohemians and a school for bohemianism, a process that is recapitulated in the strong gay inflection of the neighborhood today. The Village is a safe place for contested lifestyles, and as once did the historic presence of artists, our thriving gay community marks it as a space of tolerance and adventure.

Neighborhoods differ from ghettos by offering the right to remain but not obliging it. In the just city, it should be easy to move up and around and very difficult to be forced out. The distinction is crucial. Ghettos can embody strong cultural traditions, deep bonds of feeling and affinity, long threads of continuity, and great vibrancy. But they are prisons. While the vitality of cities depends on transitional places—on points of entry—this vitality relies on clearly marked exits. The Lower East Side of Manhattan has been a classic portal to New York and has, over its long history, offered a starting place for Irish, Jews, Italians, Chinese, and African-Americans. Because of the timing of waves of immigration, it has been a serial ghetto. But as each of these groups has been assimilated to a larger set of possibilities, it moved on, whether into the "secular" culture, ethnic neighborhoods that are elective rather than constrained, or other ghettos.

In these new neighborhoods, the problem is sometimes reversed. Like certain white suburbs (where fear of incursions by the other is raised to extremes), such places have often thrived on exclusion. In a replay of a fatal incident of some years ago, a group of kids in heavily Italian-American Howard Beach in Queens recently set upon a pair of black teens who were perceived to be "out of place." More sophisticated forms of discouraging the "wrong" people from moving in, ranging from redlining and other styles of selective access to mortgage credit, to the panoply of subtle and not so subtle signals (fancy shops with buzzer entries, doormen, baleful stares, the absence of familiar-looking people), are all intended to mark unwanted otherness and ensure its exclusion. This is a problem that will continue as we struggle to find the means to recognize the positive character of difference while preserving neighborhood continuity and preventing the city from becoming a landscape of homogeneity, cloaked in phony consumer "choices," a Disneyland of identity politics.

Continuity in place enables an oral tradition, the most efficient and democratic way of channeling neighborhood memory. Although there are dozens of books about the Village and its history, most tend to focus on its more illustrious citizens: one is more likely to read about Mabel Dodge or Dylan Thomas than about Gus, whose old restaurant in the next block we frequented almost every week until rising rents forced him out, or the commune that flourished for years across the street in the heavy stone building nicknamed the Kremlin. It is a platitude to describe a neighborhood as a bundling of stories, but the transmission of stories, their depth of interest, and each individual's repertoire give meaning and character to neighborhoods. The modernist city has been roundly criticized for its inability to produce a sufficient variety of stories, to provide enough chambers for memory, relying instead on a single master narrative of progress. Identical buildings, minimized and sterile spaces of public encounter, and alienated relations with fellow citizens are the enemies of successful neighborhoods, whatever their careful statistical organization into neighborhood units and subunits. In places like these, narratives are forced inward (or taken over by TV), and public life becomes a marginal player.

Although Margot is the senior tenant in the building, she has inherited the mantle of bard and griot from our late neighbor Jane, who, although she died several years ago, remains vitally important to us. Her memory, and her memories, are kept alive as part of Annabel Lee's culture, by the fact that more than half the tenants have been around for twenty years or more, a span that allowed them to absorb much of Jane's local knowledge and wisdom. Joan and I regularly see sights around the neighborhood that would have remained invisible without her. We pay her ritual tribute by stopping to examine every butterfly brooch (Jane's signature accessory) we see and by a tacit agreement to preserve her summer sitting spot on the front stoop. Jane set up her folding chair on stoop stage left, we stage right. We minister to Wilson's tree, a flowering pear that Jane planted out front in memory of her late husband.

Jane and Margot are reminders that neighborhoods need their storytellers, and storytellers, their listeners. Storytelling is the primary exchange of the face-to-face and crucial to the fabrication of collective identity. Such direct transactions are foundational for our politics. Translations of the face-to-face into the door-to-door or into the leaflet passed hand to hand in the street are crucial steps in a chain of associations that form a binder for civic life and limn the scale of our community, fixing the dimensions of our collective self-interest, the boundaries of "home." These activities are particularly important as a medium of resistance to a politics that prefers to approach from the other direction, via a space of total, manipulated mediation. Local activism can thrive only in a legible space of the local.

It's urgent that there be space in the city for activists and bards, for binding agents and the continuous presence of people like Margot and Jane. Rent control seems the least we can do in exchange for their Delphic importance. Good cities—good societies—are marked by the interaction of their dynamism, tolerance, equity, and mix, not by a series of physical assaults on the city fabric by highways and blank-slate urban-renewal projects or by the attacks on the social fabric that come with gentrification. These excisions of "blight"—with their pernicious medical metaphors—were resisted by Jane Jacobs and others both because they destroyed communities and because the buildings with which they replaced what was blown away were inimical not only to the recuperation of the lives displaced but also to the creation of neighborhoods with the vibrancy and complexity of those they wiped out.

But my narrative is running ahead of itself. Let's return to the beginning. In our apartment, the mandated air shaft provides daylighting and ventilation for the bedroom, the bathroom, and two little rooms that we use as studies. Since we're on the top floor, these windows provide a glimpse of sky, not to mention an occasional peek into the living room of our neighbors in the building on the other side of the shaft. Lower down in Annabel Lee, though, the windows open only onto a grim brickscape admitting at best murky light. Because of the sheltered quality of the air shaft, it is beloved by pigeons, who gather on the windowsills, streak the walls white, and coo annoyingly into the night, reaching cacophony during mating season. One of the last constructive gestures made toward us by our landlord was to place wire mesh over the top of the shaft to deter the noisome birds. This appliance is long gone, but it seems to have altered the habits of our pigeons, which have not returned.

I like living on our top floor. The view from the front and back windows is as good as it gets in Annabel Lee, which, to the south, means a prospect skimming over adjoining rooftops to embrace a large piece of the sky and—before September 11—the World Trade Center. To the north, the view from the bedroom is almost axially aligned with the Empire State Building. Seeing this shaft rising between my legs, I am reminded of the phallocracy of sky-scraping, the masculinity of these structures. Louis Sullivan was canonically succinct: "Here is a man for you to look at . . . a real man, a manly man; a virile force . . . an entire male . . . a monument to trade, to the organized commercial spirit, to the power and prog-ress of the age . . . a male . . . it sings the song of procreant power!" Indeed.

After Harry Helmsley acquired a stake in the Empire State, his wife, the much-reviled, recently deceased Leona, inaugurated a program of illumination for the top of the building, a practice continued by the current owners. On the Fourth of July it's red, white, and blue. On St. Patrick's Day it's green. On Valentine's Day it's pink. And on Gay Pride Day (Leona can't be faulted in her sense of solidarity with all the citizens of the city) it's lavender. For us, this cultural signifier carries other messages as well. Promptly at 2:00 a.m., the lighting is switched off, and we are reminded ei-ther that we're up too late or that we've actually managed to stay up late. The illuminated top also provides us with a pretty thrilling means of calibrating the thickness of clouds and fog and of pre-dicting the weather. We're twenty-seven blocks south of the Em-pire State, and there are impressive occasions when we can't see the building at all, others in which it's visible only dimly, others still in which the clouds scud across its face. Most dramatic are lightning strikes on the mast of the tower.

Living on the top floor also means that there's no risk of being disturbed by tenants on the floor above. In a wood-framed building like ours, this is a significant advantage. Of course, sound is trans-mitted upward as well (we were plagued for a time by the noise of an amplified band rehearsing on the second floor blasting up the air shaft), but the direct concussion of footfalls above us is avoided. We are less protected from smells emanating from below, but these tend to be benign cooking aromas (a salivary rebuke to our own laziness in the kitchen). Walking on the stairway itself is more of a problem as there can be powerful pet smells on the second floor that cannot be circumnavigated. But odors have Proustian powers. There are certain commingled scents in New York buildings that still carry me back to visits to my grandmother's apartment in Brooklyn fifty years ago—Clorox, capon, camphor.

The sound of our neighbors trudging up the stairs (I remember being shocked when one on the third floor shouted "Pick up your goddamn feet" through his door late one evening) is also not something we have to live with: the higher you are in a walk-up building, the fewer people walk by. Perhaps our own most startling sonic transgression was one that didn't occur. Awakened from a sound sleep by a phone call from our outraged downstairs neighbor who was livid over loud music, we assured her (she remained skeptical) that the noise was coming from somewhere else. Such are the mysteries of sound transmission in a building with hollow wooden floor and wall construction and numerous chimney and service shafts.

This hierarchy of thinning vertical traffic would be reversed if a building were entered from the top. There are a number of such places, beginning with underground buildings that appear throughout history—the subterranean cities of the early Christians near Göreme in Turkey, for example. In the pueblos of Chaco Canyon, although the buildings are aboveground, principal circulation is along the rooftops, and one enters through an opening on the roof, using a ladder rather than a stair. More recently, there was a vogue for cliff-side hotels, which had their lobbies on the roof, from which guests then descended to their rooms. This reversal also occurs in hill towns where the conventional spaces of public circulation—the streets—are so precipitous that they confer a kind of reversibility of orientation to the space: only the circumstance of your activities determines whether you approach your home from above or below.

Most cities, though, are structured by right-angle vertical

circulation, weighted by gravity. Moving in the city means constantly changing the axis of movement. In general, lateral movement is confined to a single plane, what's called grade, the ground level. However, in cities like New York we have an effective second grade in the underground system, and the subway defines another circulation datum, a horizontal lamination. But the subway only takes you from point to point, and this lower grade is experienced discontinuously. A more thoroughgoing freedom of experience is available to us only at ground level, where we are constantly presented with choices and potential variations in route.

In a city of relatively uniform height—which is to say virtually all cities up to the latter nineteenth century and most parts of most cities today—there exists another potentially negotiable grade at the level of the rooftops. Since rooftops are precisely that—tops, termination, protection—this potential has been obscured. Because circulation in multistory buildings is fundamentally one way—which is to say from the bottom up—the condition at the top is invariably different from that at the bottom. Rooftop circulation is the domain of Fantômas, of cat burglars and fleeing criminals, of lovers, and of those acrobatic enough to negotiate the gaps between buildings.

A number of North American cities, Houston and Minneapolis among them, have extensively incorporated so-called skyway systems, networks referred to by their advocates as "streets in the sky" but that are actually webs of corridors located at second-story level that join office buildings in downtowns. A variant on this is an underground network like the ones found in Montreal, Rockefeller Center, and the World Trade Center. The most extensive such places are in Japan, where they are woven into the labyrinthine subway and rail lines that structure cities like Tokyo and Osaka. Unlike their American counterparts, which become desolate—and which often close—at the end of the working day, these teem with activity at all hours.

The motivation for these systems is multiple. Houston and

Minneapolis suffer from seasonal inclemencies, and their networks permit office workers and shoppers to move about the city without exposure to extreme heat or cold. The skyways have also been promoted as solutions to the "problem" of the street, which is to say, its public character. In the 1960s, urban streets were firmly associated with crime and seen as the habitat of the undesirable elements of the urban population—the poor, the wrongly colored, vagrants, non-shoppers, those without a place in the corporate order that was producing the new downtowns. But, as has been widely observed, these walkways suck the life from the street. Thus a number of cities are now considering removing them in order to recapture the street's banished vitality.

The idea of such parallel networks of circulation for the privileged is actually an old one. The Medici built the famous Corridoio Vasariano in Renaissance Florence as a private skyway to permit them to pass from the Uffizi over the Arno to their palatial digs without descending and mixing with the public. The arcades of eighteenth-century Paris that so fascinated Walter Benjamin were privately constructed shopping galleries designed, again, for persons of means to pursue the pleasures of consumption unbeleaguered by hoi polloi. Such places are the ancestors of both skyways and shopping malls, spaces that interiorize and privatize the space of the street. Although they may share a morphological—even functional—kinship, these are very different from the seductive quasi-interiority of places like the great souks of Fez or Istanbul or the narrowed, shaded streets of Seville. Here, the primary network at grade is intensified by commerce and sheltered from the elements but remains continuous with the larger urban fabric.

"Controlled environments" are another of modernism's great obsessions. One of the sources of the environmental crisis that so besets us today is a paradigm that seeks to isolate a building not simply from its social but from its physical surroundings. Extravagant amounts of energy are spent to keep buildings—as well as skyway systems, shopping malls, and domed stadia—at a constant temperature year-round via entirely mechanical means. The folly is not simply a touchy-feely isolation from the authenticities of nature, which can admittedly be cruel, but a larger disciplinary presumption that seeks to extend the centralized authority (central air, central government) of power ever more comprehensively. It is possible that this particular hubris may have pushed Gaia to the tipping point.

Fundamentally, this risk is ideological, not technological. The Enlightenment was in love with states of nature, with imaginary social origin points that allowed people to assess progress and to model idealized social relations in the future. Some saw these states bleakly (like Thomas Hobbes), imagining a time of "war of all against all" in which life was "nasty, brutish, and short." Others, like Jean-Jacques Rousseau, imagined a paradise of simplicity, abundance, and consent. Although Hobbes and Rousseau stand at the headwaters of very different political traditions, each produced philosophies for the management of human relations via an environment of pervasive governance.

If Rousseau is the more obvious source for the modernist fixation on the restoration of an Edenic environment, Hobbes functions as its thinly concealed unconscious, the steely control behind the curtain of bowery fabulousness. Architecture embodies these opposites in a variety of ways and spreads its own influence via compelling formal prototypes. For example, the Crystal Palace designed by Joseph Paxton for the Great Exhibition of 1851 in London was a gigantic, shopping-mall-scaled entirely glass and iron structure—a prodigious greenhouse—designed to display the fruits of the world's industry. It was historically decisive both for the enormity of the space it brought under control and for the transparency of its enclosure, the glass membrane that allowed it to be simultaneously visually continuous with nature and isolated from its exigencies. Its heirs include such loopy visions as Buckminster Fuller's climate-controlling dome to cover midtown Manhattan and, more obscurely, the 1956 "Ocean Liner City" by the French architect Wladimir Gordeeff, a huge air-conditioned housing mall designed to allow white colonials to live comfortably in the Sahara, as well as the malls, airports, and atrium hotels now found everywhere.

Skyways share in yet another fantasy of control, one with origins in the late nineteenth century, when a great wave of speculation about the form of the modern city took place. Inspired by the advent of the skyscraper and by proliferating technologies of movement— including trains, cars, elevators, and aircraft—architects and other visionary types arrived at a depiction of their integration that has become a sort of imaginative default for depictions of "cities of the future" to this day, even as the proprietorship of this vision has devolved from the optimism of such architectural utopias to the bleak dystopianism of Hollywood at its big-budget best (a distinction many would argue is meaningless). At the practical level, it remains the informing ideology of most traffic planning.

The picture that emerged from this new diversity of movement systems and radical extension of the apparatus of speed was one in which every means operated in its own exclusive horizontal plane. Cities were imagined as a series of laminations with each mode stacked above or below the others. Subways were underground, cars at street level, pedestrians a level above that, elevated trains above that, helicopters and autogiros buzzed over that, and dirigibles and airplanes flew over the rooftops. The laminations were to be skewered together by the elevators that moved up and down the towers that inevitably constituted the architecture of the brave new city.

The logic of the system was based on the belief that these various modes of movement were in fundamental "conflict" and that the task of planning was to radically reduce and manage the sites in which cars and trains and pedestrians might meet. This would guarantee not simply the safety of the smaller, less energetic party to the conflict but, by creating a space of exclusivity, ensure the unimpeded flow of each means. The whole not only answered to a paradigm of efficient movement but also verticalized the logic of zoning, producing a city stratified by use and right of access, a city that sought to distribute everything and everyone to its proper place in all four dimensions.

The invention of the elevator had a striking effect on the production of hierarchy in the vertical axis. In the nineteenth century, the tops of apartment buildings—the fifth or sixth floors—were the preserve of servants (or artists or students) who lived in small spaces under the roof and were obliged to climb up and down. With the elevator, there was not only an equalization of value based on universal convenience; there was a shift of privilege from the kinesthetic to the scopic. Desirability came to be associated with view and with a sense of commanding the uppermost, a value based on a combination of military, theological, privacy, and prestige matters. In a city like New York, the finest place to live in a tall building is the penthouse, which conflates the pleasures of the view with the idea of a private house set in open land. Penthouses re-clarify the relationships of residence to plot, taking advantage of what amounts to a second grade. The outline of the building site—obscured by ground-floor adjacencies—reappears in horizontal, buildable form.

Yet one might also imagine a city conceived quite differently—more like the pueblos in Chaco Canyon. If a city were imagined with two principal grades—one at the top of buildings and one at the bottom—the form of the city would be dramatically transformed. Standing on our rooftop in the Village, I can survey many other rooftops. On a summer day, I often see sunbathers soaking up rays on what is affectionately called "tar beach," since the majority of rooftops around Annabel Lee (and Annabel Lee itself) are covered in rolls of roofing paper, sealed with hot tar, heated over propane flames and applied with mops. Such "built-up" roofing is an inexpensive, reasonably effective, but fragile and ultimately primitive technology. It suggests that in most of our buildings, roof is residue, invisible space, mere barrier membrane.

But the roof is invisible only because we are accustomed to looking at it from the point of view of the street. If one were to fly over the city at low altitude, the roofs would be our urban foreground. It is precisely this kind of visibility that is opened up when we incorporate a distaff way of seeing—like a helicopter or spy satellite. This possibility has led, in Los Angeles and elsewhere, to the painting of enormous house numbers on rooftops to facilitate police surveillance and coordinate strategies of search and capture throughout the city. Paul Virilio has argued that the view from above has reconfigured the very epistemology of space, remaking the world as a target.

Imagine, instead, that our rooftops were parkland, that the area of ground occupied by buildings was, in effect, simply displaced upward. Imagine that the city enacted legislation requiring that the equivalent of 100 percent of the surface area of New York were to be green. A 100 percent requirement would not simply oblige green roofs. It would also demand that compensatory greenery be added to make up for such ungreenable areas as roadways, runways, and other unplantable places. Perhaps the requirement would be satisfied with road narrowings, cantilevered gardens, or green floors in buildings (utilities on the order of the mechanical floors that occur in almost all tall buildings). Perhaps there would be a market for the exchange of green rights (similar to the current trading of pollution credits) or the construction of towers devoted to the provision of fungible green space.

If such aerial parkland were linked by bridges or by a more continuous building form, an entirely new kind of public space would be created. Top and bottom would have their relationship recast. An apartment dweller might, of a morning, leave her place and go up the stairs to the second grade. A leisurely stroll through an aerial parkland might bring her to her workplace or to her friend's apartment, where she would reenter the building and walk downstairs. At lunchtime the process might be reversed with a walk downstairs to the street and then back up afterward. Needless to say, such a fantasy requires a fairly dramatic rethinking of the nature of property lines and the character of vertical connections.

Although no existing city has two grades like this, there are enough images of the condition to suggest what it might be like.

During World War II, large industrial installations were camouflaged by constructing a naturalistic second grade on their roofs. This was done in order to create from two separate planes (the factory floor and its roof) the illusion that there was only one so that aviators would be perspectively duped into believing that the roof of the factory was continuous with the surrounding ground. Roof gardens were also very popular with architectural modernists in the interwar period. A pretty good example of such rooftop green space can be seen on two of the low buildings at Rockefeller Center, though few people know about them or have access because they are effectively private spaces.

Setting aside the circulatory possibilities of such a second grade (as well as the risks of any such doubling to the life of the street), there are plenty of other reasons to make building roofs green (many of them eloquently advocated by Corb). They would surely be beautiful—in a city of towers, large numbers would look down on them—and they would provide leisure space for tenants of their buildings. They would also have a profoundly mitigating effect on the so-called urban heat island problem. Thermal images of the city taken from the air reveal that the city's temperature can be as many as five degrees higher than that of surrounding areas. The culprit here is the endless expanse of brick and asphalt, which absorbs, stores, and reradiates heat, not to mention the endless heat generated by internal combustion, air-conditioning exhaust, and the other hellish excreta of the fossil-fuel economy. By greening roofs (and shading streets and expanding park space), we can counteract the thermal behavior of the city and reduce the urban contribution to global warming. The capacity of what Olmsted called the urban "green lung" would be vastly increased.

By absorbing and storing rainwater, green roofs can also eliminate a major source of groundwater pollution and depletion. Aquifers are recharged by rainwater percolating down into the earth. Because the major portion of our cities is built of impermeable materials, water has little opportunity to enter the ground. The current method of handling this impermeability is to collect runoff in drains and sewers and transport it in pipes—often via sewage treatment plants—to rivers or detention ponds. But transporting rainwater to rivers means we effectively lose it forever. By contrast, retaining it in the second grade or elsewhere would ensure supply and—for cities like Mexico and New Orleans that are built on drained sites—would keep buildings from sinking. Urban runoff is also a very efficient way of collecting the variety of toxic pollutants that form in the streets. Simply washing this runoff into the waterways at the end of the storm drainage system contributes to the rise of pollution far downstream from the source. Green roofs, in concert with local management of storm runoff, have the potential both to reduce the spread of such pollution and to serve as a source of water supply for trees, plants, and even ourselves. There are already excellent organic technologies appropriate to the scale of neighborhood, block, or building that can cleanse captured water—even sewage water—so that it can be used for bathing, flushing, or irrigation.

One of the platitudes of big-city life is that people live in such a state of anonymity and alienation that they don't so much as recognize their neighbors. In our building we know who lives in all eleven apartments. We are cordial to all and friendly with a few and have some knowledge and lots of opinions about each. With most we have little in common except the fact of our common living place, so there's no reason beyond civility and our mutual struggles with the landlord for us to have relationships.

When Jane was still alive, our neighbors on the second floor would often prepare meals or fresh coffee for her, and they had a system of signals—involving a newspaper stuck in the railing of the stair—to indicate when the plates were ready to be exchanged. Presently, a couple of Annabel Lee pet owners have special relations, part of a social network that includes a permanent klatsch at

the dog run in Washington Square and all the complex interspe-
cies interactions that take place en passant in the street. Several
gay couples in the building share political and social news. The
rent-controlled tenants have a special bond based on both tenure
and circumstances. Older tenants—in both senses—share affinities
of longevity.

As I descend the stairs, I see lots of evidence of what's going
on, who's painting, who has a new air conditioner or stereo, who is
having a party, who is having a fight. The hallmark of good apartment behavior, though, is respect for privacy. Even the circuit of
gossip functions as a filter, relieving the need for direct confrontation, concealing uninvited knowledge, but—based on the funda-
mentals of trust—allowing an informal mediation of complaints.
Our recently departed photographer neighbor had lived across the
hall from us since we moved in. Although our relations were ami-
cable, in all this time we had not been in his apartment nor he in
ours (beyond standing in each other's doorway). Indeed, we've been
in the apartments of relatively few of our neighbors, and even fewer
have been in ours.

Part of the reason is that we ourselves are less than terribly
social and rarely entertain at home. And our neighbors—though
many are very nice—are not people we would necessarily have chosen to live with. What we have in common is the building and, by
extension, the neighborhood. This shapes the major areas of our
social intersection. We are united in reviling our landlords, a contempt that they return fulsomely. Our interaction is thus much
concerned with building services and repairs, organizing never-to-
happen rent strikes, and snide samizdat focused on the latest outrage or intransigence perpetrated by the owners.

We are also united in our affection for the neighborhood, for
its physiognomy, lifestyle, and sense of soviet solidarity. It seems
fair to say that all of us came to the Village by choice (with the possible exception of born-in-the-building Margot), although some of
the older, rent-control-dependent tenants might not be entirely
free in their decision to remain. To some degree this is true of us as

well. Our rent is protected by the rent stabilization law. When we moved in, our rent approximated the market, but increases over subsequent years have been restricted to a rate set biannually by a municipal board, following a predictably raucous public meeting pitting tenant and landlord groups against each other. Thus, although our rent cannot be described as low, it is now lower than the unregulated rents governed purely by the mechanisms of the market.

The rent stabilization and control laws have another important effect. Because we—and our neighbors—are bound to the building economically, we enjoy a certain social stability. In terms of local politics and the psychology of participation, this essentially elective investment has a positive result, increasing our stake in both the building and the neighborhood. Such long-duration presence also has the effect of making us all more knowledgeable from both a historical perspective and that of detail about the place in which we live. Our stability thus leads to a heightened and strengthened sense of participation, to an increase in loyalty, to a cementing of community.

The circumstances under which we moved into the building are an oft-told (mainly by Joan) part of the mythology of our marriage. We had been living in a series of temporary situations and had been hunting for permanent digs for some time. I had fixed my desires on a gigantic loft on the Brooklyn waterfront in an area that is now fashionable but which was then marginal. The space was completely raw (no floors, plumbing, heating, and so on), was far from public transit, even farther from shopping. One day while we were there, an armed robbery took place on the ground floor. So what? It was huge and offered panoramic views of the East River and Manhattan. That we had no money to fix it up, that my own construction skills are limited, and that the inconvenience of the location and potential endlessness of the renovation would have been a horrible burden did not figure in my delusional calculations.

Fortunately, I was eventually dissuaded, and in a stroke of luck Joan found an ad for the apartment in Annabel Lee and acted with

alacrity to secure it. Freshly painted and perfectly located, the top-
floor apartment was an excellent coup, so I—less than graciously—
gave up my architect's ambitions of massive loft lebensraum and
we signed the lease. We had never seriously considered buying a
place, which might have made more sense. We had no money, and
besides I, child of the 1960s, tended to Proudhon's "property is
theft" school of thought and simply (foolishly, as it turned out) had
no desire for ownership. Rents in New York were still relatively low,
and I was habituated to frequent moves. My landlords over the
years had been better and worse, but none had been impossible.

Our time in Annabel Lee has schooled us in many intricacies
of the sociology of property relations. On the one hand, we hesitate
to make expensive improvements to our apartment (we endlessly
debate a major renovation of the bathroom) because we would be
"giving" them to our landlord. We (rather I) also hold to the increasingly unsupportable fantasy that I will strike it rich soon and we
will move on. On the other hand, we are tightly bound to our building and its community and to our neighborhood and its civic life.
Contrary to the regnant Republican rhetoric, we are proprietary
without property. Our sense of citizenship and belonging is the
product not of ownership but of affinity, interaction, and social reciprocity. Protection by the city's rent regulations serves to deepen
our sense of collectivity at the level of governance as well as to reinforce our feelings that ideas of equity still configure policy.

The real estate boom of recent years has thrown into relief the
accelerating spatial inequity of the city as well as the obscene income gap that has seen more and more wealth concentrated in the
hands of fewer and fewer people. Manhattan is turning into a
gated community, the soft white center of a city that increasingly
relegates diversity to its periphery. This begs the questions of how
housing "affordability" is to be maintained and how such housing
is to be distributed spatially. Despite free-market pieties, we have a
long national history of subsidizing housing, be it through mortgage interest deductibility and other forms of tax relief for owners,

direct subsidy (Jane Jacobs proposed a novel form of this), public housing construction, vouchers, or rent regulation. Political rationale and rhetoric may change, but the necessity of subvention remains constant.

The city's current policy is to move from a general system of rent controls, and the public construction of housing, to a "public-private partnership" model where state subsidy is directed to landlords and builders in exchange for the *voluntary* provision of lower-cost units. The latest formulation of this policy is called "inclusionary zoning" and works by offering developers the opportunity to make their buildings larger than would normally be allowed in exchange for the provision of a certain number of "affordable" units on-site. To date, the results have been mixed. While new apartments have been built, their number is well under the number of affordable units lost to the market. And despite the clear advantages of mixed-income projects, the design of many has created localized ghettos, with the lower-cost units in legibly separate (and inferior) buildings from the primary development. As with other forms of bonus-based subsidy, the city exchanges one quality considered fundamentally important—in this case the control of building bulk and access to light and air—for another—low-cost units—thus breaching its own most fundamental paradigm of good city form.

By protecting continuity, rent control is the social equivalent of landmarking. Of all the issues that are consequential locally, the preservation of the physical fabric of our neighborhood is probably at the top of the list. There are multiple reasons for this. First is that the fabric of the Village is singular and beautiful. The eccentric streets and historic buildings are concentrated and extensive, unique in America. Second, preservation has become, in New York—much as environmentalism has become nationally—a form of displacement for many other political issues, such as who is to control the planning of the city and whose interests will be served. Although we are blessed with an abundance of local historians who can dilate on the origins of every brick, quoin, and paver, there's a larger sense that the Village fabric is not simply a work of art but the embodiment of a web of culture and folkways that should be valued for itself.

A big struggle at the moment concerns our local waterfront, specifically several soft sites that are in danger of being developed with very large buildings that the preservation community might describe as "out of character." The poster children for this threat are three adjacent and widely hated fourteen-story apartment buildings on the river, all designed, in his typically crisp and elegant style, by Richard Meier. They are held inappropriate because they are of larger scale than the predominantly low-rise character of the neighborhood, because they are unabashed in their white-steel-and-glass modernism, and because they tip the balance of waterfront development away from an irregular, predominantly low-rise scale and rhythm into a version of Riverside or Lake Shore Drives or Copacabana, driven by the logic of their views rather than by the neighborhoods behind them.

Although this is less openly expressed (and has no legal standing in any of the planning hearings that will influence the future of our waterfront), there's a giant subterranean sentiment that the buildings are also out of sync with the idea of the Village as raffish, diverse, progressive, and a bastion against the remorseless trendiness and fashionability that has the city (and, more and more, the Village itself) in a stranglehold. This reading has surely been helped by the raft of A-list celebrities (among them Martha Stewart and Heather Mills) who have flocked to Meier's buildings and paid the astronomical prices that have helped to push the cost of everything else—from real estate to yogurt—into the stratosphere.

The Meier buildings and several others nearby (including a funky, overscaled, and underdetailed pink number built by the artist Julian Schnabel, packed with a changing roster of stars, many of whom flip their digs for millions after a brief stay) beg the primary question of historic preservation: Should physical objects be the only focus? At its origin point—which most date to the failed fight to save Penn Station in 1960—the physical focus was logically foregrounded. Penn Station was a vital piece of our civic heritage, a great and grand building torn down for a horrible replacement station, a horrible office building, and a horrible arena purely to max out the site's income potential.

The event, however, was galvanizing and led both to the ongoing formalization of landmarks legislation and to the protection of thousands of structures throughout the city, both individually and through the designation of entire districts, including SoHo, the Ladies' Mile, and much of the Village, as historic. The institutionalization of landmarking was also a kind of psychic turning point for New York, its coming of age as a historic city, not simply a grid for uninhibited and eternal transformation. Landmarking represented an epistemological break with the sentimentality of avarice dear to so many commentators on the character of New York, who celebrate the boldness of the Schumpeterian "creative destruction" that knocked down the magnificent mansions of the robber barons to build the magnificent apartment houses of lesser millionaires, a city that—like a shark—had to move on or die.

The benefits of the change were mixed. By identifying the city with its forms rather than its processes, landmarking was a blunt instrument. To be sure, it recognized the permanent value of the city's architectural achievements, their singularity and their irreplaceability. Over centuries of development, New York has produced a series of climax forms, architectures that have reached an effective state of perfection. Like the squares of Georgian London, the canals of Venice, or the boulevards of Paris, the nineteenth-century brownstone rows of Manhattan and Brooklyn, the stepped skyscrapers of the 1920s and 1930s, and the apartment bluffs overlooking Central Park or the Hudson River are our native achievements, the result of singular processes of development and the outcome of the specific social, historical, cultural, and creative character of New York. The city may not be a tree—as Christopher Alexander famously wrote—but it does have affinities with the forest, with its stages of complexity and evolution and with its homeostatic outcomes.

As basic urban constituents, these climax forms are at the crest of their own refinement. They are also, in both their invention and the recognition of their importance, the outcome of a series of compacts between the city and its citizens. These forms fairly bristle with a sense of nativity—of indigenousness—and, reciprocally, they give identity to the city imagined historically and are integral to the description of the city as it is, objects of the kind of conceptual striving that invents new New Yorkers. Like the tales told by Margot or Jane, these buildings are bardic, transmitters of values held in common and in trust. Naturally, evolution produces its dead ends, and as history happens, the terminal achievements of tenement or penitentiary construction are to be saved as cautions, curiosities, or sites of useful adaptation. Both the Frick mansion and an anonymous tenement on the Lower East Side are now museums.

To the degree that it tasks itself with representing an idea of the general good and with the defense of a peculiar species of rights, landmarking has also fitted nicely with the political culture of the city and its fundamentally adversarial structure. New York has endlessly reformulated the reconciliation of private rights and public interest, and the history of the city is, inter alia, one of the continuous adjustment of the balance between the two. At some times—perhaps most dramatically during the era of Robert Moses with his prodigious output of "public" works—the initiative has been in the hands of nominally public agencies. More often, though, the preferred model has been laissez-faire, with the municipality entrusting a variously regulated environment to the tender mercies of private initiative.

Nowadays, this relationship is sanctified by the inevitable public-private partnership, a turn of phrase designed to cover the domination of initiative by the private sector and its eager enabling by government. Our billionaire mayor is part of a general national devaluation of direct public initiative, viewing government intervention (at least at home) as an impediment to the sure genius of private capital. Indeed, the visionary responsibilities that might logically be seen to fall to planning agencies are lodged instead in the deputy mayor for economic development, from whose office all major physical initiatives flow and who is the facilitator not of public projects but of private ones, themselves deemed—by the fact of their profitability—to be in the public interest. The 2007 departure of the former captain of the universe Dan Doctoroff from this post to become head of Mayor Bloomberg's private business is a typically flagrant example of an ethically blithe interlock of interests. In this schema, the Department of City Planning takes on a role of urban design—making development initiatives look good via the strategic use of architecture after the fact—or that of zoners, regulating neighborhood densities and uses for compatibility with the growth regime by fixing levels of up-zoning. The top-down efficiencies of this division of labor—and a renewed interest in planning at the large scale—have (during the Bloomberg regime) focused especially on the West Side Rail Yards in Manhattan, the Atlantic Yards in Brooklyn, and Ground Zero, all three of which, because of their ownership by public authorities, are loosely regulated and less susceptible to legal intervention by opponents. The cycle of advise and dissent, in which environmental and urban self-determination—the exercise of the right to the city—is channeled through protest rather than proposal, is reinforced by this top-down approach.

Here, too, the progress of the city is gauged by strictly economic criteria. The mayor frequently cites the zooming rise of real estate prices as the index of our success. This is Republican logic, the rising-tide-lifts-all-boats, trickle-down theory of general benefit. Increased property values will produce—along with increased consumption by those with vastly expanded incomes—increased revenues for the city via taxes that, in turn, can be used to benefit the large segments of the population left out of the upward spiral of development. Here's the vision: Manhattan becomes that gigantic gated community with a narrowing range of economic activities and a growing inhospitality toward those without the pelf to buy into its increasingly fabulous lifestyle. It's a simple but invidious fallacy: there's nowhere to trickle down to if there's no one but millionaires left.

The neutron bomb approach to preservation makes the same

misassumption. While I question few of the decisions taken by our
Landmarks Preservation Commission to protect buildings or districts, I am struck by the one-dimensional process. Restricted to
an aesthetic lexicon, preservation re-creates the city as a museum,
a repository for itself. There is bluster from the right about preservation as a "taking," an interference with the private right to dispose of private property. The real effect is the opposite. Aesthetic
preservation increases real estate "values" by assigning rights strictly
to architecture. Here, preservation becomes the expressive man-
date of gentrification.

This deracinated idea of "context" has become a leading value
of urbanism. All physical additions to or alterations of a historic
structure must be vetted for compatibility, a concept generally in-
terpreted so inelastically as to scare off anything beyond literalism.
At the scale of the neighborhood or district, the test of context is
applied generally with the greatest architectural timidity and urban
brutality, suppressing the anomalies that have resulted from the
uneven spatial development cycles of boom and bust. Little thought
is given to the evolving contexts that serve as the origin points for
a building's wider meaning or to the real constituents of neighborhood life. An extreme case is Willets Point in Queens, right next to
Shea Stadium. With wide, rutted, half-paved streets and minimal
infrastructure, Willets Point looks like something out of the developing world, home to dozens of businesses, primarily auto body
and repair shops. But its ecology is singular and symbiotic, thriving
on the dereliction of the place. The city proposes to tear it all down
and replace it with a "mixed-use" development. While auto repair
may not qualify as the "highest and best" use of this well-situated
site, the city is unable to offer any other place for the businesses to
lodge. Declared economically redundant (like the tenants in rent-
regulated apartments), many will simply die.

In SoHo—flagship historic district, casebook example of gentrification, globally recognized symbol of successful "adaptive reuse"—
the test of contextualism is used to line up cornices, promote
soporifically retro architecture, even—in a truly bizarre twist—

enjoin the planting of street trees, judged not to have been present at SoHo's creation. What *was* present at creation were a series of uses that are now completely incompatible with the character of the "historic" neighborhood. Thirty years ago, when I moved into a loft in SoHo—a seven-story walk-up!—my grandmother, remembering it as a place of factories and sweatshops, was shocked that I would choose to live there. She had contextualized my choice in terms of the "authentic" origins of the place and lacked my fine architect's understanding of the joys of living in a big empty room. For her, the meaning of SoHo attached not to the robust delicacy and yummy proportions of its cast-iron facades but to its culture of use. She remembered young immigrant women at their sewing machines, heard the clatter of machinery, sagged at the thought of the hours and the heat and the miserable wages. Clacking Manolos passing the Bellini quaffers at Cipriani simply didn't compute.

Preservation banishes this from its calculations and draws its lines myopically. While nobody misses the sweatshops, many lament the rapid decline of the city's industrial economy, now seemingly headed for extinction. There were no trees in SoHo because the incessant trucks and wagons and the piled bales and boxes in the street wouldn't have allowed them to survive. Strange to retain and aestheticize this historic condition without a thought for the consequences of such impoverished historicism. There was surely a moment in the more recent history of SoHo—before the stifling manipulations of policy enacted on behalf of money—when the earlier idea of use might have morphed into something valuable. The mix of artists, craftspeople, small manufacturers, and researchers, as well as of commerce oriented to their needs, was something that flared briefly before the inexorable operations of the invisible hand, gloved in municipal authority, grabbed it by the throat and killed it in favor of shoe stores and groovy pads for dot-com-bubble boys and girls.

Not long ago, I was on a panel discussion and had occasion to remark on the fact that tax time was tense because we had the paradoxical hope that our income would be low enough to keep us under the threshold for rent stabilization decontrol, an outcome that could force us to move. After the session, a member of the audience approached me sputtering with rage. He worked in the real estate industry and, after allowing that he strongly defended my right to my opinion, said that people like me, who wanted to "drive a Cadillac and only pay Ford prices," were the problem with New York. I began to demur, but the man was so apoplectic that discussion was impossible.

There was no bridge to this religious absolutism of the market, which reposed total faith in the wisdom of its pricing mechanisms. In comparative terms, our apartment is expensive, whether as a fraction of our income or compared with rents nationally. Over the years of our tenancy, we have paid an aggregate rent that is substantially in excess of what our landlord paid to acquire the building in the first place. To be sure, Annabel Lee is wonderfully located but has, for years, been shabby and barely maintained. We accept this, to a degree, because we understand that the rent rolls in the building have, until recently, produced a poor return, far less than would be available were all the apartments rented at something closer to the market price. Whether an increase would produce more attentive behavior on the landlord's part is a matter of speculation, as is trying to calibrate the potential relationship between rising profit and improved services, especially at the margins. In the real estate man's calculus, value has nothing to do with intrinsic quality or the particulars of the exchange, simply with scarcity or fashion. The market theory of value gives quality and appropriateness short shrift since it is only able to describe a reasonable profit as what the market will bear.

In his passion for abstraction, the real estate man also ignored the historic role of the commons in defining the nature of the reasonable. Without the law, we'd have had no way to force our landlord to patch our roof after we were inundated with leaks (we had to get an order from the Housing Department, which took two years) or to repair the ancient boiler when it sputtered and died in the middle of the winter. Nor, without the building laws, would there be windows in the rooms that face the air shaft. Our landlord is a classic because he appears to be completely without altruism—which, because its nature is to be uncompelled, is no basis for a contract—or any sense of obligation beyond that which is literally prescribed. Like the sputtering man at the panel, he seems without any ethic of reciprocity beyond the struggle for advantage. From his point of view—and the market's—such Hobbesian behavior is simply logical.

Although the landlord can't be relied on for much, he dependably slips a rent bill under the door at the end of every month. Occasionally, our bill was mixed up with that of our now departed neighbor across the hall. Since the envelope was unsealed, we, of course, opened it up to see what our neighbor was paying. In New York, where the extraction of value from real property is a major industry, everyone is obsessed with what everyone else is paying for shelter. Because of the durability of the city's rent laws—enacted as a wartime measure in the 1940s—people pay radically divergent amounts, and our rent-controlled neighbor was paying something like a fifth of what we were, perhaps a tenth of "market value."

Nevertheless, we expect a certain morality. The system—at this point—is patently inequitable, resulting in people of means who enjoy tiny rents, elderly people stuck in huge unmanageable apartments, and a giant excluded class forced to rely on the tender mercies of the market. That such a system persists is in part due to the political clout of the very large number of people who enjoy its benefits and to a perverse feeling that there is something fundamentally right about a system that—at least in theory—recognizes people's different abilities to pay. It's a symptom of the way we're inured to the city as a place that deploys space based on a radical set of advantages and disadvantages. "If you can make it here," you must deserve it, and vice versa.

To poor residents of the city who are daily obliged to witness the spectacle of hyper-consumption, gnawing resentment is surely a part of daily life. Yet they continue to function with remarkable equanimity despite it. Likewise, we somehow manage to avoid the paralysis that might ensue were we truly consumed by the

injustice of our neighbor paying 20 percent of what we do and enjoying the same benefits. This is partly due to our élan as New Yorkers,
that insufferable sense of living at the center of the universe, and
partly due to our willingness to channel inequalities into dreams
rather than rage, a luxury we can enjoy from our middle-class comfort (my walk is very different from one in Morrisania or East New
York). Thus, many of us continue to expect to hit the jackpot on
real estate (as so many already have). As the neighborhood and the
city become more and more inhospitable to diversity and mobility,
this hopeful sublimation will die hard.

There are limits on people's ability to see the bright side of
inadequate circumstances. Living in the Village, we enjoy access to
a panoply of urban pleasures and know that we are in the center of
what is, in most ways, the embodiment of a desirable urban neighborhood. Our rent-regulated stasis is tolerable because it marks not
just an inability to move but the impossibility (as we see it) of moving
anyplace better. In the slums, the sense of the long term must appear
not as an advantage but as a sentence. We celebrate the tenacity
of self-help institutions in these places and romanticize their
desperation-induced forms of comradeship, but they are fundamentally different from our own. No matter what our difficulties, in
the Village we look at our circumstances as fundamentally positive
and see our activities as work toward a kind of perfection. In the
slums, such perfection can be achieved only through departure.

The rent system is one that largely bypasses the idea of the
civic or of citizenship, of duties uncoerced. Thus our landlord—
like so many in the city, including the largest—takes no real responsibility for the participation of his property in the larger urban
ensemble. That our building has long been one of the shabbiest on
an otherwise lovely block has only recently come to concern him,
the result of a sudden impulse to make improvements that can be
passed along in higher rents and of a raft of violations issued by the
Buildings Department. Likewise, while the sidewalk out front is in
reasonable repair—the owner's obligation in a city in which sidewalks are legally private, not public, property—the tree that shades

it is a matter of complete indifference. The devolution of civic responsibility for trees and sidewalks into the hands of adjoining landlords results in the ridiculous absence of trees on even the city's most prosperous thoroughfares. My bile rises when I pass the unshaded sidewalks of the corporate skyscrapers of midtown because even these entities—worth billions of dollars—are as indifferent as my landlord to the public realm. Contrast this with well-bowered cities like Paris and Hanoi (influenced, happily, by the colonizer in this particular). The missing trees in midtown have the same source as the cracked sidewalks of Bushwick: the landlord doesn't give a damn, and the city doesn't think the matter important enough to make him.

Our rent-controlled ex-neighbor Carl was in many ways an exemplary neighbor but also—like the landlord (and us)—a creature of the system. Over the years we heard very little from his apartment other than the late-night bounding of his cat down the hall. The cat was purely inferential: although we often heard it running back and forth on its little cat feet and saw the occasional empty cat-food can in the garbage, we'd never seen the cat nor, in my memory, even heard it meow. What happens behind closed doors is fundamentally invisible. Of course, we got an occasional glimpse when our comings and goings coincided. These sightings were often amazing: to put it mildly, Carl was a pack rat of clinical proportions. Behind his door we caught views of an apartment stuffed to the gills with every imaginable detritus, old newspapers climbing to the ceiling, piles like skyscrapers, global disorder.

I've known a couple of other people with similar propensities. Inwardly, I'm appalled by them. On the other hand, my sense of tolerance insists that what one does in one's own space is one's right. Unless, of course, it affects me. Putting aside my dismay and anxiety for the state of Carl's mind (is he so disordered that he will turn out to be an ax murderer?), I did have worries that this debris was the potential source of a conflagration as well as the breeding ground for the ubiquitous New York roach. Of greater concern was our neighbor's history of failure to confine this flow of stuff to his own apartment. For years, his rubbish tended to spill into the hall-way, in the form of piles of paper and broken furniture stashed at the end of the hall.

We tried a variety of means to try to tame this proclivity. I'd frequently take his trash and pile it in front of his door. Some-times, I'd take it down to the street. I'd type up notes addressed to all Annabel Lee tenants in which I'd complain how unsafe and unneighborly it was to store trash in the halls and how especially galling it was to us who, living on the top floor, were obliged to descend past it all. This had absolutely no effect. Only when the landlord warned of the impending arrival of a fire marshal and threat-ened steep city fines did anyone take notice. The improvement was immediate but evanescent, and soon rubbish began to creep back into the halls.

The hallway—what is sometimes called a semiprivate space—is a fine instance of the delicate negotiation strategies that character-ize civil life in the city. Our particular hallway is ugly and grimy: a largely symbolic mopping once a week is the landlord's best effort. Its dangling lights, peeling paint, and general decay do not appear to interest him. As tenants, we are torn between our dismay at the hallway's ugliness and our sense that the hallway is the landlord's responsibility. This yields a paradox. We abuse the hall because we feel abused by it. We don't participate in its maintenance, because to do so would provide our landlord with something that he should be providing to us. We engage in the same kind of "irrational" behavior that residents of the "projects" are so often accused of: fouling our own nest.

The matter of garbage collection is also constrained by the system. Trash is picked up from the curb three times a week by the city. For most of our tenancy we placed our bagged trash in the hallway the night before, and the handyman took it down early in the morning. Under the best of circumstances, this meant that the hall was full of garbage overnight. In practice, though, we generally put out our garbage when the bag was full, which meant that the hall was virtually never without bags of garbage. Recycling day was worse. Baled newspapers, plastics, and metals used to be picked up from the curb on Fridays, and on Thursday evening a big, dirty blue plastic city-supplied garbage can appeared in the first-floor hallway. The porter did not carry recycling down, so tenants were obliged to do it themselves. What happened was newspapers tended to appear in the hall long before the end of the week. Often these bales—as well as shopping bags full of cans and bottles—began their migration to the front hall days before pickup. We gleaned a certain amount of information about our neighbors from the archaeology of these piles (second floor put out three empty wine jugs this week . . .), but the general impression was simply that of depressing disorder.

Our relationship with Carl reached a crisis point a couple of years ago. He had not been much seen in the building during the previous year, having, we understood, moved in with his girlfriend. Although it is illegal to sublet a rent-controlled apartment, he got around this by bringing in a "roommate." It was some months before we met this new neighbor, who'd already gotten on our bad side by leaving vast quantities of unbagged trash on the landing. He also played loud music (the primary incivility of apartment life) and had visitors around the clock who often rang our bell instead of his.

His behavior became the talk of the stairs, challenging Annabel Lee's live-and-let-live lifestyle. Because of our proximity to the problem and our own scrupulosity, it fell to us to do something. At first this consisted in pounding on the wall when the music was too loud (a signal that was understood). Later, I Scotch-taped a cigarette butt, one of many ground out on the stairs by the unseen tenant or his friends, to his front door, only to find it taped to ours the next day. Once, we tied his bags and reorganized his garbage in anal rows as a signal. Presumably, he found us priggish fools.

Things came to a head when we left a note on his door, detailing his crimes. Sometime the next day came a pounding on our door. Joan was at home alone. She asked who it was, and it was the neighbor in a rage. *How dare you leave me such a note. You probably left it because you're racists!* Joan replied that such a motive was unlikely as we had yet to see him and had no idea what race he was (he turned out to be from the Philippines). This slightly placated him, and Joan opened the door and had a stern word with him. The result was a marginal, though transitory, improvement in the rubbish situation.

He quickly reverted to his old habits, and the porter who had been taking trash down to the street three times a week soon began to refuse to deal with him. For a time, the result was a series of complaints to the landlord, who snapped that the only alternative would be *to fire Lester,* the hapless, kindly, underpaid, elderly black man who looked after the halls. Our landlord is a master of Hobson's choice.

After some days of standoff, the landlord arrived at a solution. Notices were posted in the hall letting the tenants know that the landlord would no longer collect trash from our apartments and that tenants would henceforth be required to take their trash down to the first floor. The landlord had won again, giving us the alternative of leaving our garbage on the landing indefinitely, while we attempted some legal or administrative action, or carrying the trash downstairs.

We had mixed feelings about this. If the tenants chose to cooperate, there was a certain aesthetic and hygienic gain, especially to those of us on the upper floors. On the other hand, having to deliver the garbage to the ground floor ourselves was undoubtedly a reduction in service, and this was a prime territory of our ongoing struggles. We understand our relationship to our landlord not simply as a legal one but as a social contract, which is to say, a political contract, and saw this behavior not only as adding inconvenience but as an assault on our tenant rights.

Our neighbors on the second floor (rent-controlled tenants of long duration) have long chosen—as a gesture of contempt—to throw their trash into the light well in front of the landlord's basement office, and this began to seem like a good idea. After all, why should the trash be piled in our space when it's the landlord's obligation to get rid of it? It seems both fair and reasonable that the collection point be in front of his door, not ours. At the moment, on non-collection days, many tenants leave trash at the top of the steps leading from the sidewalk to the landlord's office. From time to time we do this ourselves. I assuage my guilt at contributing to the disorderly appearance of the street by making sure the trash is neatly bagged and by the justification of a signaling affront to the landlord, another pathetic display of pique at a bad system.

If I leave the building around nine, it sometimes happens that I meet the landlord on the way in. In fact, the landlord is two: Lou, with whom we deal about day-to-day matters, and Rose, his elderly mother. There are also several supernumeraries, including a bookkeeper and the recently arrived Jim, who is marginally more courteous and approachable than Lou, whose personality was revealed to us at the beginning of our relationship. When we rented the apartment, we signed the lease at Lou's legal office downtown, where he was then practicing criminal law. The visit proved a compact preview of the style of intercourse we would become increasingly familiar with over the years: constant interruption by phone calls always given priority, unabashed denunciation of other tenants, and an unself-conscious, blustering grandiosity.

Over the years, my relationship to the landlord has sometimes verged on the psychotic. The landlord seems to take pleasure in getting my goat, and increasingly I have been unable to restrain myself. A recurring topic was the "roommate" in our neighbor's apartment, who, we tenants concluded, was dealing drugs. The landlord was eager to get our neighbor out, although not because of this particular nuisance. When a rent-controlled apartment is vacated, the law allows the rent to float to market, in this case at least three thousand dollars more than our neighbor was paying. The landlord's venality (or business acumen, depending on your point of view) led him to try to recruit me to testify in court to the effect that our neighbor did not really live in the apartment. As an inducement, he offered to paint the hallways (which, at that point, had not been painted in over a decade), repair the floors, and fix up the graffiti-streaked vestibule.

Given how depressing it can be to return to this filthy environment, there was something tempting about the offer. But tenant solidarity, a kind of Anne Frank refusal to rat out a neighbor, and the desire that the landlord get no benefit were far stronger forces. I told him that I did not trust him to do repairs (it is an incredible ordeal to get anything fixed in Annabel Lee), but that were he to renovate the public areas of the building first, I would regard it as an act of good faith and would reconsider his request at such time as the building has been put into reasonable shape. Lou saw right through this.

Although such a crude con would never fly, it did provide me with another opportunity to tacitly insult the landlord for his self-ishness and lack of civic demeanor. I get on this particular high horse with some frequency. I lecture him about the historic character of the neighborhood and the need for everyone to do his part to make the block beautiful. I ask him how he managed not to acquire any sense of public responsibility in law school. I point to other buildings on the block that are kept in clean and decent order. He finds me ridiculous.

This time, I pressed my case and asked, in a mildly provocative manner, why he had been unable to break the lease of someone engaged in an illegal sublet. I suggested that my theory was that he must be covering up the fact that he is in cahoots in the drug trade. It turned out that he had been prevented from recovering the apartment because Carl had claimed that the dealer and his prior subtenants were his roommates (his own gaming of the legal system), but there was the imputation that something darker was afoot. What it might have been I have no idea. Most likely, nothing.

The situation upstairs grew worse and worse until the offstage Carl was finally forced to call the police. I arrived home one day to find the "roommate"—who was not simply dealing but apparently manufacturing drugs—being led away in handcuffs. One would have thought that the first law of drug dealing would be to make yourself as inconspicuous as possible. His flamboyantly annoying behavior was his undoing, and he was soon replaced by two well-mannered young women, Carl's new "roommates."

Our most violent encounter came eight years ago. At the time, I was teaching in Vienna and commuting once a month. After my first big extended illness, I decided to resign the job, which had become both tiresome and very tiring. I was walking down the stairs, suitcase in hand, on my way to fly over on what was to be my last trip, the first I had made since getting better. It was a lovely spring day, and I was in a fine mood. In the vestibule, I met Rose. I mentioned I was traveling to Vienna, and she—a European refugee—and I chatted about the charms of the city, especially the excellent pastries to be had at Demel, the legendary café. It was rare to have such a remarkably civil encounter, and I left with the thought that such intercourse might continue to be possible in the future.

On my return, however, I found a legal notice, the result of the landlord's having reported to the rent stabilization authorities that I had offshore income which he suspected I was not reporting on my taxes. His motive was simple. Under the rent stabilization regulations, when a rent has risen above the level of two thousand dollars a month (which ours had), a means test can be applied to tenants. Any making more than $175,000 a year for two consecutive years lose the rent protection, and the price rises to the market rate. Hearing about my job in Vienna, the landlord reasoned that there was a possibility that Joan's salary, my salary, and my earnings from my architectural office (a negative number for years) exceeded the cap.

I simply understood him to be accusing me of a felony: tax evasion. Being scrupulous about such matters and having paid taxes at the virtually confiscatory Austrian rates for years (which, as they are deductible from U.S. taxes, I would have been a fool not to report), I was totally enraged. Joan was also very angry at the sneaky way a pleasant conversation had become an opportunity to impugn our integrity, so we went downstairs to confront the two of them.

The landlord has learned to play me well. I immediately fell into my high ethical mode, and his smug response only further enraged me. He goaded me on by saying that if I was so angry, he'd clearly touched a nerve—further proof that he was right. I responded that how dare a slimeball like him accuse solid citizens like us of being crooks. He reverted to his legalistic formulations, pronouncing that he was well within his rights to do so, and again suggested that my anger was prima facie evidence that he was correct. I turned to Rose to tell her how awful she was to have converted a civil conversation into yet another attempt to screw a tenant. At this point the landlord was laughing hard at my out-of-control, ineffectual anger.

I was now screaming with rage and decided to let loose with what I thought was the most insulting thing I could say: "People like you give anti-Semitism a good name!" My attempt at casting the landlord as Shylock, however, had not the slightest effect, and in the face of his continuing laughter I left, slamming the door behind me, and went to sit on the stoop to calm down. Joan, who'd stayed behind to confront the landlord's ridicule, suddenly swept all the papers from his desk onto the floor. This shocking act by someone known for her quiet demeanor silenced him immediately. After telling her that he thought such behavior beyond the limit, Joan told him that we felt the same. He wondered then how I dared impugn his religion, and Joan told him that it was precisely because I held my co-religionists to a higher ethical standard that I was so enraged. She left and joined me on the stoop. We eventually replied to the rent authorities that our income was below the limit and that we felt this episode to be another example of the landlord's ongoing harassment. That was the end of it. For a while.

Smaller incidents abound. One day, fed up with the disgusting condition of the stair hall, I posted a letter to the landlord asking that it be cleaned and painted and suggested that, should he fail to do this within some reasonable period, I intended to paint it myself. I proposed to the rest of the tenants that anyone interested might think about joining in the Tom Sawyer–esque fun or at least making a contribution toward the paint. None of the neighbors took this very seriously. Lou did. He responded by threatening to take me to court. This was almost temptingly comical enough to prompt me to begin painting at once, as I could not imagine a judge who wouldn't castigate him for the frivolity of such a suit. A lawyer friend told me that I was actually likely to lose the case, since a tenant has no right to interfere in what was clearly the landlord's space.

Thanks to Joan, though, we have made a little progress. After the leaks in our ceiling dramatically increased in number and every rain brought fallen plaster, puddles on the floor, streaks down the walls, and the ruination of a particularly prized piece of furniture, Joan filed a complaint with the rent board and the Buildings Department, which duly dispatched inspectors, who found that the roof was indeed leaking egregiously and, moreover, that our window frames were dangerously rotten. The landlord was ordered to perform repairs to both and given a deadline, and we were granted a small but appreciable reduction in rent until the repairs were performed. The day before the legal deadline, roofers appeared and began the work.

These battles are endless. Perhaps ten years ago, the antique doorbell-and-ring-back system in the building had its last gasp. At this point we were paying the highest rent in the building (not to mention living on the top floor, which entailed the most inconvenience going down to let visitors in or to fetch postal deliveries taken back to the branch, a round-trip walk of twenty-four blocks), and the landlord obviously felt a vague sense of differential obligation to us. So, rather than shelling out to replace the defunct system, he tried to fix only *our* bell. It rapidly proved impossible to repair just a portion of the failed wiring, so he strung a wire out one of our rotting living room windows down the front of the building to the vestibule, where he affixed a crude bell. The power for the system was provided by a battery that sat on our windowsill. There was no means of letting someone in other than by either going downstairs or opening a window and throwing the key down in a sock.

Of course, the system didn't work: the wire blew away, and the leads became detached from the buzzer almost immediately. Dozens of angry phone calls and letters ensued, over a period of many months. Finally, after a year of such complaints, the landlord had the system repaired, although it has now—for the zillionth time—reverted to a state of differential dysfunction, working for some apartments and not for others. A similar battle was waged over the landlord's flat refusal to permit the installation of television cable in the building, which went on for years (despite Joan's zinger to Lou that he would probably have refused telephone service back in the day) and continued, after that victory was finally won, with his lengthy obstruction of efforts to upgrade the system to digital. Installers at various levels of the cable company chain of command roll their eyes and gaze in stunned perplexity at a landlord's claims not to know where the wires enter the building or where they run.

While Lou and Rose are probably extreme cases, their behavior is consistent with a structure that governs their ability to make money from all of us. What I regard as their lowest-common-denominator attitude toward us and their minimal approach to maintaining the buildings is shaped by the letter of the law and an asymptomatic relationship to it. Lou and Rose appear as almost parodic exemplars of what used to be called "bourgeois morality." Their seeming disregard for their tenants is simply a translation of business ethics into social behavior, while our expectation that they will treat us with kindness or generosity or that they will take an interest in the larger life of the neighborhood reflects our insistence on speaking to them in an essentially incompatible language, one that does not figure in the discourse of contracts and legal obligations.

We come down hard on Lou and Rose because they are the human faces of a system dedicated to self-interest. But, really, they are small-fry and take the heat for much larger operators who function more anonymously. After twenty-five years, we see them more as difficult relations than as emblems of the depravities of capital. Real estate is New York's leading economic enterprise. Landlords are merely foot soldiers in the defense of the primacy of property values, of a view that sees every site and building in terms of its extractive potential. The business model of governance, fervently embraced by our billionaire mayor, keeps its eye on the bottom line, thereby guaranteeing that the "right people" make money.

Increasingly, the state is willing to deploy its most violent environmental power—condemnation—on behalf of private development and to bypass deliberative review. While politicians bemoan the culture of welfare and cut back its benefits, they offer enormous handouts to needy corporations, subsidizing the private office market through either tax relief or bulk bonuses and simultaneously displacing responsibility for the public realm onto private actors. It is a system that has turned Manhattan into a frenzied development zone, driven the average price of an apartment into the stratosphere, and produced the widest income gap—and the smallest middle class—in history.

By contrast, the kind of landlord-tenant drama we enact with Lou and Rose, featuring their ability to eke out small sums from us and our corresponding efforts to extract small repairs from them, is probably the eternal price of bohemia, of the right of a marginal, if glorified, part of the population to enjoy its lifestyle in the heart of the city. And we willingly, complainingly, play our part.

THE
STOOP

Beyond the front door lies the stoop, which performs a variety of social functions. First, it is a fine, filtering, intermediate space, modulating the transition from the public life of the street to the private life of the building. The short ascent offers a sense of arrival that proceeds through two ritual stages: the vestibule—home of mailboxes and buzzers—and the front door, scene of the special transactions of arrival, the fumbling for keys, the first glimpse of the bills, the shifting of packages from one arm to another to facilitate the key-in-lock and push to the door. Because of the brief enforced pause, and because everyone in the building must repeat the same process coming and going, the stoop is also the site of many holdings of the door, vettings of strangers reading the bell, schmoozings with neighbors, sidelong glances at kids, tourists, and homeless people. Our stoop is particularly inviting to the homeless as the vestibule at the top—unlike most of the others on the block—has only a single inner door and provides an accessible sheltered space.

Along with being a meeting place, the stoop is a space of spectatorship. A street lined with stoops is a kind of lateral stadium, ideal for viewing the passing parade, whether formal ones like the giant Gay Pride and Halloween Parades (until their route was changed a few years ago) or the more informal quotidian version. Hanging out on the stoop allows the sitter to observe the dance (Jane Jacobs's ballet) of daily activity, to notice what is out of the ordinary, to provide the kind of public presence that prompts neighborly behavior—cleaning up dog poop, greeting people, taking care of the beleaguered plants and trees, and just generally fixing memory on the street. We Annabel Lee tenants certainly think we have first claim to our stoop, especially during parades when competition for seats can be fierce. Our danders rise when we find people drinking or sleeping on the stoop or when our way is blocked by rows of smoking kids or when cell-phone talkers seem oblivious to the fact that the stoop is not exactly public space.

Such territoriality is often reinforced by architectural means. The building next to ours—a co-op—has a cast-iron fence at street level with a latched gate at the bottom of the stairs. Although this gate is never locked, it does clearly extend the building's claims on privacy down to the sidewalk. That building also has an inner and outer door in its vestibule—both keyed—which turns it into a tiny lobby, preventing strangers from camping out and providing a more weatherproof environment for getting the mail. It also prevents the graffiti that our vestibule invites, not simply by its accessibility, but by its shabbiness and, ironically, by the cruel, overbearing lighting provided by a bright yellow sodium lamp, more suitable to a prison yard than a quiet street.

Joan and I once sublet an apartment on the Upper West Side from my uncle Ralph, in a place called Pomander Walk (named after a Broadway play that had been a hit at the time). This was a mews of tiny apartments constructed in the 1920s and designed to look sweetly "Dickensian." Reached at either end through an unlocked gate and up a long flight of stairs, it was unbelievably charming and very private, unknown even to many longtime neighborhood residents and architectural aficionados. Each of the little row houses (containing two apartments) had its own stoop, and the collection of these stoops formed the armature for a lovely summertime social ritual, organized by a group of elderly widows who were long-term tenants.

This was nothing less than a floating cocktail party that made a circuit of stoops and often lasted well into the night. After passing these gatherings (and receiving greetings that grew increasingly cheerful as the evening wore on) for a few weeks, we decided we should make an appearance. For our inauguration into the society of stoop sundowners, we prepared a large tray of cucumber sandwiches, a treat to which we had become greatly attached.

Unfortunately, we were not yet sufficiently knowledgeable about the Pomander Walk parties and arrived at 5:00 p.m. on a day when there wasn't one. We walked up and down the mews looking for some sign of festivities and finally rang the bell of Mrs. Runstein, their organizer.

We ate a few sandwiches in her orientalist living room—shades of Maxime Du Camp—thick with carpets, divans, and hammered brass, took the rest home for dinner, and prepared to try again later in the week. Of course, we became the talk of the Walk, and our failed effort was seen as a fine piece of neighborliness. It was a pleasure to be the butt of ongoing jokes about wandering with our tray in search of conviviality. The intimate society of the Walk was surely a product both of the extremely congenial physical circumstances that enabled this ritual and of the presence of a tight-knit community of long standing. Such settings are quintessentially urban, possible only in an environment that blurs the line between public and private space by providing a useful, tractable variety of intermediate conditions. The mews and the stoop are special because they are neither the public sidewalk nor the private yard but something in between. The planning of the city must take the creation and protection of such places of blurry proprietorship very seriously.

The mews house is a rarity in New York (there are several rows in the Village, including one nearby that formerly housed stables), but the type is superb. I've long been especially enamored of the so-called *longtang* houses found in Shanghai and other Chinese cities. These are complexes of two- and three-story row houses on networks of pedestrian lanes, entered off major streets. Not only are they islands of calm; they are brilliant social condensers where a walk through can find islands of kids at play, old folks clacking mahjongg counters, potted plants on the sidewalk, birdcages and drying fish hanging from the eaves. The type originated in the nineteenth century as a composite of European and Chinese styles and can be found in a wide variety of architectural expressions. Unfortunately, they now tend to be both overcrowded and centrally located and are being demolished at a tragic clip. Indeed, I can remember many trips with Chinese friends to see specially prized examples only to find holes in the ground and construction cranes. "Ah, but it was here last week!"

That the type doesn't appear in New York is the product of the prohibitive economics of scale, the hegemony of road traffic in figuring architectural morphologies, a lack of a vibrant tradition of such building, and the precedence of other spatial prototypes. To introduce them now in our neighborhood would be to reinforce the kind of uneven development that makes the Village so great but would flaunt the ethos of the maxed-out building envelope. And sites of suitable scale for anything but the most miniature versions have ceased to be available. But the type is brilliant and desperately needs to be reborn as part of the global housing repertoire. It might still have a life in New York as part of a densifying retrofit of more loosely developed parts of the city.

Although both Joan and I are children of the suburbs, neither of us has lived in one since we left home to go to college, and both of us now think of them as nightmarish, estranged from urban sociability and too dependent on cars and commuting, something for which we have no taste. We did do a brief stint in suburbia while I was teaching in Austin, Texas, where we lived in a motel-like complex on the edge of town. We both remember the daily sense of amazement and the twinge of disorientation produced by the unmediated entry to our "unit." We simply parked the rent-a-car in the space opposite the door, turned the key in the lock, and suddenly found ourselves standing in the living room. We never grew accustomed to the missing decompression of the sequential entry up the front stairs, through the vestibule, up the inner stairs, and into the hallway of the apartment.

For years, Annabel Lee's stoop was the special territory of our neighbor Jane. Jane lived in the smallest apartment in the building, at the back of the first floor, a space with little light and no view. As soon as it was warm enough, she set up her folding chair on the stoop, from which vantage point she read, did crossword puzzles, kept an eye on comings and goings in the building and on the block, and participated in a very rich social life. As one of the block's senior citizens, she knew everyone—including children and dogs—and was constantly engaged in conversations with passersby, often sharing her encyclopedic and up-to-date knowledge of block matters. She kept a supply of dog biscuits on hand, and when she sat out, one always saw leashes being tugged by dogs hastening toward the reliable treat.

Jane was the quintessential public citizen (or "public character" in the Jacobs locution). She not only lived in and was enlivened by the urban medium; she was essential for the perpetuation of our urbanity. Through her crucial role as collector and transmitter of memory, her key position in a network of local politics and cooperation, she became our symbol of interchange, kindness, and congeniality. She was an active presence at the community garden by the library down the street. She paid scrupulous attention to the health of the street trees and plantings on the block. She once—her most legendary act—propelled herself from her chair to thwart a mugging across the street. Jane died in the course of a beloved part of her urban ritual, felled by a heart attack on her way to the farmers' market in Union Square.

One beautiful day, I was sitting opposite Jane's spot on the stoop when I noticed two guys walking down the street in the parking lane. As they passed Wilson's tree, the bottom of which Jane had strung with a cat's cradle of string to protect the flowers from dogs and litter, one of them reached down and snatched a piece of paper that had been thrown on top of the marigolds. I saw then that he was carrying a paper shopping bag into which he put the scrap and watched as he went to the next tree down the block and did the same.

I find such acts deeply moving. Indeed, it is the fabric of such small behaviors that makes urban life possible, even beautiful, and that saves us from the Hobbesian jungle that for so long has been the preferred national metaphor for urban life. In his *Paths in Utopia*, Martin Buber wrote, "I sometimes think that every touch of

helpful neighbourliness in the apartment-house, every wave of
warmer comradeship . . . [is] an addition to the world's community-
content." Yes, indeed.

We've all encountered that little message in the airplane bathroom: "As a courtesy to the next passenger, please use your towel to
wipe the sink." Airplanes are interesting hothouses of civic behavior. Cramped and homogenized, preventing you from leaving your
seat to go to the bathroom without disrupting the comfort of your
neighbor, trapping you in immobility with no wiggle room, air travel
is possible only because of an implicit compact of good behavior.
The forms of such neighborliness are calculated minutely—in
inches—in an environment that reduces the issues of public and
private—of neighborliness—to nearly degree zero in the contest
for arm or leg space, in the niceties of sleeping next to strangers, in
the imperatives of keeping the place neat, never mind being on
dogged guard against row mates with incendiary shoes.

A revelatory moment for me came several years ago when I
was standing in an aircraft lavatory. I'd finished washing my hands
and used the towel to wipe the stainless steel sink. I kept wiping
until all spots were gone from both the sink and the countertop
and then went on to the mirror. Suddenly I found myself on the
floor, wiping it clean with a fresh towel. With a jolt, I realized that
I was crouched in the bathroom of a 767, a paper towel in my hand,
washing the floor, and wondered whether I had slipped into a neu-
rosis deeper than usual. I do not think this act was purely unselfish,
since my assiduousness was not simply a service to the next passenger but an address to the previous, inconsiderate one, even
though it would go unseen and unappreciated.

The aircraft lavatory is a miniature behaviorist laboratory, a
stimulus-response setting of rich precision. There are several clear
incitements to clean: the little sign asking you to, the condition of
the lavatory, one's own sense of community with other travelers,

native altruism, and, of course, the possibility that one will be directly implicated in the dirtiness of the lavatory by the next user, even if it's not your fault. In general, the system works. It can be overwhelmed by overcrowding, and the lavatories at the end of a trip on a child-filled jumbo jet often approach the toxic, but people do very often behave thoughtfully.

But to me the most astonishing piece of such collective good behavior is the virtually universal compliance of New Yorkers with the "pooper-scooper" law. Although New York City has had a "curb your dog" law on the books since 1938, it was much observed in the breach and, even when obeyed, still yielded stinking piles in the street. In 1978, the state enacted the Canine Waste Law, requiring people in all cities of over 400,000 in population to clean up after their dogs. While the health and aesthetic problems of this form of pollution were widely acknowledged, there were objections to the legislation, including claims that because it was a state law, it violated the principle of municipal home rule. On hearing of the law, one dog owner said she planned to "read Thoreau to [her] cocker spaniel and teach her civil disobedience." (In the run-up to the law, I myself had undertaken the "Poop Press Project," which had entailed fixing a star-shaped cookie mold to the end of a stick to transform the noisome waste into street art, an attempt only intermittently effective.)

The law was also unsuccessfully challenged for its constitutionality in a suit by Orthodox Jewish plaintiffs who claimed it violated their freedom of religion because they were forbidden to pick up litter on the Sabbath. In rejecting this claim, the court commented: "Plaintiffs' theory is that a religious individual may litter on the Sabbath, but cannot be compelled to pick up his litter. If it is permissible to walk one's dog on the Sabbath, it is permissible not to defile the streets. Works of necessity are permitted. . . . Since cleanliness is next to godliness, it is doubtful whether an all-seeing and benevolent deity would approve the desecration of public places in the name of orthodoxy." Although I love dogs, I can't suppress an involuntary shudder at the sight of some well-turned-out walker, her hand wrapped in a plastic bag, at the ready to pick up a steamy pile. This only increases my sense of admiration and gratitude.

The marvel of it all is that this cooperation is at heart the product not of a police crackdown but of simple compliance with a reasonable statute, very different from, say, Singapore, where the scrupulous cleanliness of the streets is achieved via overdone restrictions and absurdly cruel punishments. At some level, though, I do understand Uncle Harry's jeremiad against chewing gum—forbidden, until recently, and now regulated like a dangerous drug. Each sticky blot on the sidewalk or the subway platform seems to me not simply disgusting but a sad commentary on the solidarity and sense of order of the citizenry.

The key to a democratic urban citizenship is that cooperative behavior is elective. We obey the law because we shape it. Here coercion, the hallmark of authoritarian systems, is distinguished from persuasion, the democratic medium for producing assent. Yet this distinction is itself problematic as democracy, too, can tyrannize not only by commanding the unwilling compliance of dissenters but by privatizing exclusivities. The huge number of "homeowner associations" that characterize the suburbs—and the co-op boards that are ubiquitous in New York—all function via various restrictive covenants designed to coerce narrowly described forms of "good" behavior (no purple houses!) or—more sinisterly—to ensure that only the right people have access to these communities: no blacks, no "theater people," and so on.

It's often observed that Disneyland is an environment in which people behave well, and it is remarkably clean given the very large numbers of visitors it attracts. It's further noted that this high level of cleanliness is largely the result of visitor restraint, not of extraordinary efforts on the part of staff. At Disneyland, then, there appears to be an implicit compact among visitors to be on their "best behavior." Part of this is surely inspired by the sight of an environment that is fundamentally orderly, a place that's already clean, scrubbed immaculate each night. This suggests to visitors that it's possible for the place to *be* clean, that a personal contribution—placing that ice-cream wrapper in a trash bin—will have an immediately measurable effect. Unlike voting—the primal image of which is also placing a piece of paper into a public receptacle—no abstraction is required here. A failure to vote is personally invisible, while the failure to dispose of an ice-cream wrapper opens the offender to public disapproval.

The beach is also a place where there's clearly a relationship between our pleasure in an environment and our willingness to engage and defend it, and I have fond memories of holidays spent over the years in places like Fire Island, Martha's Vineyard, the Jersey shore, and Cape Cod. This affection springs from the beauty of the beach, from the space of leisure, and from the way in which everyday transactions are transformed by such environments. Because beaches are considered "special" (like Disneyland), behavior there also becomes special, part of a repertoire of behaviors reserved for places such as churches, libraries, and concert halls. As at these, courtesy at the beach seems to be more elaborate and more common. Shopkeepers advance tiny amounts of credit, and shoppers make a show of paying back the small change on the following day. Doors are left unlocked. Watching kids in the water becomes the shared responsibility of everyone. People chat more freely with strangers, feel greater trust.

One reason for this is the elective character of the assembled, "intentional" community: we seldom come closer to utopia than when at the beach (reflected in the immortal slogan of May 1968, "Beneath the pavement, the beach"). Because vacationers have made a deliberate, short-term decision to come to this place, there's a clear commonality of taste and interest, a homogeneity of assumptions about the basic character and purpose of the environment. Certainly, one possible reading of this outline of common interests is that it represents the shared assumptions of class, including its exclusionary component. But class can be read in a number of ways, not all pejorative. Although a city neighborhood should be open to different economic and social classes, the citizens of a neighborhood are united in the particularity of their interests, in the idea that the local has an identity. They can legitimately be said to share a set of class interests or, more precisely, a class of interests.

One might even speak of a kind of environmental or place-based concept of class, where shared interest is at least partially defined by physical character. If neighborhoods ever become truly elective and inclusionary, the reasons that they will be chosen will be, first of all, the character of life they offer. This will include both the kinds of people and activities that the neighborhood supports and the physiognomy of the place. It seems entirely legitimate to speak of a class of people who prefer a village atmosphere, a class that likes the anonymous hive of high-rises, another that prefers the bufferings of suburban space. Preference is an amalgam of convenience, conviviality, commonality, and taste, and good cities and neighborhoods recognize and support communities of difference. No platonic preference—including Jane Jacobs's roistering street—can hope to comprehend the real limits of diversity, those who *like* living in the dark or the woods or facing a blank wall. Desire is never a defect.

Another reason for the special behavior at Disneyland and Fire Island is that we see such places not simply as different but as *better*. Every neighborhood is special in that it is—by definition—different from every other neighborhood. But in the case of the vacation spot, there's an implicit qualitative valence, the idea that one gets away to a place where things are simply superior. Disneyland is so appealing to so many people not only because of the character of its literal amusements, the rides and parades and costumes, but because it offers—like Fire Island—a proposition about many of the problems that vex us in "normal" life. In this sense, the virtue of Disneyland is not that it provides respite and enjoyment, nor even that it derives so many of its pleasures—pedestrianism, street performers, parades, human scale, and so on—from the urban repertoire. Rather, it is the fundamental absence of choice that results from its distilling out everything that might upset the narrowly fixed behaviors it permits.

Troubles with the behavior or with the disquieting nonconformity of the other in Disneyland (and in cities) are addressed by a variety of filters: admission expense, appearance codes, a high degree of surveillance, a preponderance of families, and a dedication to pleasure. Disney is also a major producer of a very particular kind of entertainment, wrapped up in routines of spectatorship and involving semipuritanical restrictions (no sex, alcohol, bad language, and so forth). The historic Disney discourse—the pleasurable economies of life in a cartoon—pervades the Disneyland experience like a kind of constitution. It offers an enjoyable passivity, a place where one's responsibilities are very small—don't litter, don't cut in line—and where the anxieties of genuinely political participation are held at bay. It reformats the space of daily life as a place to spend, ratcheting up our narcotic alienation.

But Disneyland would not have become a huge success if it were simply a vehicle for the mass marketing of a certain strain of semiparticipatory show business. The genius of Disneyland—as many observers have noted—lies in its urbanism. As a nation, we are afflicted with the idea that many of the pleasures, and much of the collective purposiveness, of urban life have disappeared. Although it presents itself initially in the guise of a small town, Disneyland has a density that is unachieved in any but our largest cities. (To be sure, this is true only during its hours of operation, as nobody actually lives there and this nightly disappearance of population is part of the magic of the Magic Kingdom.)

Disneyland directly addresses many of the issues that are most pressing to city dwellers. It is a safe place, in the sense both that it is virtually free from crime and that it filters out, by price and convention, people who might prove threatening. It is a place where infrastructure is in tip-top shape, where everything that is meant to work, works. It is scrupulously clean and relentlessly orderly. And it is suffused by a utopian ethos, a carefully cultivated self-representation as an ideal community. This is signaled both by the foregrounding of the image of a fictitious but beloved small-town America and by a total dedication to providing universal happiness based on complete—and almost completely passive—leisure, a world without work.

The critique that so much contemporary urbanism is being "Disneyfied" reflects something very real, not least the co-optation of the utopian ideal by commercial enterprise and the relegation of citizenship to consumption. Here, the sanctioned forms of entertainment are produced by giant corporations—Disneyland being a model for a style of globalization that is rapidly homogenizing the planet—by creating a world culture of sealed environments, Hollywood movies, McDonald's, Coca-Cola, Walmart, and all the rest of the infrastructure of multinational capital. There is no doubt that locality is increasingly undermined by these influences, that mom-and-pop stores are being crushed by chains, that accumulations of spatial character are being blown away by the cruel imperatives of development and global finance. Dubai is the world made Disney.

Disneyland is also the model for the loss of rights that comes with this territory, a place dependent on too much policing, too few genuine choices, too much passivity, and too much differential concentration of power and privilege in private hands. Even the Village suffers from these symptoms. Local businesses and long-time residents are being forced out by rising prices and replaced by chain stores and yuppies. And the public-private model of public service is creating its own special unevenness and distortion. Eighth Street, a longtime commercial hub of the Village and once a scene of diverse retail activity, has come to be dominated by low-price shoe stores, all selling very similar merchandise, largely aimed at non-neighborhood shoppers. Of late, though, these stores have fallen on hard times (unable to compete with the national chains that have opened on Broadway and the Ladies' Mile).

Several years ago, in an effort to enhance the fortunes of Eighth Street, local merchants formed a Business Improvement District (BID). BIDs—which have proliferated in the city—are self-taxing private organizations that provide "public" services which, in the case of Eighth Street, include repairs to the sidewalks, tree planting, new streetlamps and furniture, and a variety of other improvements. The BID also employs a cadre of employees—dressed in red jumpsuits—to sweep the sidewalks and empty trash receptacles. While no one questions the benefits of these measures, and while our BID does not seem to have engaged in the same level of harassment and abuse of homeless people that the BID operating around Grand Central Station notoriously has, it nevertheless represents a decline in the public realm.

BIDs and many other private organizations focused on civic improvements—like the Central Park Conservancy—are strongly concentrated in areas of prosperity, where businesses have the margin (and self-interest) to permit such forms of voluntary self-taxation. While it can be argued that Central Park is the common resource of all New York's citizens, it is also true that it is flanked by some of the most expensive real estate in the city, property that draws much of its value from proximity to the park. The issue here is not charity, nor local efforts to improve local environments, but rather an uneven benefit of civic improvement, illustrated by inattention to the shopping streets in poorer neighborhoods and the relative lack of investment in the city's other parks. Where government retreats from its role as equalizer, from its special obligation to the neediest, and acts in a way that enhances inequality, it creates yet another form of preferential zoning.

America is often called, and is, a "public-private partnership," and democracy means constant work to address the meaning and effects of this balance. Nowadays, the construct is used to justify a contraction of the public side of the deal and to advance the empowerment not of our individual privacy but of the rights of big money. Whenever I hear the phrase, I reach for my revolver.

THE
BLOCK

At the bottom of the front stairs, I confront my first choice of the day: left or right. Over the past twenty-four years—since I've had a studio within walking distance—I have most often chosen the left, although both directions have their pleasures and liabilities and there is no particular economy of distance in either. A right turn does take me by the corner newsstand, where I enjoy the friendly interchange with the Pakistani newsdealer who sells me my *Times*, and leads to a route through the West Village, with its quaint streets and eccentric geometry. The disadvantage is that this phase of the walk only gets me so far and I am, eventually, obliged to complete the trip on either Seventh Avenue or Hudson Street, both of which are filled with traffic and neither of which is particularly attractive.

A left turn opens a more varied and interesting set of choices, a more porous street frontage, and—despite the orthogonality of a grid in the 1811 alignment—more opportunities for bobbing and weaving. It also allows a stop in what has been, for decades, a favorite café that attracts a cadre of regulars of which I have been a minor member. The routes that open up with a left turn bring me past many places—shops, parks, corners, buildings where friends live—that mark the culture of local citizenship, allow the calibration of change, and offer opportunities to describe and refine the network of human relationships that anchor me in place.

Navigating the grid on my way downtown involves a continuous series of choices, governed by a fluctuating compound of desires: speed and efficiency, variety, particular points of interest, sunny side versus shady side, and more. I tend to conceptualize my walk as an aerial navigation, as a sequence of waypoints and vectors.

Thus, a quiet block might offer the opportunity to take a long, efficient diagonal down the middle of the street, although this can be frustrated by cars parked too tightly along the curb. Seasons are important too, and summer walks are highly influenced by a decision matrix that weighs the shadier east side against the mitigating presence of street trees and the possibly greater interest of events on the west.

Inescapably, the walk takes on a narrative quality. Walking is a natural armature for thinking sequentially. It also has a historic relationship to mental organization that ranges from the Peripatetics, to the philosophers of Kyoto, to the clockwork circuit of Immanuel Kant, to the sublimities of the English Romantics and their passages through nature. Walking, considered as something more than simple movement from place to place, puts one in mind of previous walkers. From time to time, I think about Albert Speer in Spandau Prison, circling the yard, imagining a walk around the world to distract himself from the boredom of his situation and the memory of his crimes. Occasionally, I interpolate a recalled street for the one on which I'm walking: MacDougal Street does a credible evocation of the Rue Mouffetard in Paris, where I used to hang out when I briefly lived there.

Technology has dramatically accelerated the affinity between movement and the perceptual habits by which we assimilate experience. Much has been written about the revolutionary effect of cinema in constructing visual narratives of the everyday. One of film's early masterpieces—Dziga Vertov's *Man with the Movie Camera*—mesmerized audiences in 1929 by its depiction of the everyday activity of the modern city—dawn to dusk in Moscow—as the observer moved through its scenes. Vertov was polemical in asserting that film ("I am kino-eye, I am mechanical eye, I, a machine, show you the world as only I can see it") offered a perceptual revolution, revealing the world afresh, just as the microscope and the telescope had.

Among the innovations of cinema was montage, the capacity to create meaning via the studied juxtaposition of forms, places, movements, and events. *Man with the Movie Camera* is filled with associative cuts—blinking eyes and venetian blinds, washing hair and washing clothes, happy couple entering a municipal building to marry, sad couple to divorce—thereby mapping a rich repertoire of strategies for producing meaning via visual connections. The pioneer of the theory of montage was Vertov's contemporary Lev Kuleshov, the inventor of "creative geography," an editing technique by which various shots, taken at different times and different places, were combined to create a sequence that appeared to be temporally and spatially continuous. The classic example was a combination of shots of a man in Moscow walking up a flight of church steps that, when juxtaposed with stock footage of Washington, D.C., made him appear to be walking into the White House.

Cinematic creative geography is symptomatic of a complex of technologies and events that has radically remade both the way we read the city and the way the city is made. It is a bridge to the idea of psychogeography, the understanding of the gap between the mental map of the city each of us carries within us to organize our engagement with it and the physical map with its precise dimensional distributions and comprehensive recordings. It also anticipates the freedom of juxtaposition that an increasingly global culture imposes or allows. That a few blocks of MacDougal Street offer French, Turkish, Italian, Japanese, Thai, Chinese, Israeli, and vegetarian restaurants illustrates such cultural transmissibility. The Disney model, with its juxtapositions of ersatz versions of Rhine castles, American small towns, the Wild West, the pirate Caribbean, and our old friend, the city of the future, takes it to extremes, abandoning city-making as consensual accumulation in favor of the creative geography of juxtaposed simulacra from a narrow multinational repertoire.

Walking is not simply an occasion for observation but an analytic instrument. As a particular way of being in the city, strolling is more recent—the walk self-consciously detached from destination is another fruit of modernity. Walter Benjamin wrote extensively on a type already identified in the early nineteenth century, the *flâneur* or stroller, much inspired by his reading of Charles Baudelaire, the great poet of Paris transformed, the muse of the crowd, as well as by a huge literature that depicted a new kind of life in the streets. One of the reasons that this behavior was so strongly associated with Paris is that the city was itself in the throes of creating a new kind of street, the great boulevards being blasted through it by the legendary prefect of the Seine, Baron Haussmann. Although such systems of grand avenues—central to Baroque city planning—predated Haussmann (the L'Enfant plan for Washington, D.C., for example), the creation of the Paris boulevards coincided with a complex of phenomena that refigured the relationship of the social and the formal in the city.

The *flâneur* was a man (there was no such thing as a *flâneuse*, and much has been written about the troubled accession of women to their own right to the city—think only of the term "streetwalker") who was part of a crowd, whose walking was a product of leisure, who reflected in the idleness of his pursuit a degree of alienation (that most modern of psychic states), and who walked in order to observe. His observation took in both people and things, and one of the *flâneur*'s core pursuits was the appreciation of commodities and assessment of fashion (an activity that eventually opened up a ground for female participation in urban domestication: shopping). All of this was made possible by the anonymity of the crowd assembled on the newly enlarged sidewalks of Paris, an environment where goods and people were on widespread display—in boutiques, cafés, carriages, and streets, venues of the newly prosperous nineteenth-century bourgeoisie.

The practice of *flânerie* endures to this day both as part of our own perceptual equipment and in a more explicitly analytic mode. From the late 1950s into the 1970s an energetic, incisive, often zany group of activists operated, mainly in Paris, under the banner of "Situationism." The Situationists—and their leading theoretical light, Guy Debord (himself inspired by Henri Lefebvre and his seminal work on the social production of space and the practices and politics of everyday life)—advanced a critique of a society that presented itself as an accumulation of spectacles, a complex of simulations in which time and space were more and more commodified. The Situationists' Marxism was as much indebted to Groucho as to Karl, and they were renowned fomenters of festival-like events and pithy sloganeering. They were also practitioners of a special urban-analytic walking style, the *dérive*—the "drift"—which Debord described as "a technique of transient passage through varied ambiences. The *dérive* entails playful-constructive behavior and awareness of psychogeographical effects; which completely distinguishes it from the classical notions of the journey and the stroll."

"In a *dérive*," Debord deadpans, "one or more persons during a certain period drop their usual motives for movement and action, their relations, their work and leisure activities, and let themselves be drawn by the attractions of the terrain and the encounters they find there. The element of chance is less determinant than one might think: from the *dérive* point of view cities have a psychogeographical relief, with constant currents, fixed points and vortexes which strongly discourage entry into or exit from certain zones." Debord drolly formalized the practice of the *dérive*, suggesting it was best performed in small groups, that it should take about a day's time, and that prolonged rains (though not other forms of precipitation) made it virtually impossible.

Like so many observational techniques of artistic modernity, the *dérive* was an effort to draw on the resources of the unconscious to clarify elusive aspects of the everyday. Many contemporary avant-gardes have sought to liberate the creative potential of the unconscious by freeing it from its repression, and the *dérive* joins the free association of surrealism, the LSD of hippiedom, and cinematic montage as tactics for overcoming the fixity of received ideas of order and logic. And like psychoanalysis itself, the idea of psychogeography—for which the ironic *dérive* constitutes a "technical" instrument—represents a new discourse for the systematic study of its object, a new way of constructing it.

Another of Debord's great influences, the pioneering French urban sociologist Paul-Henry Chombart de Lauwe, observed in 1952 that "an urban neighborhood is determined not only by geographical and economic factors, but also by the image that its inhabitants and those of other neighborhoods have of it." A contemporary of Henri Lefebvre's, Chombart de Lauwe used a series of mappings to study the way in which individuals create their own versions of the city through the filter of their daily routines within it. Later, this idea of private geographies was influentially enlarged by the American urbanist Kevin Lynch, whose 1960 book, *The Image of the City*, asked a variety of people to verbally or visually map their own environments. Their maps produced radically different visions of place—enormous variations in order, distance, landmarks, mood, and meaning.

Walking received a similar reading from the French Jesuit philosopher Michel de Certeau, who included a chapter on "walking in the city" in his 1984 book, *The Practice of Everyday Life*. In the choices and preferences expressed in the way people navigate the city on foot, Certeau identified a set of "walking rhetorics," practices of the city's "*Wandersmänner*, whose bodies follow the thicks and thins of an urban 'text' they write without being able to read it. These practitioners make use of spaces that cannot be seen; their knowledge of them is as blind as that of lovers in each other's arms." In writing of "pedestrian speech acts," Certeau textualized walking and other everyday acts in a way that brought them into the larger theoretical ambit of the day, liberating literary and philosophical tools for urban application, and his book has long been a particular favorite among *bien-pensant* urbanists.

Each of us brings such a private map along and revises it every time we step out the door. These maps have consequences not just for our feelings about the city but for our literal ability to negotiate it. An article in the *Times* recently reported that according to brain scans taken of London "black cab" drivers—obliged to master a vast and complex network of streets—not only was their posterior hippocampus—the site where spatial representations are stored—larger than those of the general public, but the increase in size was proportional to the number of years the cabbie had been on the job. Unlike New York cabbies—many of them recent immigrants whose legendary ignorance of the city is often reflected in the mantra "Which way would you like me to go?"—would-be drivers in London are first obliged to undergo a rigorous training program called "the knowledge." One regularly sees trainees navigating the city on motorbikes, consulting plastic laminated flipbooks of maps, in order to imprint London's intricate streets on their memories.

In my own experience of Village life, I've discovered that virtually everyone I know—no matter how long they've lived here—is unable to give directions to the part of the West Village where the streets are irregular. Knowledge of this relatively small area would make up a minuscule portion of a London cabbie's repertoire and, theoretically at least, shouldn't pose an overwhelming challenge. My theory is that Villagers refuse perfect knowledge in order to retain the possibility of getting a little bit lost, one of the great pleasures of city life being the discovery of unknown places, with the chance of accidental encounters. Too much knowledge precludes this opportunity. We map the Village as more intricate, and larger, than it actually is to firm up its aura and extend its possibilities. We create it as a treasure hunt.

There are many cities more completely structured as labyrinths than New York, places where locational clarity is produced not geometrically but relationally, in terms of proximity to a landmark, a transit station, or a major route. London is one such place; Tokyo is another. No Londoner is without his or her *A to Z*, a book of maps with an alphabetical listing of streets keyed to a superimposed grid. In Tokyo, it is not unusual to be e-mailed a map on the occasion of a visit, showing the route from a nearby train station. The proliferation of GPS devices in cars unravels the inscrutabilities of navigation by issuing real-time prompts. But GPS—as well as the more primitive MapQuest—is predicated on the idea of a single, most efficient route and has the sinister side effect of letting others know just where you are so that you are never lost to the authorities.

Describing his childhood in Berlin, Walter Benjamin wrote, "Not to find one's way around a city does not mean much, but to lose one's way in a city, as one loses one's way in a forest, requires some schooling." The *dérive*, by putting progress through the city into a state of constant indeterminacy, represents a schooled "style" of being lost. It is related to the Villager always being a few streets short of a full picture, a way of being open to, and seeking, surprises and accidents, of being sensitized to the city's power to offer unexpected pleasures. Benjamin's statement draws on a hoary analogy between the city and nature, a comparison implicit in his famous description of the *flâneur* as a "botanist of the pavement." But nature is not all gardens and stately groves. The "concrete jungle" carries a less benign connotation, a place where every accident is an unhappy one and getting lost can be frightening. (David Lynch's work is filled with a strange anxiety concerning getting lost.)

The modern city produces its own style of getting lost, rooted in its special form of alienation. Here, the crowd, while it can be protective, is also a medium for both erasing individuality and homogenizing experience, for making us disappear. The industrial city has replaced old paradigms of spatial confusion—the maze or the labyrinth—with an endless sea of regularity, a place where all the streets and buildings look the same. Such is the standard complaint about modernist planning, that it's impossible to distinguish one apartment block from another; the environment simply repeats itself over and over and over. I've heard this in Shanghai, Havana, and New York, and it comes in several variations, including the hard form of the penitential project and the softer suburban version, split-levels without end. Today's favored dystopia is global, the same skyscrapers and Starbucks in Abu Dhabi, Kuala Lumpur, and London, the same suburbs in Orange County, Almaty, and Beijing.

Nowhere is this ideological geometry better embodied than in the domination of the right-angled grid as a means of spatial organization. Founded in the triple axes of Euclidean geometry, the grid is a supremely useful means of measure, a powerful descriptor of a world negotiated via increments of property, and a symbol of "rationality" itself. It is the medium by which virtually every city in America is organized and, indeed, the way in which the country itself is ordered via the famous continental grid imposed on the entirety of the western extension of the United States by Thomas Jefferson. This continental grid, perhaps the greatest piece of land art of all time, is visible with striking and relentless clarity from the air for thousands of miles.

Whatever its nominal Cartesian rationality, the grid is also a pattern of colonial transformation that, not uncoincidentally, was used by conquerors for millennia. In the United States, it has been the means for introducing the idea of private property, for subduing and subverting alien populations and their unpossessed landscapes. It was also the medium of the Spanish colonizers (and their famous Laws of the Indies), for whom the cruciform datum of the missions had additional import. It surely befuddled the Indians, who were slow to cotton on to the implications of such ownership.

The 1811 system of blocks and lots grew from an early vision of what we would now call "development," an efficient organization of logically sized properties, scaled to the prevalent architecture of the time. This architecture assumed that the size of buildings was to be relatively small and that some attached land would be used to provide small agricultural plots, access to sun and air, a buffer from neighbors, and a miniaturized "estate" for the owner. The main issue of the gridded block, however, is the result of its universality: the idea that it was to be the instrument by which nature was tamed, ordered, and made useful to the needs of human settlement. The grid was simply laid over existing topography, which either was obliterated—as in much of Manhattan (a name some suggest is derived from the Algonquin for "island of hills")—or fought back at the price of great inconvenience. Compare, for example, the contour-hugging layout of an Italian hill town with the San Francisco grid. The latter was platted over hilly terrain without the slightest reference to it, producing the sometimes charming, sometimes absurd exigencies of a system of circulation that can seriously compromise accessibility for any but the brave or the athletic.

Despite being oriented to the cardinal points, the Cartesian grid has very little functional connection to that most important feature of planetary life: the sun. By establishing a literal and conceptual parity among the four sides of the block irrespective of the climate or latitude, the grid creates four very different conditions for buildings that line the blocks it creates. In any given location, the preferred orientation optimizes control of solar access, maximizing (or minimizing) daylight over the course of the day. The situation is actually more complicated than one of an architecture automatically better or worse depending on which side of the block it inhabits. Party-wall buildings have fronts and backs, and freestanding buildings can open to any direction. Buildings can vary in height and in the layout of their rooms in relationship to the building perimeter and might (although New York City zoning is indifferent to this) be massed within their blocks to maximize solar access to the greatest amount of space within every building, a sunny utilitarianism.

This said, however, it is important to point out that daylight should not tyrannize architecture (as it did in many modernist schemes, like the sinisterly regimented proposals of the influential Ludwig Hilberseimer). Desirable levels of lighting not only vary from activity to activity—artists prefer even, glare-free, north light, and the exclusion of intense afternoon sun also precludes the vista and glow of sunset—but also change from climate to climate and season to season. More, there are important questions of taste. People with a penchant for gloom should not be left out of the repertoire of illuminations our buildings provide. As with so many aspects of the design of the city, light is something that should be available in a variety of modulations and susceptible to a variety of controls. However, the prejudice must always be for access.

One of the innovations of modernist urbanism was the "super-block," a much larger increment of organization than the traditional city block, within which elements such as housing, schools, shops, and sports fields were to be arranged. Part of the logic was to free architectural form from the tyranny of the perimeter, allowing it to respond without constraint to solar angles and prevailing winds. The superblock was designed to create a protected environment for kids and pedestrians, by routing traffic around the block's exterior. But from the standpoint of vitality of the street as the crucible and conduit of urban life and from that of the neighborhood, the bedrock of local city politics and identity, the superblock was fatally flawed.

Enthralled by efficient organization and intoxicated by the dumb clarities of the organizational diagram, modernist urbanism was filled with relational idealizations of urban increments. Super-blocks were often the morphological medium of those "neighborhood units" discussed earlier. These were to be agglomerated into larger units and organized around appropriate centers, linked with highways and other infrastructure to form a supergrid. Such schemes were prescriptive formulas for homogeneity, thwarting the possibility of, and local expressions of, difference and stifling the prospect for self-organization that lies at the core of neighborhood life.

Incorporating modernism's special prejudice for buildings freestanding in "nature" and its weird animus against the street—which Le Corbusier led with a hostility that can only be explained by psychoanalysis—the superblock became the preferred increment of urban organization. Its influence can be seen both in the precincts of numerous housing projects and in cities built from scratch—such as Brasília and Chandigarh. Similarly, the idea of setting office buildings freestanding in plazas stems from a fixation with the autonomy of individual buildings rather than from any consideration of their place in the compounded megastructure of the traditional block. Tension between the idea of the continuous street wall and the isolated building has been a staple of debate about the form of the good city for more than fifty years, and conventional wisdom in New York has now swung firmly back to the "traditional" side. When I was in architecture school, there was much talk of background and foreground buildings in a context that treated virtually all modernist planning principles as writ. Today, the distinction is often an indirect way for traditionalists to attack the preening artistry of reviled modernist "starchitects."

Much of the modern history of New York's physical form is the result of debates over light and air. The tenement laws and their guarantees of minimum access persist in regulations that set standards for the provision of windows and ventilation, room by room, in residential architecture. Unfortunately, many of these minima do not apply to commercial buildings. Although European countries now have regulations that set standards for light and air in workplaces, requiring every worker to be near a window, nothing like this exists in U.S. building regulations (although many communities are now working to produce and institute green codes). Our office buildings remain shaped by the "need" to maximize profit and accommodate big bureaucracies in contiguous spaces. The "efficient" floor plates of typical American office buildings are thus far too large, generally resulting in a ring of windowed perimeter offices for the privileged and a warren of windowless cubicles for employees of lower status, historically women, in their interiors.

Even more decisive to the macro-physique of the city than solar access to building interiors is the set of regulations that govern the solar access to the spaces outside buildings. These stem, in part, from the construction in 1915, in lower Manhattan, of the Equitable Building. Rising 540 feet straight up from the sidewalk on the south side of Cedar Street, the building was one of the city's tallest, and from the day it was completed, it inspired widespread outrage for throwing a blocks-long area to its north into perpetual shadow and robbing the street below of all daylight. This seminal moment of conflict between private and public interest led to the enactment of the 1916 zoning law, which sought to solve the problem by regulating the size and shape of buildings.

In order to ensure the penetration of sunlight to the public street, the law defined the envelope—the notional container—above a given lot within which a tower could be legally built. It articulated a series of setbacks at mandated heights, intended to produce buildings that grew skinnier as they rose: the angle defined by these setbacks was calculated in relationship to the position of the sun, and the law invented a formula that continues to be the foundation of bulk zoning regulations to this day, taking into account the width of the street below so that wider streets support taller buildings (or higher initial setbacks) and narrower streets lower ones.

The effect of the law was remarkable—galvanizing—and it was foundational in producing the stepped, "wedding cake" profile that typified a major portion of the tall buildings erected in New York until 1961, when another paradigm was introduced, favoring slabs that rose straight up behind open plazas. Architecturally, what is striking about the 1916 legislation is that it sought to articulate a logical formula for achieving a public good in the absence of a specific vision of exactly what would actually be produced. Fortunately, the architectural community—especially the great Hugh Ferriss, who produced a series of influential (and gorgeous) studies of what this verbally defined envelope might look like—was inspired by the inner logic of this constraint and went on to design and build one of the most remarkable collections of buildings in history.

Although the view from our apartment encompasses a number of buildings shaped by this legislation, the law has no direct effects on the block itself. Our block is home to twenty-three buildings (including those that have their principal entries on the two intersecting streets at either end), and these consist of seven tenements, ten row houses (most now subdivided into apartments), two relatively low elevator apartment buildings, a small hotel especially popular with foreign tourists, a large drugstore entered from Sixth Avenue, and a much larger apartment building facing Washington Square. Commerce—limited by zoning—includes a dry cleaner, the hotel and its restaurant (which has a separate entrance on the street), and one of the city's more soigné eateries—Babbo—the successor to the legendary Coach House, an old-fashioned place with a vaguely southern feeling and a favorite of James Beard's, noted for lamb chops and sherried bean soup served by a corps of elderly black waiters.

The block on which Annabel Lee sits runs from MacDougal Street on the east (where it forms the western edge of Washington Square) to Sixth Avenue on the west. Sixth Avenue divides the oldest, pre-independence portion of the Village from an area that developed somewhat later. Initially called Greenwich under the English, it was a separate village comprising farms and summer houses for the city's elites, who also used it as a haven during outbreaks of disease. Following the yellow fever epidemic of 1798 (in which 1,310 people died), the area that is now Washington Square was used as a burial ground, in order to keep the infected corpses beyond city limits. After another epidemic in 1822, many of those who retreated northward from the original Dutch settlement as a temporary measure simply decided to stay, and soon after the Village was incorporated into the city. The street pattern of both New Amsterdam and Greenwich was medieval, an irregular network of streets intersecting at odd angles and creating non-uniform blocks. The later extension of the neighborhood was planned on an orthogonal grid, joining the concatenation of colliding grids that characterized the early growth of New York.

In a city organized in grid form, the block becomes a crucial increment of both the physical and the political and social order.

Since the time of the Greeks, democracy has been understood to have a spatial dimension and so, by extension, an element of scale. In the *Politics*, Aristotle described the measure of the agora, the setting for Athenian democracy, as the distance over which a shout could be heard, about the length of a block. Plato measured the polis, the unit of democratic citizenship, at five hundred citizens. Counting the buildings entered directly off our block, I estimate its permanent population at about the Platonic five hundred, an extremely tractable size for a community that seeks to express itself through direct engagement. However, there's clearly a difference between this kind of rational urbanism, in which dimensions and numbers are produced by ideas about the practicalities of association, and the "scientific" type where numbers are the outcome of the efficiencies of control.

Given the huge city in which we live, not to mention the countless ascending increments of government and affinity by which we all are affected, there is something illusory about the importance of this (or any) single number. Still, without this legible medium of localized identity and without its clear connection to the larger network that defines our sense of neighborhood, the risk of alienation and disenfranchisement would be far greater. Although it is a subject that oscillates between the irrelevant and the seminal in contemporary political theory, the idea of the "face-to-face" as the enabler of collective democracy seems beyond dispute, if only as the last hedge against a world in which political relations are increasingly virtual. The block, in its legibility and dimension, is a crucial, enabling constituent and, in most cities, the basic organ of the neighborhood, itself the bedrock of the organization of the city as a whole.

Not surprisingly, much political and social organization in New York is based on the block, where myriad block associations engage in varying degrees of local activism and in building strategic alliances with other blocks. Our association, which meets sporadically, provides a conduit up the political chain and a medium for liaisons with other neighborhood organizations, including our community board, local politicians, the police, and government agencies, as well as with groups of more specialized concerns, such as historic preservation, parks, and social services. Whom we interact with, of course, fluctuates in influence and importance: at the moment the Greenwich Village Society for Historic Preservation, because of its strong and articulate leadership, is playing a particularly big role in debates over the future of the neighborhood. While our block associations are not exactly on the same level as, say, the Cuban Committees for the Defense of the Revolution, themselves organized in block-sized increments, they have the superior quality of being elective, spontaneous, and freely adversarial, not designed to ensure compliance with inhibiting laws or to monitor neighbors. This last is particularly crucial. In a culture of overly centralized authority (grown more so with the "War on Terror") and increasingly predatory capital, local resistance is the citizen's last defense against the big processes that shape our everyday lives.

Block associations are generally organized around not the square block but the street block, so opposite sides of the street are conjoined, despite belonging to different square blocks. This is another manifestation of the importance of the "face-to-face." Neighborliness stems from contact, visibility, and experience. We are far more likely to encounter those living on our own streets than those living a block over, more able to identify where a neighbor lives if we see her leaving the house each morning. Thus, the logic of organization by experience trumps the logic of organization by property. The direct democracy of building committees, co-op boards, and block associations exists at a scale of intimacy that does not require representation.

Nothing symbolizes the culture of the block like the block party. Once a year, the block is closed to traffic and replaced by a variety of food and crafts vendors. The street assumes a bustling, convivial atmosphere and attracts people in numbers sufficient to generate a crowd, enforcing slow going on streets and sidewalks otherwise seldom jammed. Yet the current version of the block party is, if lively, a pale version of its originating ideal, reflecting a transmutation of the scenes and formats of public life into shopping. Nowadays, most of those hawking the bonsai trees and roasted ears of corn at the fair are merchants who travel from block party to block party during the summer months. There are still a few locals, though, including our second-floor neighbors, who sell antiques both at the fair and at a variety of local flea markets.

The expressive importance of these fairs is not simply their service as containers for conviviality but their appropriation of the street itself for "irregular" use. The increasingly commercial character of block parties notwithstanding, they ritually assert a right to public appropriation of space that, every other day, serves simply as a conduit for vehicular traffic. Streets are far and away the largest area of city surface in the hands of the public. In New York City, they add up to around 15 percent (excluding sidewalks) of the total area of the city. In and of itself, the disproportion is not unreasonable. Efficient movement is critical to the life of the city. Since free assembly is the key spatial expression of democracy, free access is its necessary guarantor. In this sense, the block party is an assertion of the public's right to its public space, a day on which the streets belong to the people. Remember the old exhortation: "Vote with your feet, vote in the street."

Among modern urban theorists, Henri Lefebvre was particularly attuned to the importance of the "carnivalesque." In this, he was seminally influenced by the work of François Rabelais, the great sixteenth-century poet whose masterpiece, *Gargantua and Pantagruel*, was a virtual manifesto of ribaldry, a nonstop celebration of the joys of the flesh summed up with the stirring proto-hippie slogans "Be Happy!" and "Do What You Will!" Lefebvre's passion for Rabelais, expressed both in a study of the author and in a theory of the city that recognized the centrality of festivals to a genuinely satisfying everyday life, was something he shared with an influential predecessor, Mikhail Bakhtin. Bakhtin, a Russian formalist critic and author of *Rabelais and His World*, made an insistent argument for the connection between laughter and freedom, two threatened commodities in the Stalinist era, during which he wrote. According to Bakhtin, "All were considered equal during carnival. Here, in the town square, a special form of free and familiar contact reigned among people who were usually divided by the barriers of caste, property, profession, and age."

Our two greatest neighborhood-wide celebrations—the Gay Pride and Halloween Parades—are among the most dramatic assertions of the public's right to the enjoyment of public space. The parades often test the limits of public behavior and expression on the part of both participants and spectators. Consumption of alcohol in the street, a bit of nudity, provocative banners, and noisiness all extend, via their remnant Rabelaisianism, the margins of what is considered acceptable everyday behavior. New York's famed ethnic parades can also test the idea of tolerance in the other direction. For example, there has been a years-long battle with the organizers of the St. Patrick's Day Parade over the participation of gay groups. Although these groups are constituted from the same communities (of Catholics, of Irish) as other participants, they have been banned for behavior that is not sanctioned by the Church. The ban begs fundamental questions about private tolerance and also about the limits of private expression in public space.

On our block, the street is sixty feet wide (including the parking lanes), while the combined width of the sidewalks on either side is about twenty feet. We tend to treat these dimensions as reasonable in proportion and as logically ordained and efficient, even though the sixty-foot street (and hundred-foot avenue) date from the 1811 plan. In general, the planning and transportation establishment tends to advocate the enlargement of vehicular space, frequently at the expense of that available to pedestrians. Even in New York, there is little resistance to this, although the current transportation commissioner has emerged as a strong advocate of cycling, and bike lanes are, finally, seeing a measurable increase. New York has, however, resisted the hegemony of the car in one utterly crucial way:

an enormous, if never entirely adequate, investment in public transportation, most crucially the subway. It is central to our genius loci that we use public transportation at a rate many orders of magnitude greater than any other place in the country. One of the corollaries of this usage is dramatically higher energy efficiency, among the best, per capita, in the United States.

Localized alterations to the ratio of pedestrian to vehicular space do occasionally take place, officially under the rubric of "traffic calming," a mix of strategies to reduce traffic speed and congestion and assure greater safety for pedestrians. These strategies include the necking down of streets at intersections (and occasionally mid-block), the introduction of inconvenient one-way streets and dead ends, manipulation of the timing of traffic lights, and a variety of other small-scale interventions. Where these have been introduced in the Village, they've had a very modest effect, except in arousing the ire of the janissaries of motor traffic.

The difficulty in introducing even these minor modifications is exacerbated by the great grail of traffic engineering and the fictions that support it. The ideal of traffic planners is a smooth and ever-increasing flow of vehicles, moving at as high speed as practical, achieved by the removal of impediments (via synchronization of traffic lights, discipline of pedestrians, elimination of slower vehicles, like bikes) and by the continual increase in the space available for vehicle movement. Protagonists offer this naively simple formula: the more space we provide for vehicles, the faster and more smoothly they will flow.

This has proven not to be the case, and not just on city streets. Studies demonstrate that building and enlarging highways not only does not abate the congestion it is designed to relieve; it invariably exacerbates it. Increased supply generates increased demand. Yet despite the evidence, the road-building mentality persists. Every attempt to cul-de-sac city streets, to change traffic patterns in favor of pedestrians, or to narrow street ends is met with the same howl of protest from the authorities: this will increase congestion because urban traffic is a zero-sum game. Any reduction in volume in one place in the city will inevitably be accompanied by a rise in traffic somewhere else.

This claim is fallacious: the true corollary is the opposite. In case after case, a reduction of the space available for vehicular traffic has simply resulted in the reduction of traffic overall. What if this false reasoning and narrow interest could be set aside and the space of the block more fully governed by its residents? And what if the circulation space of the block were reconfigured to reflect a different hierarchy of preferences, needs, and uses? I have for years been engaged in a thought experiment, the product of which is the idea of a program of "greenfill" for the city streets. The idea is simple: if one lane of every block in the city were removed from the automotive system and returned to the pedestrian realm, an enormous range of urban problems could be solved.

Were my block to be greenfilled, I could imagine any number of things that might be done with the new space. As ours is a particularly heavily walked block—given its role in connecting the big West Fourth Street subway station with Washington Square, NYU, and the East Village—it would enhance the space of pedestrian movement. An additional row of trees would offer dramatically greater shading for both the street and the sidewalk. Storage for bicycles could be added at street level, a boon to those in walk-ups. The new space might also be instrumental in helping to deal with our abiding waste management and disposal problems. Solid waste—which New York generates at the rate of 36,200 tons a day—is currently dealt with in stunningly primitive fashion. Three days a week, our sidewalk is lined from end to end with a nearly continuous Jura of plastic sacks of garbage, piles of newspapers, and old furniture and appliances. The hideous and invariably leaky range lies there for hours at a stretch, frustrating movement along the sidewalk and across the street, a situation made worse by rain or snow.

The solution to this is not rocket science. Setting aside the unlikely imminence of some larger social transformation that would reduce the amount of trash produced by our crazed culture of disposability, the immediate need is to create an intermediary space for waste. In Vienna, we disposed of trash in a brace of large plastic waste containers at the end of the block—which took up what might otherwise have been a couple of parking spaces. These were designated for "biological" waste, for clear and colored glass, for metal, for plastic, and for paper. People sorted their trash diligently, and a truck—equipped to automatically hoist and dump the containers—came regularly to service the little depot. Although not beautiful, the containers were unobtrusive in the neighborhood landscape.

The system, intelligent and minimal, seemingly exceeds the imaginative and physical capability of most American cities. On the greenfill strip I imagine for Waverly Place, this arrangement could be improved by the provision of an appropriate enclosure for the bins or by some even more technically adventurous solution that would embed the whole collection of receptacles in the ground. This is a fantasy that can be strung out to even greater lengths, involving ever more elaborate divisions of labor: the collection of recyclable or reusable elements, the repair of and resale of furniture (something done systematically in Japan), the composting of organics for local use, and so on.

Seen as a larger system, greenfill (as it takes over one lane after another) might also be used for community gardens, for storing gardening and other equipment, for small playgrounds, for benches, chess tables, child-care centers, and little social spaces, and for a multitude of other uses. It might also become a vehicle to begin the full municipalization of the existing sidewalks and their incorporation into a larger system of publicly owned public pedestrian space. It is a bizarre anomaly that we freely spend countless billions on the construction and maintenance of our streets but leave the repair, and cleaning, of our sidewalks—and the crucial shading apparatus they support—to the tender mercies of private landlords who show no strong inclination to take proper responsibility for this vital duty and whose responsibility for but a fragmentary increment of the block creates conditions of uneven repair and character.

There is not exactly a biblical injunction that specifies the proportional division of the cross section of the block, nothing that requires that cars be given three times the space of pedestrians. Of the four lanes reserved for vehicular traffic, two are parking lanes. On our block—as with most blocks in New York—there are no meters, and parking is available on a first-come, first-served basis. The city, in effect, provides half the area of the public space on my block for the storage of private cars, and approximately forty will fit when all spaces are occupied. The diversion of public space—some of the most valuable real estate on the planet—to the private interests of the least efficient and most dangerous and dirty means of movement in the city is a fundamental affront to the real needs and habits of New York's citizens, the majority of whom do not own automobiles.

WASHINGTON SQUARE

A left turn brings me to Washington Square at the end of the block. The square is anchored by its famous triumphal arch designed by McKim, Mead & White and erected to commemorate the hundredth anniversary of George Washington's inauguration. In 1917, Marcel Duchamp and John Sloan climbed atop it and fired cap pistols to declare the independence of the "Republic of Greenwich Village."

Washington Square is our neighborhood park. It serves as, among other things, a center of New York youth culture—a gathering place for kids, musicians, buskers, and marijuana dealers. Flanked on all sides by buildings of New York University—with a mix of apartment buildings, churches, and a stately row of Federal-style houses—it also constitutes a de facto academic quadrangle. As joggers circle its perimeter, addicts and the homeless hang out, many waiting for meals served up by adjoining churches. One corner is given over to chess players, their tables with pieces set up and clocks primed, ready to hustle would-be Bobby Fischers.

Toward the center of the park is the neighborhood dog run (recently metamorphosed into large-dog and small-dog versions), providing a social scene for both canines and their owners. On the south side, a couple of strange, hardened mounds are the domain of skateboarders. On clement days, two elegant, fenced-in playgrounds quickly fill with toddlers and their guardians. In summer, grassy areas abound with sun worshippers. A very large circular fountain in the center of the park (which sees water only sporadically) is the scene of various performances, both artistic and political. There's always a play being rehearsed or NYU film students with their signed-out cameras making something in Super 8.

Pretzels and knishes are sold. Cops amble through. There's one of the only public toilets for miles.

One reason the park sees such intense use is its location at the heart of the Village. Another, however, is that lower Manhattan is among the most underserved areas of the city in terms of green space. The borough as a whole has .0025 acres per person of open space, well under half the average for Brooklyn, the Bronx, and Queens, and less than an eighth of the average on Staten Island, where people tend to have private green space as well. The reasons for Manhattan's lack of open space are both cultural and historical, having to do with burgeoning population, changes of use, pressures of development, and the fact that the idea of public parks as a natural part of cities stems from the mid–nineteenth century, somewhat after the Village had grown to a version of completion.

On Saturday, August 2, 1997 (I remember this date because it's my birthday), Washington Square Park was closed to the public. It was a beautiful day, unusually cool and dry for the New York summer, just the kind of day made for strolling or lounging in the park. Unfortunately, at every entrance, fierce-looking, black-clad private security guards—like giant ninjas—prevented anyone from entering. The reason? A film was being shot. The entire neighborhood was swamped with trucks and lights and stunt cars and what seemed like hundreds of people shouting into their walkie-talkies and inviting people "encroaching" on the production to cross the street.

Of course, many were charmed with the prospect of having movie stars in their midst (this film had, among others, Robert Duvall, Téa Leoni, and Morgan Freeman), but I was outraged. I've grown to hate the almost ubiquitous film productions that use the city as backdrop, particularly in our neighborhood, which is so picturesque and so filled with signifiers of "New York." I feel my blood pressure rise as I pass the ranks of mobile dressing rooms and supply trucks, all with their exhausts belching and their noisy generators running to keep overpaid stars cool or warm. I hate the officious production assistants asking—insisting—that I cross the street so the filming of some moronic commercial can proceed without interruption. I especially hate the groaning catering tables spread with nutritious snacks placed curbside in case anyone involved with the production wants a nosh: but none for you! To me these spreads always suggest Reaganism—abundance for a few, illusory trickle down for the rest.

Any company that wishes to film in New York must receive permission from the Mayor's Office of Film, Theatre, and Broadcasting, which exists to encourage such uses of the city. There are a number of reasons for this municipal role. Certainly, New York is the nation's leading center of artistic production of all kinds, and to be seen as such is central to both its substance and its image. The argument most frequently employed, though, is economic. The city's unemployment rate is currently well over 9 percent, so the jobs productions provide are a priority. It's not just in film that economic arguments have come to dominate the discourse of urban improvement. Whether in the form of zoning bonuses that give away public access to the sky or film licenses that deny the use of parks or streets, the administration always seems too eager to understand public good in the narrow terms of revenue, even the illusory promise of a tax benefit years down the road.

What is the nature of public proprietorship of public places? What are the limits of the public's right to control the content of the activities that take place in those spaces? How free is expression to be? Setting aside the obvious fiduciary responsibility of government to secure revenues to supply public services and the corollary duty to stimulate employment, the primary standard by which government stewardship must be judged is the degree to which it either hinders or encourages public access to public places. Such a standard implies that these sites be provided in the first place and that they be distributed throughout the city in such a way that no one is deprived of access because of geography. But a "right" to public space suggests that there be some public standard about what kinds of activities are supported by these community properties. While there may be near-universal consent about the value of strolling, sitting on a bench, or taking a swim, the issue becomes murkier when it comes to bocce courts or cricket pitches or, for that matter, baseball fields, which require a large area to provide for the enjoyment (discounting spectators) of relatively small numbers.

Let's take this argument a little further. Assume that *Deep Impact*—like virtually every "drama" from Hollywood—is a movie that entails violence and gunplay. Does the public have a right to control the expressive or "artistic" content of activities taking place in its spaces? Activities that fall under criminal statutes—selling drugs, soliciting for prostitution, stealing plants—are easy to prohibit. Other sorts of activities are not as simple to sort out: kids selling lemonade, for example. Graffiti certainly straddles the line and is hard to pin down. Tagging the arch with indelible spray paint is out of bounds, but what about chalk drawings of *The Last Supper* on the pavement? Or consider musical and dramatic performances that are tolerated, if not protected, forms of expression, unless, of course, they overstep nominally criminal bounds, as when the musicians play too loudly or a performer bares it all.

The legitimacy of this sort of expression in public space is bound both to art—which has exploring limits as its role—and to the nature of place. Because Washington Square has historically been the site of protest and performance and because this sort of behavior is emblematic of the Village, the square provides a certain latitude that other public places in the city may not. There is, however, something very problematic about what is, in effect, zoning for free speech—Hyde Park Corner–izing—or what Herbert Marcuse described as "repressive tolerance." One of the crucial behaviors of a democratic public is the constant testing, extension, and defense of such expression. And part of this testing is the sort of investigation of the relationship of propriety and place that happens all the time in New York, whether at the level of individual behavior—performing, panhandling, protesting, or simply sleeping in the street or the park—or in more collective acts. Private interests, too, constantly test the limits of public propriety—for example, in seeking to arrogate areas of the sidewalk for cafés, or running clubs for raucous crowds, or stressing the street with idling limos, or covering buildings with advertising.

Two relatively recent protests come to mind. In the summer of 2004 while the Republican convention was taking place at Madison Square Garden, organizers applied to hold what was forecast to be a huge rally in the Sheep Meadow of Central Park. The Bloomberg administration—nominally Republican—turned the event down on the grounds that such a large gathering was likely to have deleterious effects on the freshly restored grass of the meadow. This may or may not have been the case, but at least the mayor's argument was posed in terms of conflicting public rights of assembly, albeit only one of them explicitly political in the partisan sense. The question was cast in terms of the propriety of numbers, although the issue of whether there should be limits on the number of people gathered to picnic on the lawn never came up.

As an alternative site for the gathering, the administration offered a stretch of highway on the west side of Manhattan, rejected by the protest organizers as being ill configured and marginal, away from any likely audience. Although the highway was actually closer to Madison Square Garden than Central Park was, it had a decidedly inferior symbolic character to that of the city's premier public space. Both sites, however, shared one difficulty: they were designed for other uses—leisure and traffic—than large rallies. The same was true of another logical candidate for the gathering of purposive crowds—Times Square. Its most celebrated occasion, the mass gathering at New Year's Eve, requires the area to assume a state of exception from its normal purpose, the movement of people and vehicles. Like our local parades, the protest against the Republican convention, in which members of the public wished to utilize a public space designed for something else for a special expression, represents a crucial instance in defining the limits of public expression in general.

In the case of the convention protest, a compromise was finally reached that allowed the protest to morph from a rally to a "march" past Madison Square Garden, but with no stopping to gather for speeches or for the creation of a stationary mass, a fixed, if temporary, form of assembly that certainly carries a different weight and meaning from that of a crowd in motion. What this event ultimately revealed is that New York, in fact, lacks a large plaza that is not freighted with functions, whether circulation or leisure, that prevent it from becoming a logical arena for mass gatherings. Of course, the existence of such places—think of Red Square, Tiananmen Square, or the Zócalo in Mexico City—guarantees nothing, and they are not necessarily less contested in practice, as the massacres of 1968 in Mexico and 1989 in China attest. Still, the presence of these environments of almost purely symbolic public function constantly begs the question of their own meaning in a way that Times Square—for which a single exception of celebration is sanctioned—does not. What a shame that Ground Zero could not have become such a democratic gathering space, the ultimate riposte to fascist terror: free assembly.

There is a group of cycling advocates in New York called Critical Mass that, in its signature style of action, assumes a permanent right of mobile protest. On a regular basis, groups of cyclists gather for mass rides through city streets. These processions perforce take place at a speed that is less than the "limit" on vehicular traffic and therefore constitute—in the eyes of the police—a form of disruption. Large numbers of demonstrators are often arrested for, in effect, exercising their legal right to use the street for its designated purpose, the movement of wheeled traffic. The introduction of speed as a category in vetting acceptable public behavior has interesting (and largely uninvestigated) implications for public assembly in general, since it demands the drawing of very fine and often arbitrary lines. The idea that a demonstration is threatening for being slow is an affront to the idea of public assembly as the exercise of free exchange, something intrinsic and sacred to it since the days of the agora. There is deep perversity in the effort to control the modal distribution of affinity, framing a difference between fifty cyclists and fifty schoolkids or tourists on a bus. By coercing more narrowly symbolic behavior, the authorities limit the expressive dimensions of speech.

In a move many attribute to their efforts to thwart Critical Mass, the police department has proposed to require parade permits for cyclists in groups of twenty or more as well as for any cyclists or walkers in groups of two or more who use the streets in contravention of traffic laws for any activity whatsoever, including parades, races, protests, or simply chatting. Additionally, they want to require a permit for groups of thirty-five or more protesters, even if they confine themselves to the sidewalk. The police defend these restrictions on the grounds that they are "designed to protect the health and safety of participants in group events on the public streets and sidewalks as well as that of members of the public who find themselves in the vicinity of these events." Debate has focused on whether the police have the authority to impose these regulations without a vote of the city council, and on the obvious restriction of protests such regulations imply. The New York Civil Liberties Union has declared that whatever the authority of the police to make such rules, they are "antithetical to the principles and values of the right to protest that New York is associated with." The police have begun to backpedal.

If New York City has one site that is historically linked to public protest gatherings, it is Union Square, located just beyond the northern boundary of the Village on Fourteenth Street. Union Square has been the scene of popular demonstrations since the mid–nineteenth century and had also, until their eclipse in recent years, been the center of a neighborhood in which many organizations of the American Left—including such relics as the Communist Party—had their offices, meeting halls, bookshops, and presses. Union Square was the site of the traditional May Day workers' rally, a celebration sadly absent from our current repertoire of civic celebrations. During World War II, Robert Moses (then parks commissioner) went so far as to ban demonstrations there. Nowadays, Union Square's waning popularity for such events is a product both of the general decline of the organized Left and of the current configuration of the square itself, elevated to accommodate a sub-way station beneath it and designed for individual leisure rather than mass assembly. Like other public spaces in the city, it is in-creasingly home to uses that are not strictly public, including a planned new (private) restaurant that has been the object of much contention.

But its resonances remain in the collective unconscious of the city, and it continues to attract many small-scale demonstrations and other political events. After the destruction of the World Trade Center, it briefly became a sad, immensely moving, and spontane-ous shrine to the victims of the attack as well as the key gathering place for survivors and people throughout the city seeking some form of collective expression of loss. As family and friends desper-ately sought word of the "disappeared," Union Square—the first major public space north of the cordoned-off area south of Four-teenth Street—became the primary site for posting their images. While these poignant photographs—holiday snapshots, graduation pictures, formal portraits—initially appeared as a means of search-ing for information, they quickly became a form of commemora-tion and memorial. The array of faces posted over the square was like a gathering of ghosts, a mass demonstration of absence and grief.

Within a few weeks, however, the authorities concluded that this transformation had exceeded its license and removed the pictures, returning the square to its normal valence. While few imagined that the hundreds of thousands of photocopied images papering the city were other than temporary, they were an extraor-dinary, spontaneous expression of feeling by an arbitrarily but powerfully constituted public. That the posting of these images was technically transgressive was rendered irrelevant by the im-mensity of their importance—the same equation that defines the value-in-defiance of many other forms of public speech, however immediately trivial they may seem. As an artifact, the images—product of no single design and growing out of the control of normal routines of propriety—transformed the square. The ponderous, overwrought, and reductive forms of official commemoration pale by comparison, abstracted to banality.

Under certain circumstances, though, abstraction can carry very specific meanings in space. In 1985, the city was caught up in a controversy concerning the artistic use of a public space that devolved on a conflict over the meaning of abstraction. The space in question was a bit of government property, a plaza sitting between a courthouse and an amazingly ugly federal office building in lower Manhattan. Some years before, under a program that mandated the placement of works of art on such federal properties, the artist Richard Serra had been commissioned to make a work for the plaza. The result was a piece called *Tilted Arc*, a long, curving wall of self-rusting COR-TEN steel placed along one side of the plaza in 1981. It was classic Serra and resembled other such arched pieces he had erected, to much acclaim, on other sites, both in the United States and abroad.

Opinion about the piece was divided from the beginning. Some thought it a masterpiece, and others found it simply ugly. While the art world largely lined up in admiration of *Tilted Arc*, those who worked in the building in front of which it stood tended to loathing. Among those who couldn't stand it was a federal judge whose opposition became a near vendetta and eventually resulted in a decision by the local administrator of the General Services Administration to have it removed. The outcry was tremendous. The arguments pro and con were strident and generally less than subtle. Supporters decried the government as philistines and assassins of free expression. Plus, they argued that the government had commissioned the work and had a contractual obligation not to destroy it. The government claimed, limply, that it had no intention of destroying it and would happily remove it to a sculpture park in the countryside.

This became the nub of an interesting artistic debate. Serra claimed—with some justification—that the work was site specific, that to remove it was to destroy it. The government argued otherwise. Both sides, though, largely missed the most important and potentially difficult point. It was not only that many of the users of the plaza in which the Serra sat reviled the piece in and of itself but that it was the very specificity of the work and its measurable effects on the space that they objected to. First, it clearly blocked free passage across the plaza and under the adjacent courthouse, which was lifted up on columns. Second, in co-opting the plaza for artistic spectatorship, it replaced other kinds of uses—planting, picnic tables, fountains, whatever.

The site-specific argument was made in essentially architectural terms. Serra claimed that the sculpture transcended any notion of simple appearance and was, in fact, work that was intended to transform the way in which the space was used. Serra meant this argument to buttress the claims of specificity. But in making it, he also validated the arguments of his opponents, whose claim was not simply that the sculpture was ugly but that it denied them the use of an amenity that was part of New York's system of public spaces. Their argument, finally, was that public access to a public space was compromised by its use as a site for a site-specific work of art. This contention of diminished public use made the legalistic argument seem trivial. By having made social claims, the work was open to social arguments. More, by occupying social space, it opened itself to questions about its social usefulness, a category in which visual pleasure is simply one among many.

But the situation was even more fraught. Nobody would dream of demanding that the truly hideous federal building—a far greater blot on the visual commonweal than the Serra could ever be—be torn down. In effect, *Tilted Arc* took the heat for a far larger artistic and environmental failure because its presence or absence was tractable while the building's was not. This displacement is typical of the artistic and architectural conversation in New York. Critics write endlessly about narrow issues of styling while rarely tackling questions of use (the cubicles generated by the big floor plates) or the larger issues of urbanism. For example, construction awaits on a huge building by Richard Rogers on the Queens waterfront designed to house film studios, offices, shops, and apartments. It sits directly adjacent to the beautiful Queensboro Bridge, and—although the architecture will be a typically fine Rogers product—the effect of the building in its site specificity will be to forever alter the prospect of the bridge from Manhattan. How should *this* loss be valued?

After the Serra was removed (in the middle of the night), the plaza was reconstructed by a landscape architect. Where Serra's work was aggressively minimalist, her project attempted to return the space to a more traditional, parklike feel while simultaneously commenting on its strangeness via an ironic surreality. Standard-issue light poles are stretched to giraffe-neck lengths. Funny hemispherical grass mounds dot the plaza. Wooden benches curl continuously through the space, painted in a demonstrative shade of green. Surrealism has become the kitsch of postmodernity, and although the new plaza is clearly softer, kinder, and gentler than what was there before, it lacks Serra's astringent ambition and rage. But ambition and rage may not be what people are looking for on their lunch hour.

Whatever the design's artistic merits, on a sunny afternoon the benches are filled with people, schmoozing and eating sandwiches. The circulation and sense of visibility are much enhanced. In summer, a misting system keeps the plaza cool. In short, however one thinks of its reconfigured artistic content, the plaza functions much better as a space of everyday social interaction. So here is an instance where an artist's right of expression foundered on the permanent quality of its transgression against the public's right to conveniently use a public space. *Tilted Arc*'s "specific" critique of that space had the effect of making it even more uninhabitable, via its failure to critique its own conventional "plop art," sculpture-in-a-plaza formula. Self-represented as a kind of sanctioned graffiti, the wall had to take responsibility for the content of its message precisely because the content of public spaces must, in its *permanent* qualities, answer to a test of appropriate expression that free speech in its openness to exchange with contrary opinions does not. Like the marble Ten Commandments ordered removed from the

hallway in that Alabama courthouse a few years ago, it's the unre-
dressable imposition that's the problem.

This may be a somewhat circuitous way back to that film in
Washington Square, but the argument is the same. There are times
when sacrosanct matters of the content of expression should and
must enter the equation. Public space must be judged by the way
in which it advances the idea of public use by a public that is increasingly multiple. Of course, there is a public interest in the general artistic and cultural climate, and such a climate can thrive only
in an atmosphere of free expression. But the public also has an interest in discouraging certain kinds of speech (hate speech, incite-
ment to criminality, shouting *"Fire!"* in a crowded theater) and in
actively creating certain kinds of physical and expressive spaces.
There is an idea of the greater good here, the idea that speech or
construction must be judged by what it precludes.

One reason to object to urban renewal or gentrification is the
range of community activities removed by its destruction of their
physical settings, as well as by the homogenizations that result
when all but the rich are priced out of an area. The Serra seems to
fall under this rubric, narrowing the choices and expressions the
greater community of this plaza was able to enjoy. The movie, on
the other hand, is a problem for other reasons: it kept us out of our
park on a beautiful day and promoted a kind of speech that is not
in the public interest, save via the argument that free speech is
indivisible. One can, of course, argue the universal validity of private claims on public space, but we know very well that this will
not do, just as we know the merit in the old saw about the free
press being available to those who happen to own one.

I just saw (on a plane) *I Am Legend*, a blithely trashy Will
Smith vehicle in which Washington Square plays a key role. The
film is about a New York depopulated (except for zombies) by a
pandemic triggered by a cancer cure gone bad. The Smith character, who has immunity, is a scientist holed up in his posh Washington Square digs searching for the cure. The film opens with a scene
of Smith racing through the deserted (save for herds of deer) city

streets in a hot red sports car, searching for zombies on whom to test his latest batch of vaccine. Manhattan has been quarantined with orders to blow up the bridges (some fine special effects here), and I saw the film at the height of the now-lost battle over congestion pricing, of which this might be said to be the ultimate example.

The film's climactic scene is an attack on Smith's house by a brigade of zombies who overcome flocks of improvised explosive devices Smith has rigged throughout the square to impede them. We all witnessed the resultant pyrotechnics during the production (which lasted for weeks). People came from all over town to photograph zombie bodies hanging from trees and the phalanx of burned-out cars surrounding the park. In a town a little too familiar with apocalypse—both AIDS and 9/11—these sights were more than a little over the top, a few too many metaphors to bear. And the sight of the square reduced to ruin put many in mind of the current controversy over its now-just-begun renovation.

Because of this reconstruction, the neighborhood is once again caught up in a debate about the public nature of Washington Square. Since it first became a park in the late 1820s, the square has gone through a number of transformations and alterations. It began its public life as a pestilential cemetery, then became a potter's field, and, for a while, held a gallows. Later it was a military parade ground (a stratagem to favorably affect the property values of the lot holders around it) until it was finally consolidated as a public square in the image of the squares of Georgian London, greatly envied by many in early New York.

In its first incarnation as a park, the square was formally landscaped in geometric style. In 1848 (a revolutionary year) it was protectively fenced in iron and in 1852 received its first fountain. The arch that forms its entrance was dedicated in 1895. Although it is now a pedestrian preserve, traffic flowed across the square for almost one hundred years, finally eliminated only in 1965. Traffic has been an especially resonant issue because it is foundational in the life and character of cities, decisively representing the push-pull of the use of public space and structuring the basic morphology of the city. As in so much of the modern history of New York, Robert Moses was the key player in attempts to relieve the city of this anomalous interruption to the unobstructed flow of traffic. As early as 1935, he proposed a project to turn the square into a giant traffic roundabout with a scheme that came to be known as the bath-mat plan for its resemblance to that homely object. This was defeated by local opposition and World War II.

But after victory he was back. In the late 1940s, Moses launched another in a series of attacks on the Village that, despite shifting particulars, invariably included ramming roadways through the park. Moses had long since—via the public authority structure that continues to blight democratic planning to this day—devised a tight legal means to circumvent public opinion and oversight. After the war, his legal, ideological, and economic armamentarium was buttressed by two pieces of federal legislation: Title I of the federal Housing Act of 1949, the wellspring of urban renewal; and the National Interstate and Defense Highways Act of 1956. Together, these have resulted in damage to the American urban fabric of a scale to rival what we inflicted on the cities of Germany and Japan during the war.

Both programs shared the vision of a city of isolated towers linked by highways, a vision that was the hallmark of the modernist fantasy of the city of the future, most emblematically expressed by Le Corbusier's image of the Ville Radieuse, so thoroughly excoriated by Jane Jacobs. Both came with absolute powers of condemnation, allowing for the efficient acquisition of property and the displacement of residents. And both were paid for by the federal government. In the case of Title I, the Feds covered the expenses of condemnation and site clearance, and in that of the interstate act, federal funding covered 90 percent of the total cost of construction. The willingness of city after city to effectively commit suicide by driving highways and urban-renewal projects through their hearts in exchange for this money continues to be amazing and appalling.

In the Village, Moses's idea was to clear the "slums" south of the square, from Mercer Street on the east to Sixth Avenue on the west, all the way down into what is now SoHo. As part of the project, Fifth Avenue was to be extended south—either directly or as a double roadway (Fifth Avenue East and West). Opposition to Moses was immediate. The threat to the neighborhoods south of the square—then largely Italian—was met by strong resistance, and by the early 1950s the area slated for demolition had been halved, sparing the dense residential neighborhood west of West Broadway. The eastern side of the square was not so lucky and was eventually demolished, replaced by a series of classic modernist towers, two 583-foot-long slabs vaguely modeled on Corbusian Unités d'Habitation, and three high-rise towers, all part of NYU. In subsequent years, NYU has maintained its penchant for the overscaled, and its current prosperity has resulted in a program of expansion—including a brace of giant dorms in the East Village—that has made it public enemy number one in the eyes of the neighborhood.

The project for a major roadway through the square eventually petered out. Community opposition was buttressed in 1958 by a trial closure to cars that demonstrated, contrary to the dire predictions of the traffic planners, that traffic in the area actually *decreased*. In 1962, plans for a new Washington Square roadway were officially killed, and in 1965 a turnaround for buses was removed, and the square became traffic-free for the first time since the nineteenth century. Insurance that the square would remain road-free came in the form of a deal that permitted NYU to use forty feet of West Broadway (the Village portion of which—from Houston Street to the square—was renamed LaGuardia Place) for its new library. This was something of a Pyrrhic swap as the gigantic (and hideous) red sandstone cube now casts a long shadow on the square.

With the elimination of Moses's threat, the park was redesigned, its current incarnation completed in 1970. The landscape plan was not without controversy. In fact, it took the agitation of Jane Jacobs and others to preserve the great circular pool at the center of the park for gathering and performance, rather than turning it over to be used as a purely ornamental fountain. This space remains one of the world's great sites of free assembly, the core of the park's meaning and use. Yet the fountain, ironically, has recently been disassembled under still another plan to redesign and refurbish the park, in order to move it to a position directly on axis with the arch. Intense opposition to this idiocy has failed despite compelling arguments against the influence of private donations on the design, or the claim that NYU is trying to take over, or the sheer silliness of the axial jones of the current designers. Underlying these arguments is a sense that the meaning and memory of the park are bound up with the original location and character—the site specificity—of the fountain.

The assault on the fountain is the latest in a series of "improvements"—from graveyard to parade ground to park to another kind of park to roadway to another kind of park to another kind of park—that have sought to alter the use and meaning of Washington Square. In this long cycle of reactions and counterreactions, a constant has been concern about the nature of inappropriate use, whether the gathering of the dead or of the all too lively. For some, the expressive freedom of the park has always rankled—a threat to bourgeois proprieties, property values, or civic decorum more broadly. And, in truth, in its history the square has often enough come to seem like a drug emporium ("smoke, smoke" breathlessly hissed at passersby) and crash pad/toilet for the down-and-out.

Perhaps the most controversial element of the current effort to freshen the park (which does badly need refurbishment of its tired asphalt, tacky lighting, and deteriorated furnishings) is the proposal to ring the park with a fence. The original 1848 fence was removed in 1870 after the first formal redesign of the park transformed its tepid symmetries into a more naturalistic Olmstedian vision. The park went fenceless for a hundred years until a new constituency for fencing emerged. This time the impetus was explicitly driven by a perception that the park seethed with the criminal element and that defensive measures were urgently needed. These found their intellectual justification in a book that then had a huge impact on planning ideology: *Defensible Space* by Oscar Newman, published in 1972. Its writing was motivated, in large part, by the national debacle of crime-ridden public housing. Ignoring the possibility that social pathologies were not produced by, but came to be warehoused in, typical public housing towers, Newman proposed a physical solution that could be brought about by establishing clear proprietorship of space, eliminating ill-defined (and non-maintained) public areas, and replacing them with private yards and more visibly structured environments.

In Washington Square, this idea quickly morphed into a more general vision of the control of potential miscreants via the construction of a fence designed to keep them out. A debate raged, fed by a general sense of beleaguerment by high crime and urban disinvestment, and by the recurrent vibe of us versus them. The fence was almost built, but cooler heads prevailed, pointing out that the crime rate in the park was actually lower than in the rest of the Village (and the rest of the city), so the familiarity and pleasure of the square's unencumbered edges carried the day. The current impetus to fence has been more successful (if with a lower fence than originally proposed), in tune with the new millennium's penchant for enclosure and control. For some years now, the park has been surrounded by police video cameras, and the well-established panoptic regime is certain to remain, empowered by its demonstrable success in curbing drug traffic, as well as by the general post-9/11 willingness of citizens to be everywhere surveilled.

The character of Washington Square grows from its design, from its population, from the character of its edges, from how it is spatially enclosed. One of the singularities of New York is the way in which it produces and manages a wide variety of juxtapositions of scale. All cities can be described as a dialogue between homogeneity and exception, and each strikes a particular balance that is at the core of its character. Exception can be produced by a variety of means and has a variety of drivers. Much municipal legislation is directed at descriptions of "noncompatible" forms and uses—at the delineation of the limits of exception. Incompatibility can be described formally, as in limits to size or style, or functionally, as in limitations on absolutely or situationally defined obnoxious uses like loud nightclubs in residential areas, porn shops next to schools, or nuclear plants downtown.

Broadly speaking, New York's most thrilling styles of physical exception—like Washington Square—are produced historically, by the shift of paradigms and possibilities over the years and by the cyclical nature of the construction economy. The city's variegated scale is part of its genius loci, and—because so many of its striking juxtapositions are essentially accidental—efforts to codify this component of its character save after the fact are largely impossible. A laissez-faire approach is, on the other hand, actually an inscription of contemporary models, likely to lead to a uniformity of the most profitable forms. Sometimes this produces fabulous results. Lower Manhattan retains most of the original "organic" pattern of New Amsterdam, its narrow streets and irregular grid. But waves of prosperity have now made prominent a building type—the skyscraper—that the Dutch could hardly have imagined. The best of these have irregular bases defined by the eccentric shape of their blocks, stepping profiles defined by the 1916 zoning law, and tall, thin shafts—often rotated to the orientation of the uptown grid—in order to max out their area and to figure in the San Gimignano dance of status on the skyline. Many have been converted to upmarket residential use because their skinny towers are now too small for the expansive layouts considered necessary for contemporary offices.

In the Village, the layering is more intense and includes large areas of very old fabric, alterations caused by, among other things, the interpolation of tenements and apartment buildings in pre-zoning and pre-preservation days, remnants of the industrial waterfront, excisions by urban renewal, corridors carved by the insertion of avenues and subways, the presence of specialized institutions, and the effects of the progressive movement of the center of town northward, including a substantial intensifying commercial presence during the late nineteenth century and early twentieth. Its variety is also the by-product of dramatic shifts in population, of the waves of rich people, immigrants, bohemians, students, gays, yuppies, and others who have left their marks on its culture and physiognomy.

Maintaining both the social and the physical character of this mix is a main focus of neighborhood activism, and although the battles of affordability are largely lost here, we take reflexive objection to projects that too greatly tip the scale or remove relic textures. Two of the bitterest recent battles have been over a very tall and ungainly dorm being built by NYU—an institution that has long had an amazingly deaf ear for community concerns about its aggrandizement—and the demolition of a much-loved old church that the Catholic authorities have sold for development. In other parts of town—including Williamsburg in Brooklyn and the Lower East Side—gentrification and supportive zoning have caused innumerable towers to sprout from the low-rise fabric. While I admit to the visual excitement of the occasional well-designed shaft shooting out of the uniformity, I also recognize that each of these poses a peril to established communities and threatens an eventual reconfiguration that is likely to yield a more general, and generally unhappy, urban condition.

LAGUARDIA
PLACE

Reaching Washington Square, I face another decision: which of four parallel streets to take south. A square-skirting right turn takes me down MacDougal Street, the most heavily commercialized and busy option. Over the years, MacDougal has remained raffish and student-oriented. Its predominance of small storefronts has ensured it as a home for small businesses, including a multitude of cafés, pizza and falafel parlors, head shops, newsstands, candy stores, Indian jewelers, bars, and restaurants. Sullivan and Thompson Streets are similar but a bit quieter and less commercially dense. Each has its particular appeal, both in its Village stretches and in its run below Houston Street, where it enters SoHo. Sullivan Street has a couple of chess parlors, and I like to walk it periodically to reassure myself that they are still there. The survival of such economically marginal but culturally vital uses serves as a canary in the mine shaft, on alert against the gas of gentrification.

One route-driving criterion, especially important in the summer months, is the possibility of walking in the shade. Because my morning walk is southerly, the shade cast by buildings on the east side of the street—remembering that the general scale of building is fairly low—disappears by an early hour. This means that until late afternoon, when the west-side buildings take over, shade is provided by street trees that spread their canopies directly overhead. The frustratingly uneven distribution of trees in the city—particularly their absence on most major avenues—demands careful calculation for a bowery stroll.

Because of urban renewal and the anomalous municipal ownership of a wide strip of land along the eastern side of LaGuardia

Place, the buildings between West Third Street and Houston are substantially set back from the street. The space between is devoted to landscape, and after being improved in fits and starts over the years, it is now completely green. The eastern edge of the space is occupied by a one-story commercial strip—a continuous building in the first block with small shops and restaurants and a freestanding supermarket in the next, a rarity in the city and now threatened by NYU expansion plans. The east side of LaGuardia is divided into two superblocks that replace what were formerly nine city blocks, bits of Brasília in the midst of nineteenth-century New York.

In the summer, the temperature along this green strip—a model piece of greenfill—is always several degrees lower than that of the surrounding streets. The greenery, which for one block includes a thick ground cover of ivy and for the next is shared by community garden plots and Alan Sonfist's *Time Landscape*—a nice art piece that purports to restore its small plot to the landscape native before the arrival of white settlers—covers most of the surface and contributes to the cool atmosphere. It even produces a rare and refreshing smell. This linear landscape provides relief from unremitting hardscape and functions as a fragmentary park. The city has a number of these linear landscapes, most more formalized. One of the most important of these—Sara D. Roosevelt Park (which replaces the block between Chrystie and Forsyth Streets)—is on the Lower East Side, running all the way from Houston to Canal Street.

Chrystie-Forsyth arose as the result of the demolition of the housing blocks between its two eponymous borders, a classic Robert Moses project and one of many—including hundreds of beautiful parks, playgrounds, and beaches and 600,000 units of housing—that make his legacy ambiguous. Chrystie-Forsyth dates from an era—and a sensibility—in which modernist ideas about the introduction of green lungs into the city, and the removal of overcrowding via the wholesale demolition of "slum" housing, were largely unquestioned. Indeed, the urban-renewal project south of Washington

Square and the green spaces between buildings and green strips along their borders are a last gasp of the project of urban renewal in its classic, tabula rasa incarnation.

Still, there's something remarkably pleasant about this part of the city, and it's a relief from the uninterrupted construction of the grid. There are many places in New York in which the altruistic logic of the "slum-clearance" project can be clearly seen and clearly seen to make sense. From the core of the Lower East Side—now the object of remorseless, breakneck gentrification—one can look down streets crowded with airless tenements toward handsome housing projects built by labor unions and understand the impetus to replace unsanitary, ill-repaired, crowded "slums" with generously dimensioned and well-built structures to accommodate sunshine and breezes, and to integrate buildings and green spaces.

Unfortunately, the models have been received too purely and are too predicated on a zero-sum game, ensuring that the embrace of one involves the erasure of the other. But the history of the city, as suggested, has produced a special authenticity—a genius loci via a formal hybridity that is the result of the centuries-long sequence of renewed paradigms jostling for priority and of the fact that the slate can never be wiped clean. The unique character of New York is the product of a series of juxtapositions of elements that might imply a continuous picture of the city—the city of row houses, the city of towers in the park, the city of street walls, the city of freestanding houses, and so on—but that are distributed throughout the city as larger or smaller fragments of a more demanding whole. The future of the city lies not in the superposition of the next great idea throughout the town but in the careful articulation and expression of these differences.

The sequence of spaces from Washington Square down La-Guardia Place is a reminder that public space is something that is both physical and genuinely accessible, an extension, rather than a denial, of the street. This interleaving describes the objectives and ambitions of the collectivity, as well as the willingness of government to acknowledge and defend them. Unfortunately, historical ambivalence about the public sphere, along with the tirelessly tiresome mantra that private arrangements are superior, has led to a blighting of the ideology of shared responsibility and collective harmony. This is also expressed in the ambiguously hybrid arrangements that force even well-meaning institutions into perilous "balancing acts" that involve utilitarian decisions about the "greater good," decisions that always entail doing some "lesser evil."

For example, Cooper Union, a remarkable East Village institution that has provided superb, free higher education for more than 150 years, has had to sell off some of its neighborhood landholdings in order to top up its teetering endowment. Fiduciary logic insists on the highest bidder, and as a result the school now sits opposite one of the ugliest, most inept buildings in this part of town, a sealed glass tower for the mega-rich with a giant bank on the ground floor. Similarly, north of the Village, in Chelsea, a block-square Episcopal seminary that comprises magnificent, if crumbling, Gothic Revival buildings was embroiled with the surrounding community over its plans to replace its one (awful) modern building with a relatively tall condo. The logic here is for the new structure to finance repairs to the rest of the campus. Designed to the scale of the fiscal context, the project is, however, out of scale with the physical one. Recently, though, the news has been good, and the seminary has agreed to a compromise. The same scenario is currently playing out with plans to replace our local hospital—St. Vincent's—with a new building, to be largely financed by turning over the warren of older structures it currently occupies to a developer, who will replace them with the usual super-luxe condos.

The city increasingly conducts its business via the same Peter/Paul principle. Since it was first formulated in the 1960s as part of the city's repertoire of zoning tools, the so-called bonus system has come to be one of the main instruments for the direct subsidy of private development by the municipality. Initially created as a means to induce specific amenities—parks, through-block passageways, arcades, and so forth—the system is a formula for exchanging some putative public good (like a plaza) for a public ill, almost invariably building bulk that exceeds the underlying zoning. The exchange is fraught by nature, since there is always a predicate of harm in the arcane formulations by which the Solomonic cost-benefit analysis is expressed. Thus, the bonus system has been used not simply to create specific forms of public space but to induce developers to build in areas (like Times Square and the Theater District) that were considered "blighted" or below capacity. Such bonuses are often part of larger packages that include tax holidays, municipal condemnation, publicly financed improvements to infrastructure, and liberal air-rights transfers.

The current variation of this system—still in its infancy and not yet substantially proven—is the idea of "inclusionary" zoning mentioned earlier. As the incredible pressure on Manhattan increasingly drives the poor and the middle class to the "outer" boroughs (or outta town), development has also accelerated in areas of the city long neglected. Much of Brooklyn—the Heights, Park Slope, Carroll Gardens, and so on—has already been Manhattanized, and every borough is experiencing greater or lesser effects of the great bubble (though the sub-prime crisis that has devastated the housing market is only just beginning to be felt here). Recognizing that the city is experiencing a huge net loss of "affordable" housing, the administration is promoting a new bonus system whereby bulk is exchanged for the inclusion—either in the project under development or elsewhere—of a certain number of lower-cost units. This might be described as a form of market compulsion, predicated on a rational-choice theory of economic behavior. That is, to work, the system must persuade a developer of the certainty of greater profit if he or she decides to take the bonus deal.

The city is now engaged in an extensive project of re-zoning, inspired by the need to manage widespread pressures for development (and by the frequent failures of current zoning to accommodate demand or to prevent egregious outcomes from the exploitation of a system that couldn't have anticipated the city's transformation). The net result will be an aggregate increase in the literal volume of the city, the selective protection of certain high-value areas, and the large-scale transformation of large swaths of the city—including the waterfront and a number of remaining concentrations of industrial zoning—to relatively generic residential and office use. While there is some wisdom in this approach's attempt to induce the market to provide the lower-income housing it has no particular inclination to offer, only time will tell whether a truly serious number of units will be produced and where the ongoing negotiation over where the structure of such deals will fall on the continuum of beneficence and theft.

This same idea of the "public-private partnership" has been extended to park space, which, according to current municipal writ, means that parks must pay for themselves. This is partly the legacy of the dark days of municipal bankruptcy (FORD TO CITY: DROP DEAD read the headline as New York sought assistance from the Feds), when empty coffers meant "deferred" maintenance of everything from streets to subways to green spaces. Mainly, though, it's the result of a combination of social parsimony and Republican ideology, the idea that all government is bad government and therefore not to be trusted with money. This abdication often masquerades as "prudence" under a "pay-as-you-go" or "lockbox" style of dedicated revenue. Most of the new park and public space currently envisioned is shunted through this self-financing rubric, and all of it is meeting with varying degrees of community resistance.

The new Brooklyn Bridge Park—constructed by the city on a fabulous site on the East River lined with abandoned piers—went through a cycle of protest over how much area was to be handed over to developers for luxury apartments. Farther upriver in Greenpoint, a smaller riverfront park is to be built by developers of upscale housing in exchange for zoning bonuses. The argument centers on the degree to which the neighborhood behind the phalanx of waterfront towers will have access to the new park, as well as on whether the exchange of shadow-darkened afternoons for a smallish piece of green is a fair one. Closer to home, debate roils over the fate of the huge Pier 40, now a parking facility and heavily used sports fields, which the city considers the linchpin of its scheme to provide a self-financing mechanism for Hudson River Park. Outcomes remain unclear as developers jostle to control this giant public asset.

Most contested of all is a project proposed for a rail-yard site in central Brooklyn by the developer Bruce Ratner (with architecture by Frank Gehry, confirming the truth of the old saw: If you want to build a bad building, hire a good architect, and If you want to build an outrageous building, hire a distinguished one). Here the issue is an enormous increase in scale and density (predicted to become the highest in the country). If built as proposed, the project's buildings will tower over the low-rise neighborhoods around them and, along with the professional basketball arena that is also part of the project, will produce huge increases in traffic, pollution, and strain on municipal resources, including transit and schools. In exchange, the public will receive "development" of an unbuilt area, the new arena, and a relatively modest amount of park space, an increment that is hardly enough to serve the thousands of new residents. The whole project, like many of those promoted by city hall, takes advantage of the fact that most of the site is already in the hands of a state authority, thereby allowing the process to evade much formal public review. Protests have been vehement (with telling divisions between newer, "gentrifier" residents of the area and older, poorer ones), and the project is likely to be somewhat modified. Developers very frequently present enormously overscaled proposals to give themselves leeway to scale back, often to something still unreasonable.

For most of the twentieth century, architecture has been spoken of principally in the language of functionalism, and even today some version of utility continues to be the default for "rationally" explaining the meaning of building. Everyone knows the famous, variously ascribed slogan "Form follows function." This aphorism, which suggests that the physical character of a building should be primarily dictated by the uses to which it is to be put, is architecture's main claim for appearing logical and scientific. Behind functionalism—as opposed to traditional aesthetic styles of judgment—is the idea that architecture can be objectified. The criteria by which a building is judged are quantifiable via some scientific measure—efficiency, thermal behavior, psychological well-being, and so on.

This positivist analytic mood implies not simply that building could be described by a series of reliable measures but that, like rationality itself, the form of architecture itself could become universal. The famous 1932 exhibition at the Museum of Modern Art in New York—from which the sobriquet the International Style emerged to describe architecture characterized by white walls, great simplicity, a certain whiff of the technological in its image making, and an assembly-line approach to urbanism—was a high-water mark in the codification of a particular style. This was also the peak of a fundamentally colonial mentality, the idea that this concretization of a Western formal and social order would suit and benefit everyone on the planet. Ironically, the origins of this particular strain of modernism derived, in part, from the prismatic inspiration of the whitewashed architecture indigenous to both the European and the African sides of the Mediterranean. Like the "primitive" sources beloved of so many artists of the time, it represented a return of the repressed, not to mention oppressed. One feels this same tension in the anxious binarism of many colonized cities—like those in North Africa—in which the "irrational" medina is doubled by a non-identical twin, the gridded new town of the French or Italian suzerains.

To be sure, the triumph of this minimal style was more parochial than its publicity let on. Like the art of the time—which included both Mondrian and Georgia O'Keeffe—modernity in architecture was diverse. The victory of the minimal style represented the triumph of one particularly well-organized camp within a far broader conversation, one that included Antoni Gaudí, Alvar Aalto, Michel de Klerk, and Frank Lloyd Wright, among many others, who anticipated the kind of formal plasticity and geometric complexity that is so important to architecture today. That this victory proved decisive was because the forms of minimalist modernity dovetailed so precisely with the expressive requirements of

global capital, not to mention the various modifications of the Cal-
vinist welfare state, and the ultimate triumph of the American
style of democracy and production: what's good for General Motors
is good for the country, and what's good for us is good for the world.

The fantasy of the melting pot was the galvanizing metaphor
of the American experience: *e pluribus unum*. This idea of democracy lay in the progressive surrendering of differences until all were
reduced to a self-similar distillate of Americanness, an enterprise
we are now pursuing abroad with such disastrous consequences in
Iraq as we demand, at the point of a gun, why Sunnis, Shiites, and
Kurds who want nothing to do with one another can't just get
along. Although we put the happy spin of the universal on all this,
the same processes of purgation were practiced by totalitarian systems in their own effort to produce the "new man." Rationalism
and scientific understanding joined with radical views of the nature
of equality to give rise to the idea of a universal—and statistical—
subjectivity. If we were all to be the same in our needs, tastes, and
aspirations, it seemed only logical that our architecture be the
same as well. The consumer system could handle any superficial
local inflections: put the orientalist arches in the skyscraper lobbies
of Dubai or see that the Hong Kong CEO is satisfied with the feng
shui of the boardroom.

The sources of the economist turn behind the rise of minimalist styles of expression were overdetermined. These were, after all,
the years of Fordism, mass production, the rise of the Taylorist efficiency expert, and the infinite replication and studied imperma-
nence of the consumer object. These were also the beginning of
the years in which the corporation, arrogating the colonial thrust
of the first-world nation-state, became unabashedly transnational.
Minimalism was seen as both a suitable (and inexpensive) expression for triumphalist global reach—not just an anonymous default
mode—and an apt style for housing (later incarcerating) the universal culture and the replicant citizens of the welfare state. Early
"good-for-you" ideas of the therapeutic benefits of rationalism, twisted
by totalitarianism and greed, have now frankly devolved into the

good-for-us regime of the clash of civilizations, whether fought out in Baghdad or South Central.

Under the rhetorical veneer of science, modernity has always had an ethical problem. The informing idea of functionalism is what is called elegance by engineers and scientists—the notion that the best solution to a problem (whether applied to a mathematical proof, a machine, or an organizational diagram) is the most succinct. This conceit collapses the technical, the ethical, and the aesthetic, which powers the idea exponentially. Postmodernism, with its counterattack on behalf of ambiguity, indeterminacy, relativity, and difference, has been an important rejoinder to the oppressive side of universalism but has often occupied a slippery ethical ground, undermining ideas of consent, pulling too many moral punches, and coddling styles of ambiguous meaning. And yet the destabilization produced by its critique has been vital in disconnecting the reflexive link between a particular kind of architecture and the production of a particular kind of society.

That the mood of modernity was fundamentally therapeutic is not what distinguishes it from its predecessors. What does is its combination of a post-Enlightenment politics of equality, a special concern for scientific "objectivity," and a focus on the body. To be sure, architecture and its theory have incorporated similar ideas for millennia, directing its power at the elevation of the soul, taking its standard dimensions from our own, organizing social relationships according to its diagram. But the rise of "humanism" represented a fundamental epistemological shift, a new style of instrumentality in which architecture was increasingly identified with medicine, itself a series of practices that differ in style and approach but uniformly promote the idea of "health." (Perhaps it is useful to note that one of the acknowledged fathers of scientific medicine in America, Benjamin Rush, was insanely devoted to bloodletting.)

This medicalization of architecture can be seen in the movements for sanitation, light, and air that transformed the nineteenth-century tenements, in those lively debates about the most therapeutic forms for panoptic prisons and asylums, in the protective technologies of fireproofing and seismic construction, in the segregation of obnoxious uses, and in the preferred, hygienically simple, and white appearance of International Style modernism. Through the lens of contemporary ideas and methods, much of this seems at once familiar and mad. Like debates that continue to this day, this one is poignant for its combination of instrumental optimism—the wish to use "reason" to do good—and its delusional faith in what David Harvey has called "spatial environmental determinism."

This preoccupation reproduced itself both at the scale of individual buildings and at the scale of the city—at the scales of the human body and the body politic. Moreover, modern architecture saw itself both as a bridge—a channel—to nature and as a part of it. Blurring the boundary between architecture and the natural world yielded transparent buildings that allowed "nature" to flow through them, buildings lifted on *pilotis* to free the ground plane and permit nature to pass under them, buildings attuned to solar angles and prevailing winds, buildings that sought to blend inconspicuously with the natural (or social) landscape. Today, interest in these interactions has matured beyond mere symbolism into the movement for "green" architecture, to buildings with a genuinely scientific understanding of their pivotal role in the health of the planet. It has likewise led to revivals of interest in traditional geomancies, like Vastu and feng shui, which welcome assertions, like the Gaia principle, of our connectedness with nature and are likely sources of useful placebo effects.

By the second quarter of the twentieth century, two distinct modern urbanisms had appeared, both of which grew from the convergence of the critique of the industrial city and the sense that the contemporary city represented a dramatic imbalance in human relations with the natural. The first of these was the "garden city," given its classic formulation by the Englishman Ebenezer Howard in *To-morrow: A Peaceful Path to Real Reform*, in 1898, reissued four years later as *Garden Cities of Tomorrow*.

Garden cities were meant to "cure" the problems of the industrial metropolis via radical decentralization—the creation of an archipelago of small towns of village character and low density, surrounded by agricultural fields and forests. Because of their intimate scale and general greenness, they were to be incubators of citizenship and health. Although Howard's ideas were much inspired by the broad critique of modernity made by William Morris, John Ruskin, and others who sought a restoration of an individual, agrarian, and crafts-based culture they identified with the Middle Ages, the garden city was foundational for a subsequent history of efforts to build compact, sustainable new towns. It was also remarkably prescient—in the Howard formulation—in conceptualizing the next order of organization, networking these towns by transport and communications media, an extremely relevant model for today.

The second great model for the new city sought to create cities of huge scale but along more putatively rational models. The classic example is Le Corbusier's 1922 "Contemporary City of Three Million." Like the garden city, the City of Three Million sought to redress the estrangement of the city from nature. But instead of a compact arrangement based on traditional village architecture, Le Corbusier's city distributed its population in enormous towers, arranged in a precise Cartesian grid within a vast park. Uses were rigorously zoned and residents obliged to pass through an endless Eden to get to the office towers at the center of town, where commerce and sociability were to flourish beneath a giant plinth. The whole arrangement was enabled by the automobile—a technology not yet invented in Howard's time—which was to allow citizens to move swiftly from place to place on a system of highways (although Corb wildly underestimated the infrastructure required).

Corb soldiered on with this urbanism, attracting followers through his prodigious publications, polemics, and leadership role in CIAM—the International Congress of Modern Architecture— founded in 1928 and best known for its 1933 manifesto "The Athens Charter," which codified the elements of functional urbanism. In

1925, Le Corbusier translated the City of Three Million into the Voisin Plan for Paris—the ur-image of urban renewal, a scheme vast enough to make Haussmann look like a piker. Corb proposed to excise a huge area of the existing fabric of the city and replace it with a brace of his cruciform towers. As tenaciously as he clung to these ideas as social and architectural projects, Le Corbusier recognized that their practicality hinged on strong and sympathetic centralized power (an insight that had a later, very sour incarnation in his shameless sucking up to Vichy during the war). Under the influence of a form of syndicalism in the 1930s with its idea of the emergence of "natural" leadership, Corb imagined himself a likely philosopher/architect/king. Mincing no words, he wrote, in 1967, "Authority must step in, patriarchal authority, the authority of a father concerned with his children."

Le Corbusier's advocacy of what he had come to call the "Radiant City" continued to his death, and in the 1960s he published his most complete vision, drawn with seductive elegance and insanely mesmerizing to the generation of architects teaching in my school days, for whom possession of a Corb drawing or painting was tantamount to owning a relic of the True Cross. In its final incarnation, Corb's city was organized in evenly spaced residential towers housing twenty-seven hundred inhabitants, each allotted fourteen square meters of space. From here they commuted to a zone of office towers, themselves holding thirty-two hundred workers. Corb called this, aptly enough, a "vertical garden city," reflecting the tenacity of the conceptual antithesis between the idea of city and country that had by then dominated what was more than a century and a half of thinking, spanning Thomas Jefferson, Ebenezer Howard, Frank Lloyd Wright, and countless others.

In the early 1950s, Le Corbusier actually had the opportunity to design a city from scratch: Chandigarh, in India. Now built and housing a population of more than one million, the city both adheres to and departs dramatically from the Radiant City model. It is organized in a series of eight-hundred-by-twelve-hundred-meter superblocks—or "sectors"—each meant to accommodate various neighborhood functions. The division permits, and even demands, efficient functional zoning (Sector 17 is the commercial area, government facilities occupy a special precinct at the "head" of the town, industry is somewhere over the horizon). The city's infrastructure is deployed in fiendish hierarchy. Housing is produced according to a set of space and income classifications that make the caste system look republican. Movement space is overwhelmingly generous and organized in a sevenfold order (V1, V2, V3, and so on) of horizontal laminations according to vehicular speed. Revealingly, an eighth V had to be added by Corb's successors to accommodate bicycles and pedestrians, modes for which the master had little use.

But Chandigarh is at least two things the Radiant City was not. It is low, and it is in India. As a result, the importance of the street—despite obstacles of width, division, and dispersal of commercial activity—asserts itself with complex and colorful tenacity, especially in areas of greater density. Street life in the sectors occupied by the walled villas of senior civil servants is largely the province of their security guards, who sit at their gates, cradling their ancient Enfield rifles. The blooming, buzzing confusion of Indian traffic—while substantially dissipated by the mad surfeit of roadways—gives the city a sense of confusion and bustle that Corb would have found appalling. Like all cities, Chandigarh is put to the test of habitation by people whose traditions and desires cannot be repressed by mere architecture.

Chandigarh notwithstanding, the Radiant City's reductive repertoire of isolated towers, separated uses, a green ground plane, and the replacement of a street network by a system of highways crystallized the form of an operation that was to take place all over the world under a variety of guises. The most familiar of these is the destroy-it-to-save-it, excise-that-cancer mentality of urban renewal. In New York, private developments like Peter Cooper Village, Stuyvesant Town, Parkchester, and Co-op City, as well as Housing Authority projects in their hundreds, are formal adaptations of its narcotizing images. They're social adaptations, too, in that their populations are uniform in the only sense that really counts for modernity: class, which, especially in a society like ours, tends to repeat divisions rather than obliterate them.

Washington Square Village, the two long NYU housing blocks in the urban-renewal precinct east of LaGuardia Place, is clearly inspired by another of Le Corbusier's most indelible icons: the so-called Unité d'Habitation, of which several were built, the most notable at Marseilles. The Unité was intended to be a self-contained neighborhood, a verticalization of the gridded urban landscape that formed Corb's vision of the city of the future. As materialized in isolation, the Unités are gorgeous, brilliantly composed concrete structures, filled with ingeniously designed duplex apartments that interlock sectionally to provide cross-ventilating exposures on both sides of the buildings. They also provide playfully sculpted communal roof terraces for kids (palely imitated in Washington Square Village's curvy enclosures for its water tanks and elevator penthouses) and are raised off the ground on *pilotis*. And they contain an additional element of the Corbusian canon that was less successful, the so-called street in the sky, Corb's attempted displacement of the real version.

Corb's loathing for the street suffused his ideology and infected the larger discourse of urbanism for years. The "street in the sky" was meant to replace the conventional street by providing its services *within* individual buildings. In the Unités, one floor—about halfway up—is dedicated to shops and offices, the idea being that tenants would ascend or descend from their apartments to transact their daily commerce in the sheltered confines of these dedicated spaces, never having to leave the building. As with virtually every other street in the sky, it was a complete failure in both social and economic terms. The principal reason for this was that each Unité was predicated on an erroneous presupposition of a community of interests that would draw tenants together. This idea was very much the product of a utopian socialist ideology that was formative for Corb (and many others) and, in particular, of the work of Charles Fourier.

Fourier was part of the great nineteenth-century impetus to translate ideas about social reform into concrete reality "on the ground." Generally speaking, such ideas sprang from the sense of social tractability that grew from the Enlightenment. Fourier's particular invention—which he developed with the architect Victor Considérant—was the so-called phalanstery, a collectivist community housed in a single building. Ironically, the model for its ideal architecture was derived from the image of Versailles, the home of a political system that was the very antithesis of Fourierist cooperation. Versailles—a megastructure *avant la lettre*—did, however, house a "complete" community, and there was a strong resonance in the appropriation of its palatial and exclusivist form for the use of "the people." Thus, revolutionary politics has had its own long history of struggle between lifestyle fantasies of self-sacrificing austerity and the transfer of luxury from the thieving rich to the deserving poor. The idea of constructing perfect societies within legible boundaries was a powerful one, and it resonated throughout Western culture in the nineteenth century. The democratic nation-state, the company town, the bourgeois idealization of the perfect sanctuary of "home," all participated in this amazing project of inventing and controlling harmony (no coincidence that one of the most famous American intentional communities—still in physical existence—was New Harmony in Indiana). Le Corbusier was radically influenced by this ethos of social manipulation and bought into the architect's most historic fallacy: that rearranging space could and would lead to rearrangements of politics, culture, and the soul. The Unités were ultimately doomed by the inflexibility of this vision, although they were, along the way, brilliantly successful elaborations of a modern architectural type: the apartment building.

Corb was surely correct in the idea that a large apartment building should contain a mix of uses. The idea of a day-care center on a breezy green protected rooftop, or of a dentist's office or architect's studio mixed into the residential fabric, is logical and vitalizing, an antidote to the pervasiveness of single-use zoning.

However, Le Corbusier's desire to completely disengage the street in the sky from the system of streets that potentiates the most important social qualities of the city was self-limiting, not to say outright destructive. The good city is always a balancing act between the fluidity of association and the stability of elective affinities. Like the tenants in Annabel Lee, those living in the Corbusian Unités were not thrown together out of some preexisting bond of solidarity (except perhaps architectural taste). Although they, as I do, might enjoy bumping into neighbors on the street or at the grocery store, none of us would want to be constrained to conduct all our everyday affairs in their company, nor assume an automatic congruence of taste or interest.

Perhaps this is the moment to bring up what might seem to be a contradiction in this argument: my sympathy for aspects of the messages of both Corb and Jacobs. The last few years have seen a great revival of interest in the work of Robert Moses (so long having channeled Corbusian ideas), and there have been a number of exhibitions, books, and articles that have taken a provocative line about him. These almost invariably postulate a Manichaean struggle between Moses and Jacobs, representing them as purely antithetical forces, bent on mutual annihilation. The bloom in Moses's reputation is partly the result of the administration's fixation on "big" projects, people's frustration with the slow democracy of community planning, a general sense of the ineptitude of the municipal players, and a re-appreciation of the remarkable constructive contributions made by Moses: the parks, beaches, playgrounds, and sheer numbers of housing units. "A little more Moses, a little less Jacobs" has become a slogan for many.

But what did Corb actually think about New York? In 1937, he published *When the Cathedrals Were White*, an account of a trip to the United States during the previous year. The book lies squarely in the tradition of the insemination of deep desire in the city's pliant body under the guise of observation. The French have a particularly long tradition of this, ranging from Tocqueville to Corb to Baudrillard to Lévy—even Certeau. Indeed, both Certeau and Le

Corbusier launch their observations by gazing at the city from the tops of skyscrapers, as tired a trope of analytic spectatorship as Gotham offers. Certeau uses the occasion for a rapid descent to earth, to the space of individual pedestrians. Corb's frame remains lofty, and while he is thrilled with the dynamism and verticality of the city, its cleanliness, and its grid, he finds it unplanned and uses New York as an armature for an argument about massive transformation according to his theories. His hope is that this is doable in America, a country without a past and with a raw, naive energy up to the massive job.

Corb's prescriptions for New York were predictable—bigger, freestanding, Cartesian skyscrapers; massive consolidation of building to open up the ground plane; separation of pedestrians and cars to expedite flow; purgation of the picturesque "romantic" anomalies of the historic, "provisional" city; and massive population growth. Each, however, was prompted by observations that were often on the money. In chapters like "There Are No Trees in the City" and "A Million and a Half Cars Daily," Corb attempted to defend the primary interest of people on foot. But his idea of a stroll through the city was indistinguishable from a walk through the countryside, and this elision, this mechanized ruralization, is at the nexus of the modernist problem with cities. Corb wanted those trees to form a near-continuous forest with buildings far apart. He thought that the conflict between pedestrians and cars could be solved by eliminating the rows of front doors on city streets (each a potential stopping point for a car) and consolidating them at massive towers, where thousands could enter at a single point. These ideas would have destroyed New York and have long given a logic to many who worked hard at the job.

The obligatory associations of us Annabel Leetrists are produced by a narrow terrain of common interest: the upkeep of the building and the ongoing struggles with the landlord. Beyond that, we largely go our separate ways. But we all share a sense of delight in the numerousness of the choices offered by our neighborhood. Although I can imagine living in an environment in which there are firmer, more energetic bonds with my neighbors—a co-housing arrangement or something closer to the all-student building with its own food co-op I shared in the 1960s—this is a matter about which I prefer to have a choice. It is, however, one of many options that are essentially unavailable to me within the constraints of the market system and my own preferences about where I wish to live. If I had my druthers, I would surely live in a building that provided better common spaces, used alternative energy sources, and had a better, more sustainable system for waste management and remediation. I would like to live in a city that did the same, a giant Unité.

Notwithstanding all this, I am a fan of both Washington Square Village and the buildings on its neighboring superblock, Silver Towers—three beautiful and refined Le Corbusier–influenced concrete apartment buildings designed by I. M. Pei. I like them for their formal qualities as well as for the extensive green space they create within the tight fabric of the Village. To be sure, walking along the east-west sides of the superblocks can feel somewhat unrelieved, but the ample shade they offer is a plus. Each of the buildings in Washington Square Village is lifted up in two places to permit existing streets to pass beneath them, and traffic is restricted to cars using the parking lot below the large green space they frame. In particular, the sequence down University Place, along the north side of Washington Square, through the pedestrianized block between the NYU library and the old building housing its business school, under the first Washington Square Village building into the green between it and its twin, then under the second building and across the street to the Silver Towers and finally across Houston Street to Wooster and the density of SoHo is something both unusual and stimulating, not simply in its serial spatial compressions and releases, but also in its pedestrian predominance, its quietude, and its variety of architectures.

The buildings of Washington Square Village and Silver Towers are museum-quality examples of the two great apartment typologies of modernity: the tower block and the slab. Both illustrate their strengths and disadvantages when introduced into the urban fabric in their pure state. The difficulty with slabs, solved ingeniously by Le Corbusier in his Unités, is the competition between circulation and ventilation. The most efficient way of using a slab is to move through it in the long dimension, although this often excessive length can be redressed—if not very economically—with frequent vertical cores. And the most efficient circulation system, in terms of the ratio of total to potentially usable area, is to double load the corridor, put rooms on both sides of it. This leads to the typical condition of slab blocks, apartments that have their rooms lined up along a single exposure, often with an interior hallway (paralleling the public one) to organize them.

Designed this way, a long slab produces a very long corridor, a canonical modern image of alienation: endless identical doors in artificial light, always over-warm, under-ventilated, and faintly smelly. The two-sidedness of the building prevents cross breezes in individual units and presupposes equal value in the two exposures from the standpoint of both solar access and view. Slabs need to stand free to function, and the superblock and the slab are symbiotic, one providing unimpeded space for the other. The slab form can function wonderfully in the right circumstances: the United Nations (in which Le Corbusier had a formative hand) stands free in its own superblock, one side overlooking the East River, the other the panorama of Manhattan. Facing east and west, however, the building must deal with dramatic solar loads, especially on summer afternoons. The main building at Rockefeller Center—a slab vertically attenuated to the proportions of a tower—is oriented to the north and south and commands fabulous views up- and downtown. The south side is the sunny one here, but unlike the UN Secretariat it has windows that can actually be opened.

Virtually all buildings in New York are designed without any special response to the particulars of solar orientation. This means that—inescapably—if there is a favored orientation (it isn't arbitrary that the northerly latitudes prefer the south), there must also be a *dis*favored one, whether in relationship to sun or prospect. Modernist architecture—most emblematically, the sealed and uniformly skinned glass skyscraper—continues to find its eloquence in an efficient minimalism, the aesthetic dilution of the philosophical universalism at the core of its unconscious. The price for this has been an architecture oblivious to both cultural and climatic contexts: the paradigm of the hermetically sealed tower that produces its own environment—uniform in lighting and temperature no matter what—extends the fantasy of autonomy behind the phalanstery and the Unité. Even the current generation of "green" office towers in New York cannot seem to surrender either this image or this behavior but seeks to achieve it by nominally more sustainable means, by doubling the glass wall to insulate it rather than opening the window.

The elaborate indifference to the fate of the planet in contemporary architecture is nowhere more visible than in the apparitional skyline of Dubai. Rising from the desert in *Sorcerer's Apprentice* profusion, glass towers compete to top one another in scale and formal novelty while providing space and function of utter uniformity. To keep them cool in the torrid heat, incalculable barrels of oil (not exactly scarce thereabouts) must be burned. One of the more dispiriting aspects of this oblivious potlatch is that the region has, over the centuries, produced a variety of simple heat-mitigating architectures that consume no nonrenewable energy whatsoever. Thick walls, shaded courtyards, small openings, wind-catching towers, cooling pools, rational orientation, and other similarly simple, logical devices have not simply ordered genuinely indigenous morphologies but also tested and refined principles of enduring relevance.

The received version of modern architecture, with its social simplification and technical sophistication, has gotten it exactly backward. Genuinely sustainable architecture must begin with the simplest technical solutions (sunshades, cross ventilation, correct solar orientation) but conduce the most complex social relations (variety before uniformity). Invention will come not simply from the fevered acts of lonely imagination but from the constant reframing of questions raised at the intersection of climate, culture, technology, politics, and taste, by the understanding that architectural meanings are produced, not inherent. At the moment, innovations in green architecture are impeded by lingering stereotypes of low funk, failures to challenge conventional formal and organizational typologies, and a refusal to model systems at appropriate scales.

One of the most reproduced images of contemporary architecture depicts the dynamiting of the Pruitt-Igoe housing project in St. Louis in 1972, an event sometimes bruited as symbolizing the death of modernism and the accession of post. The demolition was the first of many across the country, seeking—like the urban renewal that produced the projects in the first place—again to solve the problem of poverty by demolishing the homes of the poor. But the reflexive association of the "modern" architecture of the projects with the undeniable pathologies they housed depends on a dangerous fallacy. In both proportion and layout, the buildings of Pruitt-Igoe—designed by Minoru Yamasaki, the architect of the World Trade Center—were almost identical to those of the buildings of Washington Square Village and only marginally more parsimonious in finish and detail. The differences were twofold: one was filled with desperately impoverished single mothers and kids and the other with well-paid college professors and their families; and one stood in penal isolation, while the other sat at the heart of a vital and thick community.

Silver Towers represents the other modernist morphological prototype for the high-rise, the point tower, a vertically proportioned building with its elevator core at the center. Such buildings reduce the need for long corridors and yield a four- rather than two-sided configuration. In its most elongated forms—like Silver Towers or, in extremis, the incredibly skinny "pencil" buildings of Hong Kong—there is a sequence from lobby to elevator to foyer to apartment that completely bypasses the lateral interlude of the corridor. As I've suggested before, movement from public to private space always entails various mediating elements, both social and physical. In New York, the filters tend to be extensive and include multiple doorways, buzzers, doormen, stairs and elevators, corridors, stoops, vestibules, modulations of enclosure and of light and dark, identification protocols, locks, and bolts.

This suggests another of the differences between Pruitt-Igoe and Washington Square Village. Much of the mid-century debate about urbanity—which included not just Oscar Newman but also Jane Jacobs—was focused not merely on altruism but on crime. Immemorially, the privileged have understood the danger from those classes on which their advantages depend, and the history of the state and its institutions records the shifting methods by which the threat has been managed. From slavery to serfdom to the minimum wage to welfare, the risks rising from structural inequality have been crucial descriptors of the nature of governance, of the deal struck by the social "contract." Each of these deals has produced characteristic institutions, both social and spatial. What the reformism of postwar liberalism attempted to achieve via the construction of housing projects like Pruitt-Igoe, the more frank disciplinarians of today attempt via a vast increase in prison building.

Crime is a by-product of failed environments, within families, neighborhoods, schools, or societies. Much of the debate between liberals and conservatives in the United States is colored by arguments over the etiology of criminality, the degree of individual or collective responsibility for antisocial acts. The shifting relations between therapy and policing mark the progress of this debate and underlie changing ideas about the forms and arrangements of the good city. It is no coincidence that the explosion in prison construction has been paralleled by an explosion in the construction of gated communities, not to mention the current frenzy to secure the national borders against intrusions, by terrorists and by other "aliens." Ironically, in urban planning, this has led to a reversion to faith in physical forms, to the mentality of idealization that was so characteristic of modernism at its most utopian.

The most successful planning ideology in America today is the so-called new urbanism. This movement, formalized via a charter and a congress self-consciously modeled on those of CIAM, advocates a return to the practices of "traditional" urbanism and identifies itself with many of the precepts associated with Jane Jacobs: block form, low scale, pedestrianism, and other elements of what most thoughtful exponents of the city espouse today. In theory, the "new" urbanists idealize what Jacobs did: the tractable, intimate neighborhood, an urbanity of lively sociability based on the life of the street.

However, the focus of the new urbanists is the suburbs, and their critique is telling, if not exactly original. They anathematize the alienations and inefficiencies of sprawl, savage the uglinesses of the strip, and call for a remaking of suburbia in the image of a town. Across the country, they have successfully persuaded hundreds of developers to reformat their templates to create denser, neo-traditionally styled "neighborhoods." But they have done almost nothing to transform the ecology of suburbanism, to revise its social and economic space. The overwhelming majority of new-urbanist projects retain the almost purely residential, exclusively middle-class character of suburbia, simply substituting one formal paradigm for another. Instead of curving streets, cul-de-sacs, and half-acre lots, these developments offer grids, tightly spaced houses with front porches, and a town center instead of a shopping center containing the very same shops.

Although at one level these developments seem to embody the Jacobs writ, just beneath the bright surface they are its antithesis. With their monochrome styling, restrictive covenants, and homeowners' associations, these places are bulwarks against deviancy. Fortified against accident, they are precisely the kinds of deracinated garden cities that Jacobs so abhorred. In her first masterpiece, *The Death and Life of Great American Cities*, Jacobs famously declared that "the city is not a work of art." What she meant was not that the city couldn't be judged beautiful, that the project of its formal embellishment should be set aside. Rather, she was assailing the narrow motives and resources of modernism and, by extension, the idea that the city could be reduced to any single set of practices or techniques, whether of observation, construction, or participation. To be sure, Jacobs luxuriated in the complex and graceful choreography of the life of her block—surely an urban art form—but her city was also a place of intense confrontation. When Jacobs seized the microphone or tore up the official minutes at public hearings, she knew that this, too, was part of the dance, part of the never-ending struggle that is itself at the core of the very nature of the good city: the struggle for diversity; the struggle for self-organization.

SOHO

Crossing Houston Street, LaGuardia Place becomes West Broadway, main street of SoHo, an acronym that collapses "South of Houston" with a groovy London referent. The story of SoHo is probably familiar to you, if not the New York version, perhaps a similar one. SoHo is the nation's poster child for gentrification, a place that went from semidereliction through a period of radical vitality to the height of trendiness (and its own special style of cultural dereliction) with incredible rapidity.

SoHo is bounded by Houston Street to the north, Broadway to the east, Canal Street to the south, and Sixth Avenue to the west. West Broadway (there is an East Broadway in Chinatown) is the main drag. It is also the dividing line between the two distinct morphologies that characterize the neighborhood. To the west is what has always been a residential neighborhood, an amalgam of tenements and row houses that was long predominantly Italian, and the remnants of this community are still anchored by St. Anthony's Church and an associated monastery. The legendary Vesuvio Bakery was a recent casualty of rising rents, but some key shops hang on, including Joe's Dairy, which still makes delicious mozzarella every day. This part of the neighborhood extends across Houston Street into the similar textures of the Village—the area that Robert Moses had in his sights during the battles of the 1960s.

A fair number of original residents are still ensconced in the tenements of SoHo thanks to the rent laws. But, as many are older, their presence has gradually given way to that of Wall Streeters and movie stars. A symptom of downtown's decline is the publication of movie-star maps with a density that appears to exceed that of Beverly Hills. I frequently see celebrities on the streets. (I recently sat on a toilet seat still warm from the impress of Calista Flockhart's bum.) Yet although their direct economic role in the neighborhood has been dramatically reduced, old-timers are part of the touristic appeal of the place. They form a cadre of street users, bench sitters, and window hangers, a model for the kind of sociability celebrated by Jane Jacobs. In their common heritage, regular relationship to the church, shared habits, and working-class memories, these residents have a much tighter and more local complex of affinities than their bobo successors, who, nevertheless, do participate in some aspects of their style. Until it closed at the beginning of 2012, Auggie's, the café favored for many years for my mid-walk cappuccino, managed to remain a meeting point for the old population and the new, a connection sustained by the fact that a number of the members of the "new" population have now been living in the neighborhood for thirty years, veterans of the days when they were themselves in the minority.

The more physically singular part of SoHo lies on the other side of West Broadway, the twenty square blocks of the cast-iron district. At the turn of the last century this was a manufacturing area, and its construction (and character) coincided with the widespread use of a mid-nineteenth-century technical innovation, cast-iron facades and columns. For structural reasons—cast iron is strong in compression, weak in tension—these buildings tended to be composite, with side walls of brick and beams and floors of timber. The iron technology not only permitted the beautiful decorative quality of the elaborately cast iron but also allowed the facades of these buildings to be very light and to have very large windows. These are also the buildings that hold so many examples of those glorious straight-run stairs. Increasingly abandoned by industry, these lofts were discovered by artists who, beginning in the 1950s, took over the large open spaces when no one else was interested and the rents were accordingly low. For a relatively brief period, the artist community flourished in its marginality and evanescent specificity within this physical and economic niche. To be sure, there was a cultural and generational affinity, but there was also a sense of pioneering, as well as the rapid beleaguering caused by the fact that their status was illegal (this part of SoHo was not zoned for residential use) and later by the pressure brought to bear by the real estate industry after loft living was legalized and the neighborhood began to flourish.

Inevitably, early SoHo developed communal institutions that marked the artist community as distinct. A limited number of bars, young art galleries, the collectively run restaurant Food (where the great Gordon Matta-Clark worked behind the counter), and other art-oriented spots sprouted up. But during the halcyon days of SoHo, these were modest in both number and ambition and contributed to a salutary sense of isolation (never mind that the Village was only a few blocks away). Indeed, in this early period, the art community coexisted nonthreateningly with remaining industrial uses as well as with the existing neighborhood. Eventually, the city stepped in to "rationalize" the illegal occupation by creating an artist-in-residence category in the zoning code, thereby allowing certified artists to live in nonresidential buildings—a form of protection akin, in its effects, to the rent laws.

The idyll was short-lived, and the specific pathology of its destruction need not be recounted at length. As the artist community grew in size and cachet, galleries and restaurants followed, attracting visitors, tourists, and new residents eager to bathe in the hip vibe. The golden goose effect was incredibly swift. Although quite a few managed to cash in on the boom, artists were driven out as buildings were converted to condos. Many of the galleries were also priced out. Cheap restaurants were supplanted by pricey ones. Shoe stores and boutiques proliferated. The streets were jammed on the weekends with people who, with no thought of art, had come simply to shop and brunch and to look at each other shopping and brunching. We used to call the street-fair-like throng that jammed West Broadway on weekends the Festival of San Castelli (after the flagship Leo Castelli gallery, for years the neighborhood's most prestigious).

Yet SoHo remains attractive and vital, in large measure because of its wonderful architecture and the landmarks legislation that requires its preservation. Much of the singularity of the cast-iron district comes from the simultaneous particularity and uniformity of its scale. If there is a place in New York with the dimensions of a nineteenth-century European city, this is it. The five- to six-story envelope, vertically elongated by the high ceilings of the lofts within and richly articulated without, yields a sense of enclosure and texture much like streets in Paris. It is a superb proportion, secured by the buildings and the relatively narrow width of the streets and producing a section at once comfortably enclosing and sufficiently low to open to the sky. Given the multinational character of much of the current commercial activity, there is an atmosphere very comparable to, say, the 6th arrondissement with its haute bourgeois residents, remnant bohemianism, and identical shops and restaurants.

SoHo has, however, become part of a tourist archipelago where the definition of place falls into a set of increasingly generic categories. The act of touring devolves less on the particulars of geography than on the consumption of a set of prepackaged lifestyles, defined by a fixed array of goods and services. Almost every city in America now boasts a SoHo equivalent—from the Pearl in Portland, Oregon, to Old Town in Wichita, Kansas. These places are marked in guidebooks as "destinations" and are often the liveliest, most street-oriented places in town, casting their valorizing aura on surrounding real estate and offering an "alternative" lifestyle (or at least domicile) in cities with relatively few choices beyond single homes.

But precisely what style of tourism *is* lifestyle tourism? The question was brought into some relief for me by a recent incident. I was crossing the street in SoHo on a very crowded day when the two tourists in front of me were cut off in the crosswalk by an expensive Mercedes bearing New Jersey plates. Simultaneously, the two shouted the word that is standard for such occasions: "Asshole!"

Having muttered this particular imprecation a thousand times myself, I found it heartwarming that the pair had so readily adapted to the local form of expression. These were people who surely knew that we pronounce Houston Street "Howston." Perhaps they also take pleasure in yelling "merde!" in Paris (as I do).

A few days later I was walking nearby and narrowly missed being hit by two converging Maclaren baby carriages being pushed by a pair of yuppie moms who were gabbing on their cells. As I felt my leg brushed and leaped to avoid tripping, I found myself muttering "asshole." Yet it was not clear, even to me, at whom this remark was directed, and fortunately it was sufficiently under my breath to remain unheard. Still, babies and expensive dogs underfoot are the price of gentrification, and I had, I thought, appropriately transferred the curse up the proprietary food chain. Had I been heard, I'd have been thought a pathetic middle-aged character, still dressed for college, not even a scrap of Prada. I, of course, prefer to simply think of myself as young. Youth culture, like modernism, is a historical condition, not a question of gray hair.

In another sense, though, dogs and babies are signs of the life of the city. The question of gentrification is made complex by the fact that the urban qualities it produces—lively street life, profuse commerce, preservation and upgrading of old buildings—are highly desirable, the substrate of urbanity. The problem with gentrification is with its particulars and with its effects. While one might have issues of taste with French bulldogs and nanny-propelled prams, the real problem is not who inhabits the gentrified environment but who is displaced, who is left out of the mix.

A New Yorker cover a couple of years ago pictured Adam and Eve being expelled from paradise by an angry God overhead. The wrinkle was that they were poised on the Manhattan side of the Brooklyn Bridge, heading into exile from the unaffordable. Given the astronomical price of apartments in Manhattan, such banishment is now a threat not simply to the poor—the "traditional" victims of gentrification—but to increasing numbers of the nominal middle class. A recent study reported that proportionally New York has the smallest middle class of any place in the country. A boom is not always a sign of health.

This is reflected in tourism by its shifts in who and what tourists come to town to see, in the lifestyles into which they have come to immerse themselves. The model for such lifestyle tourism—developing since the early nineteenth century when the railway began to facilitate cheap mass travel—is voyeurism of the exotic, its classic text Richard Burton's celebrated *Personal Narrative of a Pilgrimage to Mecca and Medina*. Burton, an Englishman, disguised himself in Arab gear in order to make the hajj, and his account is the prototype for thousands of other documents (not the least of them, Le Corbusier's own *Journey to the East*) detailing the immersion of Westerners in the eastern or southern exotic. It is also (in the guise of appreciation for the other) a monument to the orientalist recirculation of occidental values. These journeys are always based on a kind of disequilibrium, the ability of the observer to be charmed by otherness, by "developing" cultures held to be innocent of the impress of a modernity that, even then, was seen as the foe of authenticity. This trope of finding superiority in someone else's tradition is one of the most annoying elements of new-urbanist self-regard.

The artist-in-residence exception in the zoning code requires that those who seek it be vetted by a board to determine if they can legitimately be called artists. There's a somewhat farcical, if fundamentally serious, repetition of this currently generating much heat in SoHo. For many years, the neighborhood mix has included large numbers of "street artists" who sell their wares from tables and display surfaces along the sidewalks. These street artists include both people hawking their own paintings, drawings, photographs, and crafts and vendors of cheap jewelry, T-shirts, mass-produced knickknacks, and knockoffs. Many, including the SoHo Alliance, the local BID, and numerous merchants, want them out of there, and the police occasionally crack down by enforcing the "twenty-foot rule," restricting vending within twenty feet of doorways. In 2000, the city council enacted legislation banning all street vendors along Prince and Spring Streets in the four blocks between West Broadway and Broadway, citing concerns over the narrowness of the sidewalks and the impediment—genuine enough—that vendors presented to pedestrian traffic.

The focus of the effort to control street artists has now shifted to West Broadway—a wider street with wider sidewalks—where the police appear to be intervening more frequently to move and harass those set up there. There has been a new scrupulosity about the twenty-foot rule, and a number of artists have reported being told by cops of an impending cleanup. Rumors of such a major crackdown are flying, and one officer was quoted in a local paper saying, "The community doesn't want the artists at all. The world has changed, it's not 1969 anymore and they don't want these people in front of their million dollar condos."

Two groups have coalesced to represent the street artists: the SoHo International Artists Cooperative and Artists' Response to Illegal State Tactics (A.R.T.I.S.T.). The former advocates the licensing of "fine artists" to the exclusion of vendors who are not selling their own work. The latter—whose feisty leader was a plaintiff in an important 1990s lawsuit that overturned the city's earlier licensing requirements for street artists—takes a broader (and more confrontational) view of artists' free-speech rights. Accusations of stooging for the BID and for a local assemblyman—Alan Gerson (held to be its puppet)—have been made. Gerson himself is preparing to introduce legislation to "alleviate congestion." Merchants along the street are divided.

The issue is important for the potential effect on people's livelihoods and, more broadly, as a matter of free expression. While courts have consistently held in favor of the First Amendment rights of artists and booksellers to use public sidewalks for business without formal licensing, they have also made it clear that these rights are subject to restrictions on "time, place, and manner." In the case of West Broadway, strict enforcement of the twenty-foot rule would probably displace the majority of vendors along the street as a matter of simple geometry. It would also transform the bazaar-like quality of the street and suppress the nice dialectic of high and low created by the juxtaposition of no-rent vendors and high-rent shops.

The legendary motto of the Hanseatic League was "Stadtluft macht frei"—city air makes you free. This was literally so, inasmuch as those cities offered freedom to serfs fleeing the feudal countryside, and also as a general matter: cities have historically been sites of free association and expression. If I seem to dwell on issues of free expression, it's because I think that cities are their conduits and compilers, and the issue of expressive limits is—and always must be—contested and never settled. Planning constantly revises the relationship of "public" rights and property rights, and the street is the scene where private citizens enact and adjudicate the proprieties of public behavior millions of times a day. These little exchanges are critical sites of the intensified reciprocity that Jane Jacobs identifies as the "golden rule" of the well-working city.

Gentrification suppresses reciprocity by its narrowed scripting of formal and social behavior, by turning neighborhoods into Disneylands or Colonial Williamsburgs, where residents become cast members and the rituals of everyday life become spectacle or food for consumption. As the enterprise of the city is increasingly transformed into the production of high-end lifestyles, citizens are forced ever deeper inside the system in order to participate in public life, which ceases to be a matter of right or election and becomes simply another commodity. As the architect Charles Moore wrote in 1965 in, only partly ironical, praise of Disneyland, "You have to pay for the public life."

It would be a mistake, however, to locate the problems of the urbanism of compulsion—the eradication of socially or commercially unacceptable or inconvenient choices—only within the context of upmarket gentrification. "Gentrification" is a term of artful derogation and should not be applied to more inclusive styles of reviving urban places. This, after all, was what Jane Jacobs and her idea of "integrated diversity" was all about. Also, my focus on the lifestyle impositions particular to my own class and taste culture shouldn't distract from other systems of narrowed choice, whether replicant public housing towers, suburban sameness, or the vacuum of opportunity most dramatically evident in the slums. The issue of how many Starbucks can dance in a neighborhood pales before the far greater problems of joblessness, redlining, limited and exploitative commerce, failed schools, narcotics, ghettos, public and private disinvestment, and all the other elements of the calculated pathology that imprisons billions.

The debate about public space and its nature has grown increasingly fierce as pressures on the very idea of a public realm and community property have intensified. Post-9/11 surveillance, privatization, gentrification, globalization, and other coercive phenomena represent only one side of the issue. The recognition of a multiplicity of publics in cities that are growing ever more plural, and a culture in which the politics of identity make ever stronger claims, suggest that the struggle to maintain and cultivate the spaces of collective experience is incredibly complicated and extremely dynamic. For some, this multiplicity provides grounds to argue that "traditional" sites of public assembly and interaction—streets, squares, parks, and so on—are relics of an insufficiently plural outlook, frustrating to diversity and naive about the constructive potential of commercial life. While this may be true, it ignores the importance to public life of accumulated forms and rituals. By fetishizing difference and instability in typically postmodern fashion, this argument reduces urbanity to a sea of fragments, trivializing locality. Cities support many different values, but their weight is not all the same.

The success of the loft life of SoHo, its wholesale transformation of the area, was not simply an accident of time, place, and culture but the result of the availability of a very specific kind of architecture: the cast-iron factory. The typical loft building in SoHo is a party-wall construction with floors of around five thousand square feet. In their manufacturing incarnation, these floors—holding printing presses, metal-stamping equipment, or rows of sewing machines—were most often open and undivided. Because these lofts were "row" buildings, the spaces tended to be windowless along their sides with their major openings on the street front and at the back of the building, generally facing into a narrow yard. Although some cross ventilation was enabled by this arrangement, solar access was generally only from the front and—depending on orientation—was of mixed quality.

As studio spaces, though, lofts were sublime. Big and cheap, their virtue was their openness, which allowed them to translate well from artistic utility to the lifestyle of the bobos, people excited at living in the grandeur of such reified "space." ("How many feet do you have?" is a fixture of New York conversation.) Before long, however, the appeal of completely open living began to pale for many. Accommodating an open loft to the exigencies of the nuclear family was not always easy and eventually produced a crisis: subdivision. With useful windows often on one side only, making bedrooms and other private spaces (with their legal requirement for daylighting) posed a great challenge. It also drove fantastic invention.

Part of the problem presented by the subdivision of loft space sprang from expectations about flexibility reflected in the architectural discourse of the day. When I was in architecture school in the early 1970s, the waning days of modernist theoretical hegemony, great value was placed on the idea of the flexibility and malleability of space. In part, this sprang from a vision of space democratized by placing its configuration under the control of the "user." Seeking the grail of "equipotential" space (a term introduced by Renato Severino in the 1970 book *Equipotential Space: Freedom in Architecture*), the dominant paradigm of flexibility was space that was as undifferentiated—as "pure"—as possible, a condition thought to maximize choice. The great icon of such space was the Plateau Beaubourg, as the Pompidou Center in Paris was then known.

The Plateau Beaubourg—the competition-winning entry of Richard Rogers and Renzo Piano—summarized a movement that had grown throughout the 1960s. The building was a clear riff on the work of Archigram, a group of British architects who produced a series of scintillating images of a highly mechanized and highly "flexible" architecture that could not only be transformed but—in its wigglier incarnations—even move across the landscape, or disappear into it. The members of Archigram also proposed (as did their compatriot Cedric Price) loftlike architectures populated by machines and modules in constant motion that could reconfigure space on a whim. The Pompidou Center was a classic expression of this fantasy of flexibility. With all its services (stairs, ductwork, escalators, and such) moved to the perimeter of the building—or housed in deep interstitial floors—the football-field-scaled use spaces were left uninterrupted, awaiting only the canny subdivision of curators to come.

This version of flexibility is, however, too constrained by its generic configuration, rigid boundaries, and vast extent to accommodate real variety, as illustrated by the huge-plated modern office building, awaiting its predictable cubicles. A more usefully flexible articulation of the idea of the loft (an architectural stem cell that might transform itself into any organ for living) is one that first takes into account the specific constraints of the environment—solar exposure, cross ventilation, views, and so on—and of the body, its capacities and dimensions. Instead of a metaphor of property or territory, of wilderness to be tamed and divided, a better metaphor is the city itself, an existing, resistant complexity out of which particular spaces and environments are created by aggregation and combination, by the reimagination and reconfiguration of elements that have the capacity to talk back, provoke, and resist repetitive, ready-made solutions.

Another model of flexibility that held great appeal in my student days was that of the squatter settlement or favela. These were celebrated for their "organic," self-organizing style of growth, their user "control," their malleability and technical simplicity, their many citizen networks and associations, and their outlaw status vis-à-vis official planning and legal norms. The response of architects and planners came first in the form of proposals for rationalizing these settlements via provision of necessary services and infrastructure and then in designs for elegantly simple building systems, few of which ever offered much advance on already available low-cost (if unaffordable for many squatters) technologies—concrete block, corrugated metal, timber, and so on. A later tendency inspired by these "informal" constructions was the attempt to translate their adaptability and user control into a language that might suit the housing needs of first-world industrial societies.

The result was a plethora of designs for buildings that embedded some system of expansion, walls that could be pushed out, balconies that could be enclosed, partitions that could be swung, service pods that could be dropped in. Perhaps the most articulate exponent of this approach was the architect John Habraken (much around campus during my MIT days), with his ideas about "support structures." Habraken's work was full of interest but reflected several fundamental conundrums. Designing systems of flexibility tends to limit the range of possibilities to those already designed into the system. These alternatives mainly devolved on expansion of the building envelope, reconfiguration of interior partitions, and the alteration of mechanical systems, giving rise to a very specific vocabulary of moving walls, free spaces for running pipes, ducts, and conduits, and a kind of building-scaled zoning to preserve space for growth. Most of these propositions were instantly obsolete, and—like similar architectural propositions for squatter settlements—few represented much of an advance on the flexibility offered by more conventional technologies: not such a big deal to move a Sheetrock wall.

However, this work did represent an important—if provisional—convergence of two great ideological spheres that were important to architecture from the 1960s onward. The first was the old modernist dream of an industrial, mass-made architecture, incorporating both a wishful economic logic that, it was hoped, might efficiently provide enough shelter to house the world and a long-standing fascination with the form of machines and other technical structures. This interest in the "purity" of technology, in objects perfectly isomorphic with their use, is the core value of functionalism, still the mother tongue of architecture, its one incontrovertible standard. A sense of the integrity—the innocence—of machinery was likewise embedded in the rising fascination with "vernacular" architecture. In 1964, the historian Bernard Rudofsky curated a show at MoMA called *Architecture Without Architects*, celebrating the formal qualities of a range of traditional building practices drawn from around the world.

Setting aside the endlessly troubled implications of the Western gaze on "primitive" cultures, the show had the very constructive impacts of encouraging formal diversity at a time when mainstream architecture had grown desperately, myopically monochromatic and of suggesting that "non-architects" were capable not only of making good judgments about their environments but of actually taking the lead in creating them. This resonated all over the place, propelling hippies into the woods to build yurts, focusing architectural practice on strategies for incorporating ongoing user input, and opening up a new territory—the vast terrain of obsolescent lofts, factories, and other structures—for architectural operations imbued, by definition, with flexibility's vibe. In an environment in which received structures—patriarchy, the family, the Communist Party, and so on—were under constant attack, the idea of a new frontier was intoxicating. Architecture would cease to be the end product of power. It would empower instead. It would be flexible! The world would be a loft, and its citizens would have the right tools to make of it just what they wished! Goodbye, Vitruvius! Hello, *Whole Earth Catalog*!

As a way of thinking about the city, the greatest flexibility of lofts is not in their configuration but in their use. The succession from manufacturing to studio to dwelling suggests an adaptable building type, able to accommodate dramatic economic and social transformations, not simply architectural ones. Such flexibility is crucial to the idea of an all-use city, the kind of city that will emerge as zoning becomes obsolete. In our increasingly postindustrial environment, the need to isolate workplaces and residences ceases to be an imperative. Instead, the relationship can now be enormously flexible and elective. In part, this is due to the shifting character of production, the decline of our manufacturing economy, and the rise of flexible production. It is also a by-product of the revolution in spatial relations engendered by the astonishing development of electronic technologies—computers, the Internet, and all the other instruments that permit instantaneous contact with anyone, anywhere, anytime. The concomitant dream of a more genuinely open society, one in which one's race, class, or origins are no longer impediments to mobility, is also a condition that will accelerate the city of anything, anyplace.

However, there is a more negative reading of this expressed in the bête noire of the contemporary urban condition, described variously as the "edge city," the "nonplace urban realm" (to use Mel Webber's succinct phrase from his seminal 1964 essay, which addressed the question of the increasingly parlous balance of the physical and virtual aspects of the city), or the "generic city." The idea of free location, of anything anyplace, has already generated the fastest-growing component of the American city, a suburbia that exists in complete independence of traditional central cities. Nowadays, offices, malls, apartments, and theme parks can sprout at any spot that has reasonable highway access, fiber-optic cable, a power line, and some price advantage. This nonhierarchical but intensely zoned condition means that as many people now commute laterally, within this suburban—or cyburban—texture, as do centrifugally in and out of the more traditional urban/suburban arrangement. This new "urban" form is also remarkable for the purity with which it maps market forces via its repertoire of "post-urban" formats—the office park, the highway, the gated community, the shopping mall—across a yielding, seemingly boundless terrain, stretching around the globe.

Such urbanism threatens more traditional cities both by being an alternative pattern of development and by its reproduction within the fabric of already existing cities, producing, for example, urban shopping streets lined with precisely the array of stores one might find at the mall. More and more we are obliged to conduct our transactions at one branded, multinational emporium or another, and every time we whip out our credit cards, we are drawn more tightly into the web of complicity and surveillance that marks our citizenship in the one-way culture of global capital. The system needs difference to drive consumption but is constantly refining its range.

In 1994, a tiny hole-in-the-wall business establishment—not much larger than a phone booth—opened on West Broadway. Nineteen ninety-four was the year the World Cup took place in the United States, and the little spot was a source for tickets as well as for foreign exchange, a place where tourists and visiting soccer aficionados could swap deutsche marks and francs for dollars. It is still in business, and there's something perplexing, almost quaint, about it in light of the fact that most people nowadays can more easily (and economically) get cash from the thousands of ATMs around the city—that is, if they don't use their credit cards (or euros in many shops).

I think the stand keeps doing business for the same reason that tourists exchange their actual dollars for Disney Dollars at Disneyland, a transaction that confers absolutely no advantage— no favorable exchange rate, no discount, no exclusivity of acceptance, nothing. Both exchanges are systems for establishing the authenticity of locality by offering the palpability of money—those soiled, depreciating greenbacks or those crisp Mouse-emblazoned bills—in lieu of the immaterial, impersonal electronic transaction. We *know* it's picturesque and genuine in SoHo because tourists need to change money to participate in the kind of cash economy one would expect in a "historic" district, still immersed in the ritual media of the past. The actual necessity for such transactions barely

exists, required only at the stalls of street vendors and the few sur-
viving businesses of the fading ethnic population that preceded the
artists and the yuppies and that embody the small-scale sense of
Old Europe, which new establishments strive with such desperate
calculation to re-create.

Easy motion over long distances, ATMs everywhere, and instantaneous electronic connections accelerate what Marx described as
the annihilation of space by time. Exhilarating as the idea of a net-
enabled global village might be, the appeal of the various forms of
netizenship lies in its power to supplement primary body-based
relations rather than its power to supplant them. Despite the skein
of connections and the power that many of us have to move rapidly
around the globe, the system is profoundly immobilizing, both in
the fixed-in-front-of-the-screen, never-go-out sense (like the Japanese *hikikomori*, boys who spend years without leaving their rooms)
and in the generic city version, in which no matter how far one
physically travels, the environment is the same. Yet precisely this
mobility is today the dominant form of American urbanism. We
exhale and think it inevitable that the imposition is the equivalent
of tradition.

I find this picture fundamentally horrifying. It is insanely inefficient from the environmental standpoint, totally dependent on
the automobile to function, a ravenous consumer of open space,
and a phenomenon hostile to the idea of boundaries, driven not by
the value of propinquity and adjacent relations but by a reserve
army of undeveloped space and labor power, the cheaper the better
and globally scalable. The planet becomes its own "loft," a yielding,
equipotential surface ready to be equipped with uniform climate
and culture-indifferent architectures. It is the omega point of capi-
talist rationality, the enemy of a democratic praxis based on the
idea of locality and face-to-face exchange, and clearly the antithesis of the kind of city Jane Jacobs revered.

The laissez-faire urbanism of the edge city—the successor to
what was described by Jean Gottmann in 1957 as a "megalopolis,"
or the coalescence of groups of cities into continuous conurbations—

also reproduces itself in the other great urban phenomenon of the new century: the megacity, the city of more than ten million inhabitants. There are now at least twenty-six such cities (and more than five hundred cities of over a million), the majority of them in the developing world. Their characteristic environment is the slum. More than half the population of the planet is urbanized—the rate only accelerates—and half of city dwellers live in slums. Although megacities like Mexico City or Lagos tend to be places of dense contiguity, they produce many of the same effects as the edge city. For both, issues of scale and dimension are paramount, and their extent militates against the qualities of comprehensibility, tractability, and choice that characterize good cities. All sorts of organisms are constrained by scale, reach evolutionary limits, become apraxic, unable to perform coordinated movements. Cities that become too large are likewise ungovernable and unsustainable.

The antidote is to limit the growth of cities and to struggle to make the urban fabric accommodating to choice and community. This will necessarily oblige the creation of many new cities that are radically responsive to human and environmental needs. Jane Jacobs is sometimes faulted for her apparent hostility to new development and new towns and her analyses dismissed as nostalgic impediments to the big tasks at hand. But Jacobs remains as vital a guide as ever to the elements of a democratic and neighborly quality of life and to one group of environments that have successfully supported it. The core of her message is that good neighborhoods cannot be reduced to their architecture but that architecture has the capacity to aid and abet forms of association and affinity that are at the core of such places.

CANAL
STREET

Canal Street marks the southern boundary of SoHo. Heavily trafficked day and night, Canal Street links the Holland Tunnel and New Jersey with the Manhattan Bridge and Brooklyn, connecting to the Brooklyn-Queens Expressway and the freeway net of Long Island beyond. In neighborhood terms, Canal Street links Chinatown and what's left of Little Italy on the east to the Broadway corridor in mid-island, to SoHo and Tribeca on the west, and to the Hudson River waterfront.

Like other major east-west streets—Houston, Fourteenth, Thirty-fourth, Forty-second, Fifty-ninth, Seventy-second, and so on—Canal Street is a seam in the city, a boundary that, like an avenue, demarcates by its width and by the intensity of its use. It is also a reminder that although most people now conceptualize Manhattan along its north-south, uptown-downtown axis, the founding sense of the place ran crosswise, from river to river. The genius of the city's natural configuration was that it was compactly bicoastal, that docks could run up both sides of the island, doubling its capacity as a port. In its heyday, this was enlarged by the inclusion of the near coasts of Brooklyn, Queens, New Jersey, Staten Island, even the Bronx—more than six hundred miles of coastline within the city itself. In the years before World War II, even little Newtown Creek—which branches from the East River and forms part of the boundary between Brooklyn and Queens—had a greater volume of shipping than the Mississippi River. Well into the twentieth century, the feel and energy of Manhattan was intensely lateral and the experience of shipping and stevedoring present in everyone's everyday.

Strategizing the crossing of Canal Street occupies me for some minutes as I approach it. Among my options, the West Broadway crossing is the most coherent. That is to say, it's an orthogonal intersection, with all crosswalks running straight from curb to curb. Although the crosswalk defines the shortest distance between the points of departure and arrival, the crossing is made challenging by the extremely short timing of the traffic signal, which for years was on a four-second "walk" cycle. This meant that unless one was already standing on the curb at the moment the light changed, it was virtually impossible to get across before the light turned red. This accelerated cycle has been the subject of heated negotiation with neighborhood activists, the result of which has been a two-second increase in the duration of the light.

This parsimonious timing is a particular problem for those who are slow moving, burdened with packages, or have children in tow, all unable to deploy the strategies New Yorkers traditionally use when confronted by a changing light: breaking into a trot as it begins to blink, accelerating at the middle of the street, maneuvering through intersections clotted by traffic, or the more balletic dodging of cars in motion. This intersection is not an especially good one for this—the scene of many pedestrian and bicycle accidents—due to an especially large volume of trucks, which use Canal Street as a virtual freeway between bridge and tunnel.

A block west of this intersection, crossing is even hairier. If I approach Canal on Thompson Street, which has an intimate scale I often favor over the wider, more crowded, increasingly generic West Broadway, I arrive at a geometric condition that makes getting to the other side a logic problem. Thompson hits Canal at approximately the same point as Sixth Avenue, and because of the collection of colliding downtown grids generated by the historically uneven development of the area and the skewed geometry induced by the angles of the streets, the dimensions of the crossings here are considerably broader. Negotiating them entails skipping from island to island, often back and forth from one side of the street to the other, all to take advantage of shorter distances, the timing of converging streams of traffic, or the availability of green lights or clear opportunities to dart. New Yorkers tend to regard crossing against the light as a God-given right, not simply because of our impatience, but because it also ramifies with our sense of the freedom of the city. Others see it differently. One of my strong memories of the years when I taught in Vienna is of the regular experience of coming to a corner, looking right and left, seeing no traffic, and crossing against the light. Frequently, I would leave a knot of Austrians on the curb, waiting for the signal to change. I could feel their censorious gazes boring into my back and would fall into an inner monologue about a culture in thrall to regulation and the narrowest meanings of the law. This easily extrapolated into "only following orders," thence the Holocaust, a fair amount of conceptual baggage to carry across the street.

On the other hand, this discipline before the law also enables the efficient functioning of Vienna's mass-transit system in a way that would surely never succeed in the United States. Trams, buses, and subways in Vienna work on an honor system. One buys a ticket either before getting on or from a vending machine on the tram or bus. This ticket is then meant to be canceled in another machine, either within the conveyance or at the entrance to the platform. The whole system is maintained by periodic inspections. These, however, are few and far between. I always bought a ticket. I was inspected once relatively early during my time in the city and then never again. While the early experience of inspection (your papers please!) may have inspired a slight surfeit of anxiety, I believe that my good public character would have prevailed even without it. I had no interest in beating this particular system, although I noticed that some of my more insubordinate Viennese peers—many of whom dutifully waited for traffic lights—delighted in riding "in the black."

In terms of the sort of rational analysis that is so beloved of the so-called law and economics theorists like Richard Posner and other University of Chicago types, the logical economic behavior is simply not to pay. Given the low frequency of inspection and the magnitude of the fine (which is meant to be forked over on the spot), it is more "economical" never to buy a fare but simply to pay the fine when or if it comes. That the Austrians virtually always pay can be read either as docility before the law or as the hallmark of citizenship. Yet it's clear that these are interrelated concepts: a democratic polity is marked by the degree to which such obedience is freely chosen by citizens who respect the artifact of self-governance. While I was appalled at Austrians' passivity before the red light, I was impressed by their respect for the functioning of the collectivity, including the need to pay for the public life.

One of the characteristics of the Vienna system is its modal richness, the way in which subways, commuter trains, long-distance and regional rail, trams and buses, extensive pedestrian-exclusive zones, and relatively limited automotive space—with efficiently organized and distributed parking—are mixed. The planners of the system recognize that efficiency is produced not by the sort of movement monoculture of cars-only American cities but by a sensitively tailored combination of modes sited to exploit the particular efficiencies of each and providing useful duplication and alternative.

On the other hand, the traffic engineers who hold sway over so much planning in American cities are prisoners of the limited conceptual framework within which they work. They understand intersections—like the one at Canal Street—as moments of "conflict" and thus see their primary obligation as minimizing encounters between such incompatible modes as walking and driving by means of regulation or construction. The traffic light is for them a conflict-adjudicating device, though a less than satisfactory one because the conflict is resolved only by serially disfavoring one mode or the other. When pedestrians cross, traffic halts and vice versa. This is galling to the engineering mentality because it means that the flow of one mode is always at a standstill, forced to yield to the other.

Many years ago, after a number of trips to India, a country that is revelatory in many, many ways, I began to think about another framework for urban movement, one based not on separation but on coexistence. India produces the ultimate convulsive collation of circulatory modes. In most Indian cities, the space of the street and sidewalk is used by an incredible profusion of movement "systems." Pedestrians, cars, pedal rickshaws, motor rickshaws, bullock carts, trucks, buses, elephants, bikes, and, of course, those ubiquitous cows mingle in a single space. Indeed, the cow is the conceptual enabler of this system, a beast whose absolute sanctity allows it to walk—or rest—anywhere it pleases. Chandigarh, with its eightfold organization of traffic, and New Delhi, with its vast axial boulevards, are exceptions, quintessential European responses to the frustrations of this flaunted hierarchy, corrective doses of clarity for a system that thrives on ambiguity.

What the Indian "system" produces on the ground is a seething knot of very slow-moving traffic, the antithesis of the segregated flows beloved of most traffic engineers. While I do not advocate precisely this system for New York (although I've often wondered what effect the release of a few thousand head of cattle would have), I am intrigued by a number of the things it represents. For one, this mingled traffic has a decidedly democratic character inasmuch as movement through it presupposes a continuous series of negotiations, which result in one party or another giving ground. This is possible only because the slowness of the moving mass offers time to undertake this constant making of compacts of deference. Such slowness also tends to neutralize the advantage conferred by the capacity for greater speed and, to a lesser extent, greater size.

When I think about how such a system might ramify in our environment, a few things stand out. The first is the value of slowness. Although I am not aware of any good comparative studies, it is possible that a dramatic slowdown of urban traffic would actually increase the speed of individual trips. There are currently experiments to this effect going on in the Netherlands, begun by a visionary traffic planner (an oxymoron in virtually all other cases), the late Hans Monderman. His project has been to remove from a series of towns as many traffic signs and signals as possible so that the constant default for bodies in motion is to be in motion, as there are no prefigured stops forced by the system—a traffic equivalent of Newton's first law. Success is predicated on slowness, deference, and vigilance rather than by a system of policed controls. In a parallel development, the United States is in the process of converting its system of air-traffic movement from a rigid scheme of flight paths, waypoints, and controls to a system of "free flight" in which individual pilots determine the most efficient route through the sky and assume—with the help of advanced technologies—responsibility for maintaining separation from other planes.

The Indian style of slow motion allows unregulated intersections, in which the right to move need only be ceded from or yielded to other movers after appropriate negotiation. The resulting lower speeds produce—at least in theory—a much safer system, one in which all movers proceed with dramatically reduced kinetic energy and consequently dramatically reduced lethality. I am intrigued with the possibility of a system where top speeds are around twelve miles per hour. This would create a space of relative safety for underprivileged modes of urban circulation, like bicycles, skates, and scooters. Such an arrangement would also be predicated on the human body's right-of-way as the alpha means of motion, the one to which every other mode operating on the surface is obliged to defer. And a slow system would reflect the actual speeds obtained in city circulation.

To carry the thought experiment a little further, the re-finessed mix of means also opens the way for a consideration of the nature of urban vehicles themselves. A preference for small, slow-moving media would result in dramatic reductions of the energy expended in getting around. Cars and other internal-combustion vehicles are designed with obscene amounts of power that allow them to operate in constant stops and starts, rapidly slowing down from or accelerating to very high rates of speed. A system in which motion is more or less constant and in which speeds are kept low would reduce the struggle with inertia that undergirds the way we move now. It would approach a condition of intelligent entropy.

A body-favoring system of movement would also have dramatic impacts on health. Not long ago, the Centers for Disease Control produced a study that found that urban sprawl was directly correlated with rates of diabetes and obesity. Another study has connected obesity in New York City with poverty. Although the two etiologies are of fundamentally different origins, both might be equally said to be functions of a system of corporately generated desire, one that requires a car of virtually everyone in most American cities and the other that lines the streets of neighborhoods with nutritionally vile fast-food emporiums. In both cases, the lack of choice forces people into patterns of behavior that are contrary to their self-interest but that purport to increase convenience in the name of "speed" or "choice" ("have it your way . . .").

Forcing people to deal with a system that is hostile to their health has a parallel in the relationship of cities to their means of circulation. For over two centuries—since the early days of the Industrial Revolution—cities have been obliged to play catch-up with the effects of technical innovations in transport that were designed without reference to, or thought of, their consequences for the urban pattern or the quality of urban life. The railroad had the effect of dramatically attenuating the dimensions of cities, enabling them to sprawl without end as well as to draw on distant resources, with the result that they relied less and less on self-reliant ecologies of local production and distribution. Grotesque modern examples: flying a kiwi fruit from New Zealand to New York produces four times the weight of the kiwi in greenhouse gases; moving a head of lettuce to here from California requires ten times the calories the lettuce yields to the eater. Becoming locavores seems imperative.

The railways sliced through the pliant flesh of the city, creating enormous linear barriers that carved cities into zones, spreading tremendous pollution by smoke, noise, and fear. The "other side of the tracks" is a place created by the tracks. While the social implications of this demarcation are, as Jane Jacobs points out, a defining characteristic of towns rather than cities, life along a railway embankment, cut, or trestle was nightmarish everywhere, especially in the age of coal and steam. The railway has been the enabler of concentrated, large-scale industrial activity, stitching the factories of the Victorian era to their sources of supply and distribution and formalizing a set of spatial hierarchies that enabled functional and social distinctions to be deployed on a colossal scale. Because it is a point-to-point system (the speed of the train depends on relatively long distances for acceleration and deceleration), the train (and the "limited access" highway) produced structural discontinuities that further reinforced the possibility for hierarchy and division.

The problem of Canal Street can be solved only by radical means. As early as the 1920s, when the Holland Tunnel was being built, a cross-island expressway connection had many advocates. In 1929, the Regional Plan Association drew up a blueprint for motorizing the region with a vast network of highways. In 1940, Moses—then the city's highway czar—proposed this network to Mayor LaGuardia, and it was soon incorporated in the city's master plan for new arterials. Things moved relatively slowly until the passage of the Interstate Highway Act, whereupon Moses proposed not simply an elevated cross-island expressway along Broome Street— two blocks north of Canal—but also similar highways at 34th, 59th, and 125th Streets. The devastation would have been unimaginable. Opposition arose swiftly, and the Lower Manhattan Expressway was rejected by the New York City Board of Estimate in 1962. However, the project would not die. The following year, it was revived by Moses and Mayor Robert Wagner, and condemnation began on buildings along its proposed route. The battle was rejoined—with Jane Jacobs again playing a leading role—and the thing was not snuffed for good until 1969.

As advocates struggled to save the project in some form, there were some interesting developments. At least two were sensible and became particularly resonant in the aftermath of 9/11, when there appeared to be a brief opening for major infrastructural projects downtown that might have solved Canal Street. The first was the American Institute of Architects' suggestion that there simply be a tunnel from New Jersey, passing under Manhattan, and emerging beyond the East River on Long Island. The second, originally the baby of Mayor John Lindsay, was that the connection be routed around the tip of lower Manhattan in the form of a highway. A vestige of this latter suggestion reappeared post-9/11 in a brief-lived but completely reasonable idea to connect the Holland Tunnel with the Brooklyn Battery Tunnel, which joins lower Manhattan to South Brooklyn. This project might potentially have been extended to include a tunnel to the Manhattan Bridge.

The most delirious proposal to save the Lower Manhattan Expressway, however, was the brainchild of the architect Paul Rudolph. On commission from the Ford Foundation, Rudolph proposed a gigantic Y-shaped megastructure designed to link the Holland Tunnel with both the Manhattan Bridge at the end of Canal Street and the Williamsburg Bridge at the end of Delancey Street, many blocks to the north. This project—while rendered with the panache and formal brilliance typical of Rudolph—was completely over the top. The idea was to embed multiple layers of movement systems—highways, streets, walkways, subways, "people movers"— within an enormous construction that would also include shops, housing, offices, and other spaces. Although it was "inflected" to respond to the differing scales of the neighborhoods it tore through, and although it incorporated some remnants of the historical architectures it would have destroyed, the scheme was a monstrous wall that would have exacerbated the disastrous effects of the highway it was meant to redeem.

Rudolph's project summed up a certain strain of modernism, extending that old laminar fantasy of movement organization, structured around a stack of systems optimized for flow. It also recalls the long interest in linear buildings that arose with the railroad and soon became a staple of avant-garde fantasies that still have life. Pride of place for the idea is generally given to Arturo Soria y Mata, who proposed a linear streetcar suburb for Madrid in 1882 and managed to build something like three miles' worth of an intended thirty. This was to be, he wrote (and well before Ebenezer Howard's similar description of the garden city), a means to "ruralize the city and urbanize the suburbs." Likewise, the project by Edgar Chambless for Roadtown, published in 1910, depicted an infinitely long, two-room-wide building atop three levels of underground rail lines for express, local, and freight traffic. In the late 1920s, N. A. Miliutin proposed a Soviet Union–spanning linear plan that—following Soria y Mata's rhetoric—would have solved the old Marxian chestnut of city/country contradiction at a stroke. Le Corbusier's Algiers scheme of 1933—a highway-topped fourteen-story building meant to stretch miles along the Mediterranean and house 180,000 people—was surely the most immediate precursor of Rudolph's "City Corridor." The Algiers scheme is perhaps the most memorable proposal in a morphological tradition that sought to re-create the city in the image of linear motion, civilization reorganized as a global veinous system, the circuit of capital in concrete.

Megastructures were much in the air in the 1960s and 1970s, going Corbusian cities of endless, rational replication one better by housing everything in what was, in effect, a single building, acromegalic progeny of the Fourierist phalanstery. The architectural media groaned with such schemes, most of them floated on a bit of progressive rhetoric. (Reyner Banham, historian of megastructures, distinguished them from merely large complexes by their inclusion of a "ludic" element.) Yona Friedman proposed a giant structural grid to float above Paris, leaving the existing city intact beneath it. Paolo Soleri published his beautifully drafted "arcologies," gigantic hives containing entire urban populations that—through their insane density and verticality—were to leave the surface of the earth relatively unscathed. In Japan, the architects of the Metabolist movement proposed covering Tokyo Bay with a huge platform out of which would rise a grid of giant, identical buildings. All ignored the fact that titanic forms of centralized organization and coercion would have been needed to accomplish them, the same nutty hubris so deeply embodied by Robert Moses, who actually pulled off projects at scales about which most architects only dream.

In fact, many megastructures were—and continue to be—built. Moshe Safdie's Habitat of 1967 combined linear form with stackable modular housing units, realizing a classic vision of architectural mass production, deployed in the image of a picturesque hill town. While it succeeded as architecture, Habitat failed as a prototype. Its unit costs were simply too high, and the mass manufacture of its modular components that might have driven them down never happened. A version of Habitat's economic vision, however, was already being realized, if in less visually compelling form, by the assembly-line production of suburbs like Levittown, by the dreary panelized housing projects built all over the Soviet bloc, and by the mobile home industry, which continues to churn out millions of factory-built, fully equipped, modular, road-transportable units every year.

The idea of the megastructure—with its diffuse ideology and narrow range of formal preferences—reached high water in the 1960s and 1970s with a run of academic buildings, hospitals, and housing projects that combined then-fashionable brutalist and mechanicalist taste with linear, cellular organization. These included the 1967 Brunswick Centre housing in Bloomsbury, London, by Patrick Hodgkinson; the 1963 Free University of Berlin by Candilis, Josic & Woods; Scarborough College in Toronto, designed by John Andrews in 1964; and the Pompidou Center of 1971. Like Gothic cathedrals, these buildings were striking for their conceptual and formal similarity, rapidly developing as a type rather than a principle. And while the type has had a relatively short-lived popularity, the principle—long in the air—lives on.

Perhaps the greatest megastructural proposal of them all was the 1955 plan by Victor Gruen (widely regarded as the father of the modern shopping mall) for the reconstruction of downtown Fort Worth, Texas. To pedestrianize the city center, Gruen (a refugee from Vienna) proposed to lift the city up on a series of gigantic parking lots and service facilities, leaving its principal (elevated) grade free from traffic. The formal organization of the scheme was to remain "traditional"—a series of discrete buildings organized around a network of streets, a gigantic project without the aestheticized gigantism of the megastructural academy. Although it was not built, its influence has been enormous, visible in interconnected, podium-based developments from Crystal City, Virginia, to Lille, France. It also proved surprisingly intriguing to Jane Jacobs, who wrote about it at length (and not without appreciation) in *The Death and Life of Great American Cities*. So much for the fashionable accusation that she couldn't think big!

The idea of the all-at-once distinguishes these projects from a history that extends back for millennia. The Oxford colleges—and the fabric of the medieval city generally, in both European and Islamic versions—are clearly megastructures, built environments that are completely and literally continuous with the idea of the individual building subservient to the fabric of the whole. In this sense, all cities are megastructures, legible and functional mainly in their aggregation, physically joined by party walls and roadways, by sewers and subways, and by communal and physical boundaries. The difference lies in the way cities distribute autonomy, how they break down the scale of any individual increment of construction, and how they become "complete." The debate is about domination, adaptability, variety, and consent. Traditional architectures and cities are the outcome of generations of dialogue between form and culture. The conventions—the climax architectures—of New York are confirmed by their adaptability and endurance and by their ability to support the collection of sentiments and activities we identify with urbanity. Great cities can be built in a hurry—St. Petersburg, Brooklyn, and Miami Beach happened fast. The problem of the megastructure is not its extent but its subversion of choice and the cruelties it visits on fragile but indispensable social and spatial ecologies.

TRIBECA

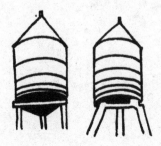

There's a commercial on TV hyping a new Japanese SUV, the Subaru Tribeca—"the end of the SUV as you know it and the beginning of the SUV as it should be." The name of the relatively indistinguishable car seems an odd choice, and the commercial makes it seem odder. Crossing Canal Street puts me in the real Tribeca (TRIangle BElow CAnal), the neighborhood that became the SUV's brand. Formerly the home of the city's wholesale butter, egg, and vegetable markets and a scintillating mix of offices, lofts, and residential residue grown over two centuries, Tribeca has become one of the trendiest and priciest neighborhoods in the city. Robert De Niro seems to own half of it, soigné restaurants abound, and those unmistakable concomitants of gentrification—high-end furniture and exotic tchotchke emporiums—lace it.

What were they thinking at the ad agency when they named the car? Does the word "Tribeca" have any meaning in the suburban territories where the SUV is to be sold? If so, what positive associations does a hyper-gentrified loft neighborhood in lower Manhattan have for potential buyers? What is the connection between any urban tissue and the status of an automobile? Subaru hedges its bets. The ad pictures the Tribeca zooming around different fragments of a quasi-urban environment that looks a great deal like Los Angeles, roaring down the freeway, passing suburban homes, gliding up a "city" street that has a sidewalk and shady trees along a massive blank cut-stone wall, somewhere on L.A.'s Bunker Hill, I think.

"Tribeca" falls on the ear like any of a dozen computer-generated neologisms that now denominate the Asiatic sedan: What is the meaning of Elantra, Camry, Acura, or Murano? The fact that each contains the unpronounceable (for Japanese) letter *r* presumably westernizes it. The names suggest origins in technical and aesthetic conditions, the world of overhead cams, electricity, accuracy, Venetian glass (metonymy for luxury?), and so on. (Could Murano be a homonym for Marrano, meant to evoke the garaged concealment of an invisible population of cars, their presence invisible from the street save when they slip out to the Holland Tunnel? Could it, even more perversely, mean to conjure Venice, the ultimate car-free city?) Tribeca sounds like one of these made-up names because it is a made-up name, an acronym pure and simple. It may also be that the ad agency is trying to parlay an association with the American Express campaign in which Robert De Niro plugs his Tribeca Film Festival.

Urban nomenclature has legs in the automotive world. The Chrysler New Yorker and the Buick Park Avenue evoke limousine luxury and sophistication. The Pontiac Parisienne suggested gaiety and style, the feminization of the subject-supposed-to-drive, and was surely meant to tone down an overreliance on raging beasts, forces of nature, vanquished Native Americans, and male buyers. But Tribeca? Why not? It conjures money, sophistication, a skosh of inside knowledge, and gentrification itself, downtown as the quintessence of upward (four-wheel drive) mobility. I look forward to spitting on the first one I see and yelling "asshole" at the driver.

The city is no stranger to this name-it-and-claim-it mentality. Newspaper real estate pages chart the creation and migration of place-names in an attempt to valorize property with superior aura. Thus the Lower East Side becomes the East Village, and Gramercy Park migrates for blocks beyond its salient patch of green. Recent flights of fancy have brought us Nolita, SoBro, Dumbo, and So-Hell, and the Sunday *Times* classifieds are a virtual lexicon of such geographical creativity. The word "adjacent" becomes a term of art for aura stretching, dropped when the edge of value rolls a little farther in the direction of the current periphery, the nameless frontier, one on which (familiar story) native identities must be replaced.

My Tribeca studio, which I occupied for sixteen years and which was the third I've had in the neighborhood, overlooked (mark this change of tense—I moved three years ago) what was—in the early nineteenth century—one of the city's premier residential squares. Like Washington Square, Hudson Square was modeled on the London prototype and was part of the vast holdings of Trinity Church (which once stretched as far north as what is now Rockefeller Center), still one of the leading property owners in the area. Despite having no further holdings directly on what used to be Hudson Square, Trinity Real Estate, the church's holding company, has reintroduced the name in its marketing, a single descriptor meant to identify its property with a place and a vibe.

Trinity has been around for a long time—it was chartered in 1697—and has long since accommodated itself to Mammon. Built by the great Richard Upjohn in 1846, the historic home of the church (its third, the first two having been lost to fire and snow) sits at the brow of Wall Street, its dark Gothic tower the perfect symbol of the Protestant mind-set that Max Weber deemed the necessary ethical prelude to the efflorescing spirit of capital, so vigorously pursued in the streets below. Trinity's nave and adjoining cemetery have long been hospitable to captains of industry since, like many other religious institutions in the city, the church has fatted itself from the get-go by playing the real estate game with a determination that puts many of its secular competitors to shame.

The nexus of Trinity's holdings is an area along Canal Street and several blocks to the north, generally east of Varick. There is a remnant square in the midst of this, but it is no more than the organizing space that feeds cars coming from several directions into the mouth of the Holland Tunnel. Attempting to cross it on foot not long ago, I was told by a policeman directing the slow-moving traffic that it was forbidden to walk across the space. The sidewalk along one side of it, it seems, functions as mere ornamental nostalgia. The "square" does possess a small Greek Orthodox church (with a diminished but active congregation) that is slated to be trashed for some higher use (and building).

The real (former) Hudson Square is a larger space to the south of Canal Street that has also been given over to the automotive system and serves to distribute cars disgorged from the Holland Tunnel to the compass points of the city streets. Uncrossable— save by brave or drunken souls—it has recently been renovated by the Port Authority, the upshot of which has been the removal of a stand of trees that were among the largest in lower Manhattan and the addition of much new paving. This was putatively to smooth traffic flow, but it has had no demonstrable effect on the diurnal queues of fuming cars and trucks emerging from or edging toward the tunnel. A couple of truly pathetic seating areas along one edge, as well as some vaguely old-fashioned-looking lighting fixtures, round out the "improvements."

As I looked down on this space over the years from my studio, many schemes for its amelioration grew to fantastical cogency under my gaze, all of which focused on reclaiming it for use by the neighborhood, by people entering on foot, now doomed by the automotive realm. Still, there are degrees of contraction. Several of my imaginary schemes divided the park between human and automotive use. Indeed, reclaiming the southern end of the space would be quite feasible with a little adjustment to the traffic trajectories and a bit of fiddling with one-way streets.

One promising possibility for the park stems from the location (behind the fine little neoclassical home of the First Police Precinct at the southeast corner of the square) of the stables of the mounted police. Lit only by the light from an open front door, a double row of stalls holds a dozen or so sleek horses. Sometimes, a sweet unexpected smell of manure seeps out to the sidewalk, where bales of straw and feed lie stacked. There's almost always a horse being led in or out, its nose ready to be stroked, reminder of a once common interaction in the city streets. My schemes for Hudson Square invariably include a paddock for these horses, grass under hoof.

More radical orders of speculation banish the cars entirely. Some schemes, however, simply accept the consequences of cars emerging from the tunnel along Canal Street, aiming east. Hudson Square is now used for deceleration, distribution, and backup space for these cars. They could, however, as easily turn directly up- or downtown without the landscaped off-ramp complex. Indeed, closing Canal Street to vehicles that use it as a shortcut from New Jersey to Brooklyn, Queens, and Long Island would have an instant and spectacular effect on the quality of life for all lower Manhattan. The lengthy closure of lower Manhattan to private vehicles following 9/11 offered persuasive—if tragically framed—evidence of the viability of such an undertaking. The recently defeated congestion-pricing scheme was another such lost opportunity for reduction.

The idea of simply removing the cars receives further embroidery. New Jersey has been building a light-rail system along the shore of the Hudson to link up the communities strung out along it. I've imagined reclaiming one tube of the Holland Tunnel for this trolley, which—as I see it—would pass through a station at the edge of the square, at which passengers could change to subways and buses running up- and downtown, or continue across Canal Street, over the Manhattan Bridge, winding up in downtown Brooklyn. Not only could such a system increase the capacity of the tunnel to move people across the river; it would—via its many potential mass-transit links—help reduce demand for car space.

My years spent working in Tribeca parallel the growth of the gigantic real estate bubble we lately occupied. Although its magnitude has caused many to speculate on its family relationship to other great bubbles—like the Dutch tulip bubble of 1637—the collapse has not had a deep effect on the downtown property market. In Tribeca, prices for lofts and apartments are stratospheric, and the lifestyle blanding of the place proceeds according to pattern. Moreover, virtually every vacant site in Tribeca is now under construction. The many formerly too small or too eccentrically configured neighborhood lots have become economic, and the possibility of putting up relatively small buildings with relatively few units has become viable. While these buildings are uniform in use, the potential for reintroducing well-considered works of architecture at this long-ignored scale is a positive thing, not least in providing opportunities for work by smaller architectural practices.

Because of these developments, Tribeca is almost finished. Given the current build-out, the staggering levels of investment, and the landmarking of virtually the entire neighborhood, it is clear that Tribeca has reached its morphological climax, that its look, at any rate, has become fixed for the ages, that further development will fit within the parameters of this particular urban endgame. This means a certain deceleration of provoking difference, since the pressure to conform to a closely prescribed visual paradigm is strong, indeed has the force of law. This is not an entirely happy circumstance and might negate the opportunities offered by an archipelago of small sites. The final architectural embellishments for the neighborhood should be the most exceptional, a kind of punctuation by relief, the last bursts of creative potential as the scene shifts.

However, the landmarks regime—valuable though it is in preserving relic textures and special works—is lethal to innovation and formulates its judgments and approvals according to a theory of the mean. Its terms of art are "context" and "respect," but its understanding of the nature of context is almost entirely physical and its style of reading reductive. On the block of Hudson south of my studio stand two buildings, each taking up most of the block front on opposite sides of the street. Both are brick, both are detailed with bits and pieces of classical ornament, both are filled with luxury lofts, both look to have been built at more or less the same moment, at least artistically. One of them actually is old, the other brand-new, a model of the deracinated, lowest-common-denominator approach of landmarking in which fitting in (the highest value for architecture in historic districts) always trumps standing out.

The city's architects know the adjudicating commission well and almost never try to push its limits. The commission, for its part, can always be relied upon to prefer an iconographic and compositional checklist—Do the cornices line up? Is the materiality like its neighbors? Are the windows detailed and proportioned like nineteenth-century sash?—to a gamble on the beauty in contrast, contradiction, elaboration, or simply originality. Perhaps it is an inevitable outcome of the decision to identify forms and spaces at climax (in the forester's sense) that conservationism becomes the agenda for everything that enters the space. The problem here is not with the idea of a civic consensus, something vital to any genuinely shared metropolis. The problem is with the predigested forms of agreement that have come to represent consensus at its most unthinking. There is a sadness particular to climax.

The idea of stages of development was once a central issue for orthodox Marxism, and countless hours—and lives—were sacrificed to the theoretical investigation of the possibility of skipping over a stage or two on the way to the egalitarian nirvana expected to follow the withering of the state. Although Tribeca has not exactly skipped a stage in its progress from working neighborhood to yuppie paradise, it was able to accelerate very quickly through one of the classical steps in gentrification, the development of a marginal, artistic community to act—as in SoHo—as the shock troops for the lawyers and arbitrageurs to come.

Tribeca gentrified after the model had already been set by its neighboring community. It was inflected in its transformation by the relatively late departure of the food markets, by its much more variegated mix of building types, and by its continued functionality for a number of long-standing uses, including government facilities, a concentration of the printing and graphic trades, and a more general connection to the civic and commercial activities of lower Manhattan. Here it functioned as a kind of extension, one that continued up Hudson and Varick Streets, lined for many blocks with big loft buildings that went up in the go-go years prior to the 1929 crash.

One of the last remaining vacant sites is a small parking lot at the corner of Beach Street, where I almost always made a sharp right turn near the end of my walk to cross along the southern edge

of Hudson Square to my studio on Hudson Street. Some summers
ago, this lot was swarming with carpenters busily erecting two historic buildings. The larger of them appeared to be a loft of cast iron
and brick in turn-of-the-century style. Next door was a little house
that looked about seventy-five years older. On its ground floor was
a desperately authentic-looking luncheonette out of yet another
era. The whole ensemble took about two weeks to build.

Who but Hollywood could have been responsible? For weeks
the neighborhood had been papered with handbills describing the
upcoming production, apologizing for any inconvenience, and generally trying to engage the community with the thrill of having a
film set in its midst. And it was kind of thrilling: the swarms of
scenographers distressing plywood into ersatz verisimilitude; the
evening the rainmaking gantries arrived and inundated Franklin
Street; the morning we saw Bridget Fonda drinking cappuccino
in Bubby's with Harvey Keitel (a longtime and oft-seen local
resident).

The flyer explained why they were doing it. The main setting
for the film was the luncheonette, scene of an encounter between
a policeman and a waitress that set the whole narrative into motion. According to the leaflet, location scouts had scoured all of New
York looking for just the right luncheonette in which all of this
might take place. After inspecting—as the claim went—hundreds
of locations, they were unable to come up with a single one that fully
satisfied their requirements for authenticity, and thus arose the
decision to make the simulacrum, a fiction more real than any of
the available realities. Although Tribeca was generally charmed
by the fake, such sets do sometimes arouse hostility: witness the
re-creation—at the cost of millions—of an "authentic" tenement in
a then particularly derelict area of the Lower East Side for the film
Batteries Not Included, in which Hume Cronyn and Jessica Tandy
are visited by space aliens. (Steven Spielberg, who produced the
film, is big on fantasy, not metaphor, and these aliens weren't stand-
ins for immigrants or developers.)

Such scenographic fictions don't come from nowhere, and a stroll around the neighborhood reveals the architectural sources for the buildings, including a loft whose facade was charmingly miniaturized and a little old house catercorner from the site, reproduced as a mirror image of itself. While such mirrorings do seem to be everywhere in culture, this one was uncanny: I've yet to see a more precise measure of the dimensions of the experience of architectural postmodernity than the space between the set and its source, between the blowtorched patina of plywood masquerading as brick and the weathered authenticity of brick masquerading as itself.

The dilemma lies in the indistinguishability. The film set was remarkably persuasive and faked out everyone, including architects I took to see it during its brief period of glory. They all loved it, loved being fooled, loved that moment when we'd pass through a door to find plywood and two-by-six bracing holding up the thin facades. Even now, I miss that set, and not just because it was a goof. Its volumes were apt to its corner, and its fake patina was remarkably rich, the product of a level of attention seldom lavished on "real" buildings anymore. In a neighborhood of expensive restaurants (De Niro owns four within blocks), a "real" luncheonette (called the Ideal Coffee Shop in the film) would have been great. The workaday atmosphere of the place—as simulated in the cheerful movie—is something that can only be recalled in a neighborhood of remorseless trendiness.

The film—*It Could Happen to You*—turned out to be not just a love story but a parable of gentrification. Nicolas Cage played a policeman who offers to share his lottery ticket in lieu of a tip with a waitress, Bridget Fonda, a beautiful, good-hearted, WASP-blond denizen of hip Tribeca. At the time their romance begins, the Cage character is married to Rosie Perez—shrill, dark, ethnic, annoying—and living in distinctly unglamorous circumstances in Queens. By the end of the film, Cage is able to escape the déclassé Perez for the distinctly more upmarket Fonda and—lottery fortune in hand—make the move downtown. The American dream!

After the film, the lot reverted to parking, but a couple of years later I found it had become a gas station. My first reaction was outrage. Of all things unneeded in the neighborhood, this topped the list, at odds not simply with local character but, I also assumed, with the lot's underlying zoning. Illegal! As I considered which public agency to contact about the crime, I remembered that I'd walked by the lot two days before and there had been no gas station. No one could have excavated for tanks and installed piping and plumbing in such short order. A commercial was being filmed—for what I'm not sure—but my bile at seeing this outpost of the petrochemical condition was certainly authentic.

The point of these movie sets (and fakely historic luxury condos) isn't that Tribeca is becoming a theme park; it's changing, for better or worse, as city neighborhoods will. And there's surely nothing outrageous about the scenographic, mimetic quality of the set. Architecture is obliged to history when it builds in town and must acknowledge established compacts about inhabitation and form. The problem lies in the disengagement, the way the corner has been taken up by the filmic "creative geography," scratch built so that its presence in New York is only coincidental, making the particularity of New York—the quality that presumably attracted the filmmakers to the city in the first place—totally irrelevant. Finally, there was no real reason for the set to be in New York at all. Except to turn New York into a set.

A few mornings ago, I passed a film crew setting up on the corner of Waverly and Gay Street—an enormously popular site that seems to be in use almost every week. The initial effect was positive: orange cones line the block, and the parked cars are gone, revealing the space in its pure architectonic state. Other cars will arrive later—movie cars—which will be either antiques to re-situate the block in a previous time or else contemporary cars, artificially new, undented, and ready for mayhem or hype. The intersection is an especially charming one. Gay Street, one block long, a picturesque crook in the middle, lined with twee little nineteenth-century

houses, is one of the Village's best. I was about to write "most typical," but it really isn't: it's one of the most exceptional.

For filmmakers, however, it functions as typical, in the same
way that the generic sets on a Hollywood back lot, sets called "old
New York," "contemporary city," or "small town," stand in for the
"real thing." They represent a kind of happy generality—like Main
Street in Disneyland—that reduces diversity and difference to a
formula. This is the true Disneyfication effect. It consists of a narrowing of range, a flattening out in order to commodify the phenomenon and render it susceptible to recombination. It makes
possible reproduction via theming, allowing Greenwich Village to
be created anywhere you want it, ma'am. Of course, such stereo-
typing is nothing new. Nor is the impulse to re-create some idealized familiar or some icon of aspiration in strange circumstances,
Victorian Gothic buildings in Bombay or Loire châteaus in L.A.
Such wanton juxtapositions are the media of the colonial, superimposed fantasies and dreams of privilege stuck into a context that
hasn't the means to resist.

What is new is the scale of the operation, the means of its
mediation, and the players. We're creating a unitary global culture,
and we risk abandoning the local invention of strategies of the particular in favor of a set of generic interchangeabilities. There's a reason that the suburbs of Kuala Lumpur look like Beverly Hills, and
it's not that the architecture is particularly well suited to the two
climates. On the other hand, if the world's elites increasingly come
to share identical cultural values, then there is a particularity to the
choice, and railing against it does no good. Indeed, it's very hard
to distinguish between strategies of grafted locality—the Village
superimposed on Beijing or Singapore or Houston—and a preservationist ethic that exults in the reproduction of historic forms within
their local settings long after they have lost their cultural and functional suitability, icons of the unrecoverable.

One can go too far with this argument. There's nothing really
pernicious about building suburbs in the old colonial style, assuming

that it's done with environmental and social responsibility. What is indefensible is the argument for special suitability and the blocking of other avenues of investigation of ideas of the local. Locality begins with social life. In the vulgar reading, influenced by Marxist historiography, we are inclined to see architecture too deterministically, as pure social or environmental production, the inevitable consequence of economic forces. New strategies of the local must be much more particular and much more cooperative.

Chosen patterns of living should lie at the root of any such strategy, followed by climate and by the biology and materiality of the region. Visual context comes next. But once these defaults are established, it's time for invention—not reproduction. While architecture has never been more artistically vital, it is suffering a crisis of utility and failing the environment spectacularly: we need a great leap forward. In New York City, logics of exposure, of minimal import of materials, of reuse, of the upper plane, of radical greening, of self-sufficiency, of the loft, of social integration, of view, of foot travel, of the recapture of public space by the city's many publics, of quiet, of environmental mediation, of energy efficiency, of equity, and of diversity are all points of departure, capable of yielding wild variety.

Scenographic re-creations are by now a commonplace of urbanism and are a means of evading authentic invention. South Street becomes "the South Street Seaport." Times Square becomes a theme park meant to evoke not New York but "New York," a promoter's fantasy bearing only the most marginal relationship to the history of the town. The city is re-segmented into neighborhoods that are produced not by histories of association and the steady buildup of forms and character but by the incremental bite of gentrification, measured by the proximity of neighborhoods already conquered. The inauthenticity is galling, but so is the inescapability of performing in a drama of somebody else's devising, whether it means being charmed by architectural mendacity or just crossing the street when the production assistant asks you to.

A last example that speaks to the genuinely sinister politics that can arise from the city seen as a set, rather than a setting, is the urban version of *The Truman Show*, itself filmed in the creepy, nothing-can-go-wrong ambience of one of the most famous new-urbanist towns, Seaside, Florida. As I was walking up Hudson Street in a funk one day, I was startled by sudden movement. Running toward me was a black man in rags with a cop in hot pursuit, his revolver drawn. A rush of adrenaline sent me into a panic of self-preservation. I don't like guns or violence, and Tribeca is a neighborhood where this sort of thing isn't supposed to happen: the sheer *inappropriateness* confused me. I was alarmed both by the apparent danger and by my complacent expectation that I was meant to be spared the sight of such daily distress in my downtown middle-class cocoon. Guilt-tripping myself all the while, I prepared to duck the bullets.

A shout of "Cut!" brought me back to "reality." Hollywood was at it again, but this time I found myself totally enraged. Crossing the street, I shouted at the crew to get the hell out of the neighborhood. As I walked fuming up the street, I met another observer of the scene, a man I know called Dale. Dale is homeless and used to spend most of his days sitting—mainly in a kind of meditative silence—on the loading dock of a vacant building on Hudson Street, where he supported himself on charity and from the proceeds of a little flea market he organizes. He is also, as it happens, a black man in rags, and his daily perch is diagonally across from the spot where the scene of cop and homeless man was shot. Indeed, he sits in the same spatial relationship to the spot as the little building that had served as its model did to the ersatz building housing the fake luncheonette a few blocks away. The film produced gentle Dale (whom the "completion" of Tribeca has now forced farther uptown) as dangerous, just as gentrification produces poor neighborhoods as blight.

The issue raised for the future of the city lies in an aggressive confusion of cause and effect. The result of urbanistic practices that too much devolve on the circulation and recombination of images is a fundamental slight to values. I believe that form has a semiautonomous life and that it deserves its freedoms. I also believe, however, that architecture and urban design are intrinsically purposive. Modernist urbanism collapsed not because of its desire for justice and health, nor even because of the nature of its too often too simple forms, but because it insisted that there was a single, universal relationship between them and a single, universal subject it served. We fall into the same error if we, like modernism or the movies, insist on the inflexible yoking of image and value, on the invariable criminality of the homeless or the imitability of the louche charm of old New York. Historic cities die when their narratives freeze into obligations or rituals and become empty sources for the global recombination of images that carries us further and further from our own truth.

I was in Istanbul not long ago and found myself at a cocktail party at the house of a local architect. The terrace commanded an amazing view across the Bosphorus where the great monuments—Topkapi, Hagia Sophia, the Blue Mosque—were visible, brilliantly illuminated against the night sky. I stared in delight at the scene but, after a while, felt a quiver of disquiet. It had to do, I realized, with their illumination, obviously relatively recent. Was I, I wondered, enjoying an "authentic" view of the historic city? I began to have my doubts about those glowing domes and minarets. Finally, I felt that this modern celebration of history subtracted something: I felt gypped out of the dark.

I feel the same thing down here. It isn't that I object on principle to either preservation or transformation, but I take exception to an ongoing winnowing of aura and theft of potential. While I love municipal improvements and delight in seeing fine buildings cared for, the incoming atmosphere gets duller by the minute. The opportunities for architectural invention that remain in the neighborhood are—one after another—being sacrificed to the lowest-common-denominator forms of consensus that seem to be the only kind of architecture the landmarkers can wrap their imaginations around.

That boring building across the street, and its numerous kin nearby, try to illuminate Tribeca by calling attention to an idea about what's best down here. But they don't. Light shined on mediocrity only reveals an architecture that has given up. As the neighborhood is reduced to a stage set for a narrower and narrower range of desires, the sense of its history drifts away. We return again to the idea of authenticity. Suspect as the concept is—and as easily co-opted for ill—neighborhoods can be found authentic in both their forms and their relationships. One of the tests of the good contemporary city is *Do we detect Disney?* Global simulation is the favored dystopia—indeed, the hegemonic cultural strategy. This is a level at which New York must resist becoming a world city.

Tribeca is almost done. The last vacant lot on Greenwich Street has been filled by a schmancy hotel, part of the De Niro empire. We're at the point where the intense activity of conversion and renovation that has left virtually no building or site untouched will soon have run its course. And dramatic improvements in public facilities, including the new West Side Highway and park and the "greening" of Greenwich Street, will provide the right kind of static, ornamental infrastructure. The big site on West Street and Chambers has been filled by a harmless high-rise like the ones across the street in Battery Park City. The City Planning Commission has jiggled the zoning for a profitable completion of the last soft sites. Landmarking is in place. Nothing "important" will disappear, and the empty lots are just about gone.

145
HUDSON
STREET

I first moved into my studio on Hudson Street in 1989. The building is a large concrete-framed industrial loft built in the late 1920s, a sturdy piece of Art Deco designed to take heavy loads. The stretch of lower Hudson it occupies holds many similar buildings that were, for many years, the center of the printing trade in New York. When I moved in, the building was still predominantly industrial (the landlord was a printer) with a sprinkling of artists and professional offices. My studio was on the top floor facing east, and through the elegant casement windows I could see past the ridge of Broadway all the way to Queens. Even better, there was access to the roof above, which offered a mesmerizing 360-degree panorama of the city, including sunset views across the Hudson.

In taking this space, I was graduating into a condition of respectability, my previous studios having been either part of lofts in which I was living or funky sublets, including one dank and dark basement with an air shaft at the back that might have admitted a whisper of breeze had we not kept the windows closed against the rats that sported daily just outside. My dramatic upward mobility was enabled by a rent that was very low by current standards and by the will-not-be-denied experience of seeing the space for the first time. And the neighbors were extremely congenial: an artist, a photographer, a paper distributor, and the back office of an architectural firm that did the unglamorous work of producing construction documents for other people's projects.

Never having held a commercial lease before, I was ignorant of certain aspects of what was entailed, including the fact that trash is collected from such buildings by private carters—the city picks up only residential garbage. Already feeling slightly snookered by a variety of add-ons in my lease—charges for sprinklers, electricity, real estate taxes, heat, and insurance—I was in no mood to pay for anything else, and when I was contacted, soon after I moved in, by a company that told me it was the one that collected the garbage in the building and asked me to sign a contract, I demurred. My first thought was, what would I be charged for next? My second that the cost seemed disproportionate to the modest waste I expected to produce. My third that the bag or two a week could be easily thrown into one of the numerous Dumpsters around the neighborhood or just left in a trash receptacle on the street.

After a certain amount of back-and-forth on the phone with the company, during which the question of my choice of disposal modalities was elevated (by me) to a matter of principle, I formally declined the service. Within an hour, two men appeared at my door, one neatly dressed in suit and tie, who did the talking, and another more casually attired and enormous, who remained silently in the background. "Are you the person who doesn't want us to pick up the garbage?" I was asked. From my high horse, I rejoined, "Why should I?" "Don't you know it's illegal not to have us pick up the garbage?" my interlocutor pursued. I said that I thought that was between me and my conscience. This went on for a while, but I finally showed them out. As they waited for the elevator, the large, silent type opened the door to the fire stair, which gave onto a tiny exterior balcony protected only by a pipe railing. Leaning over and looking down, he said thoughtfully, "Gee, I wonder what it would be like to fall fourteen floors."

The lightbulb finally went on, and I hastily reconsidered. I did, indeed, wish to sign the very reasonable contract. And that was the end of it, although a few years later legislation broke the Mafia's hold on the carting industry and required that individual tenants be able to contract with whom they wished for trash removal. Now the task is handled by giant corporate contractors, like the ubiquitous Waste Management, which advertises on TV, proclaiming itself to be green as all get-out, community friendly, and wholesome.

Prices seem to have been largely unaffected by this shift, and the garbage is still shipped out of town.

Perhaps this is the moment to reveal that there has been a certain amount of dissembling going on in this text. This book—begun a dozen or so years ago and laid down and picked up sporadically in the interim—has corresponded to two fundamental changes. One was 9/11. I saw the attack from the street as I left home to walk downtown. The towers had been visible from our living room window in Annabel Lee and were always dancing in and out of view on my walks to work. My Hudson Street studio was not so many blocks from the World Trade Center; the rain of ash and paper from the towers' destruction covered everything around, and the smell of death was inescapable. On the morning of the attack, after trying to give blood, I'd simply walked to the studio. The building was evacuated in the afternoon, and these past seven years have been filled with the unending impact of that day. If this book does not dwell on this, it is because I have been so involved with it elsewhere.

More recently—four years ago—I moved from the Hudson Street studio to a similar space about eight blocks closer to home. The reason for my departure from Hudson Street was straightforward: gentrification. The building was being converted into condominiums, priced at many millions of dollars, some going to movie stars and rockers. I'd known it was coming for a while. My downward mobility began slowly, with my departure from the fourteenth floor to a similar space on the eighth. My lease, as it turned out, contained a clause allowing the landlord to move me to "comparable" space within the building at his discretion. The switch entailed the loss of the long view, loss of access to the building's huge roof (on which a giant penthouse was being built), and the breakup of our lovely floor culture. It was one step in the landlord's top-down strategy of conversion. It was clear that the next stop on this journey was the street.

Although the landlord sold all the condos years ago for the truly astronomical prices he asked, until very recently the building remained largely unoccupied, due to legal issues relating to its new certificate of occupancy. The penthouse (now, at last, rebuilt) was one story higher than the code permitted. The conversion process lasted more than ten years, during which time the landlord sold a parking lot behind the building on which has been constructed a virtual twin of the original, long since fully occupied. Not that vacancy seems to matter. The owner of the gallery that moved into the ground floor of 145 told me recently that when one of the condo buyers for the much delayed original project backed out, the landlord was able to resell the yet-to-be-occupied space for considerably more than the original (astronomical) price. Apparently, there is a fairly brisk trade in unoccupied condos, pure speculation in the local equivalent of gold.

Shortly after the first Gulf War, the landlord at 145 hung an American flag from the suspended metal lighting grid of the lobby ceiling. Although I don't know his life story, the landlord is chronologically a member of the greatest generation. Chatting with him when I first moved into the building, I discovered that he was a donor to the National Cathedral in Washington, a handsome symbol of high Episcopal rectitude and an impressive spatial memory of my own childhood. I took him to be a straight arrow, and although I soon discovered him to be a tough guy in all matters pertaining to leases and tenancy, I never found him to be irrational, uncooperative, or dishonest. I was willing to pass under the flag in those days after the war.

The victory parade for the first Gulf War (I doubt we will see one for the second Gulf War, should it ever end) took place on Broadway, just a few blocks from the studio. I remember it well: the proud, buff American soldiery, a festival of diversity that, as if unable to cross the barrier, halted at Canal Street and dispersed to the cafés and the bars. I had the wistful thought that they might have continued their march uptown until they reached Harlem or the South Bronx, places where their skills and resources might be put to productive use, renovating houses, building schools, delivering health care.

This line of speculation led me to the idea that the "peace dividend," falsely promised by the end of the Cold War, might produce something truly dramatic in the military's sunset. Thinking about a project for this gigantic cultural, financial, and human infrastructure nurtured—engorged—over the centuries, I wondered what might be done by the armed forces that was as dramatic and gripping as warfare. The idea that quickly came to mind was the construction of new cities on bases being abandoned. This is a thought I again have in mind as a new round of base closures takes place. As cities from Fort Wayne to Fort Worth attest, the military has long pioneered urban development, providing a secure nucleus for growth.

As should also be clear by now, I am a firm believer in the project of building new cities, the only reasonable antidote to the Scylla and Charybdis of sprawl and megacities, the dysfunctional twin morphologies of contemporary urbanism. Military bases with their ready-made infrastructure, abundant territory, and skilled populations are logical—potentially decisive—sites for new town construction. The argument for a directed urbanism in which a number of cities are planned and built simultaneously also seems strong. Although there have been some tiny historic efforts—mostly under the New Deal—to think about a national project for new city construction, virtually all greenfield development nowadays is done at private initiative, and most of it tends to be at scales too small, with affects too flat, or—in the new-urbanist model—not as towns at all.

It is not beyond reason to think about new cities that are planned with the calculus of self-sufficiency in mind. This has meaningful political import in a world dominated by frail states and powerful multinationals and offers a means of taking inventory of the relationship of individuals and urban habitats to planetary sustainability, an accounting that tends to get sloughed off to higher or lower orders, to nations or individuals. By this calculus, cities, increasingly important frameworks for the exercise of democracy, become the logical increment for taking environmental responsibility. It is more than possible to think about cities that are self-sufficient in such areas as water, carbon sequestration, waste treatment, food, energy, employment, and the more diffuse set of qualities that constitute the critical mass of urban culture. A vigorous pursuit of new city construction would provide an amazing laboratory for environmental "systems integration."

I am not sure whether the flag became a political or an aesthetic problem first, but in the end they were inextricably intertwined. As with my uptown landlord, I rehearsed the "gotcha" lines I would deliver with debilitating and clarifying effect—"Why don't you display Old Glory on a proper flagpole out front instead of this cheapskate paper-clipping onto the hung ceiling if you claim to be so fucking patriotic?"—ripostes never, of course, to be delivered. As my days at 145 grew numbered, the state of the lobby became especially galling, not for any quality of its own—although (to the chagrin of generations of security guards) it was non-air-conditioned—but for something that was happening adjacent to it.

As the landlord proceeded with the conversion of the building, one of the huge freight elevators was removed and replaced by a smaller passenger cab that descended to a new lobby designed for the use of the new residential tenants. As there were no such tenants yet, this parallel lobby became the reserve of the sales agent, although we commercial tenants were occasionally allowed in during the increasingly frequent failures of our own two elevators. The new lobby was everything the old was not: cool and sleek, lavish with stone and wood paneling, elegantly frescoed. This deluxe display of how the other half would live signaled our demise: my route to the street was paved with the landlord's good intentions for my successors.

Even before the conversion, the two overtaxed passenger elevators at 145 were always breaking down. Originally the site of industrial production, the building had been constructed to accommodate heavy loads and bulky shipments, and the movement of these goods was as important as, or perhaps more important than, the movement of people. Because of industrial hours and discipline, the passenger elevators would see relatively little traffic save for short peaks at the beginning and end of the working day and at lunchtime. Thus, the building had two enormous freight elevators connected directly to a generous loading dock able to accommodate several trucks at once (as well as workers departing en masse for lunch or at the end of the day).

Over the course of my stay at 145, the passenger elevators were overwhelmed by an exponential rise in traffic. Not only were there numerous employee-intensive tenancies, but many of these dealt with streams of clients or, in the case of the photo and casting studios that arrived to take advantage of the big well-lit spaces, with a constant flow of messengers, clasping stacks of models' portfolios. The result of this increased traffic was numerous elevator breakdowns. As the worst of it seemed to come after my demotion to the eighth floor, it was marginally less inconvenient than it might have been, and many were the times that I walked down the eight flights. If I was feeling exhilarated from my morning walk on arriving at the black-hole-of-Calcutta-crowded lobby waiting on a single struggling elevator that had just closed its doors, I climbed the stairs. On other occasions I joined the crowd.

On one such day, I lived the nightmare. I've been stuck on elevators between floors before, even exiting through pried doors (never yet through the elevator ceiling), but this was the Perfect Stall. The convergence of heat, crowding, and the failure of anyone to respond to screaming and constant pushing of the "help" button made me think I was going to suffocate. Fortunately, nobody panicked. We all remained still, cadenced by periodic shouting and banging and intermittent cursing. I closed my eyes, breathed as slowly as I could, and heard the final tomb-set scene of *Aida* (sung by the sublime Leontyne Price) in my mind's ear. Eventually, we were rescued. Deaths in elevator cabins are rare, although fatal falls down shafts do occur far too often.

Still, in such circumstances, one is dramatically out of touch and out of control. A couple of years ago, the papers reported the story of a deliveryman from a Chinese restaurant in the Bronx who went missing for days. He was finally discovered alive in the cab of a housing project elevator that was stuck between floors. Had he been carrying a cell phone, he could (assuming reception) have called for help, something we were able to do from our stuck elevator on Hudson Street (at least he was able to eat the containers of General Tso's chicken he was carrying). Our problem was not that we were lost but that nobody could get us down. Using cell phones in elevators, though, begs further important questions.

Everyone knows that the forms of sociability and behavior in the elevator are highly constrained. For me the paradigm is face front, evenly spaced, complete silence. The choreography and the rules do change when there are fewer people in the cab. If I am alone and the elevator stops to pick someone up, I retreat to the far corner. On the other hand, there's a complex etiquette moving from a crowded or remote position to the on-deck and exit positions for leaving the cab. The goal is to avoid having to audibly request that any of one's fellow passengers move so that one can leave the elevator briskly—certainly before the doors cycle.

The flip side of this strategic etiquette arises in very crowded elevators (and subways) when those standing nearest the door are obliged to step out to offer passage to those at the rear. This deferral rates a thanks from passengers thus released; it also obliges the person nearest the signal plate to press the "door open" button, and someone near the door (whether in or out) to wrap a protective hand around it to further guard against premature closing. This often elaborate choreography is second nature to millions. It is a marker of urban civilization, of its resilient accommodation of new technology, of the city superego at its best.

So I continue to be struck by the unsettled nature of the compact that governs the use of cell phones. Although I have no data about the numbers of people who decline to use their phones in elevators, I am certainly able to observe the large numbers of people who do. Many enter the elevator already on the line. Others receive calls. Others make them. None of these yakkers seems to be under any constraint to speak more softly than usual, to edit the contents of a conversation, or to limit calls to matters of urgency. On the contrary, many conversations are initiated by a need to let the person at the other end know that the caller is in an elevator. This signaling of a transitional condition is also something frequently seen in aircraft. I am amazed at the huge numbers of people who—as the "Fasten Seat Belts" sign is switched off as the plane pulls up to the gate—whip out their phones to call someone to let the person know that the plane has just pulled up to the gate. I dread the impending prospect of unrestricted use of cell phones in flight.

Although—as an abidingly timorous frequent flier—I have some sympathy with the need to celebrate survival, I remain mystified by what seems like an exponential increase in the need to communicate induced by the availability of a ready new means to do so, just as new highway capacity produces increased traffic. Witness the cabdrivers who talk uninterrupted on the phone as they travel the city, or the truly huge numbers of people who speak on the phone as they walk down the street: the medium has clearly become the message, if the meaning of the message remains somewhat opaque. I am still startled at the appearance of people with operator-style headsets and little cord mics who seem to be speaking to themselves (a phenomenon not unknown in the streets of New York). Don't even start with texting!

Whatever it is, the message clearly exceeds the manifest content of the exchange. It is also clear that the etiquette of cell-phone use, while related, is not entirely parallel to the rules governing public conversation in which speaker and audience are physically present. If the willing surrender of privacy continues to be the most striking quality of cell use in elevators and in other intimate spaces, the public character of cell talk seems most importantly linked to an elasticity in the dimensions of personal space. In public conversation, the main issue devolves on matters of reciprocal infringement: on whether my conversation is carried on too loudly to prevent other conversations or, by extension, whether my conversation infringes on the right of quiet enjoyment. This question is clearer in the theater than the street, but the principles are the same.

This idea of a flexible bubble of personal sovereignty is at the core of urban civility. There is an urban right to privacy that extends to the public realm. The affront can come in many ways: men with their legs aggressively spread in the subway, preventing the use of adjoining seats; train passengers who place their luggage on the seat next to them; unbathed cabbies; drivers who "block the box"; boom-box blasters; smokers driven outdoors who huddle at building entrances, fogging the door. We all have our pet public peeves and understandings of the rules, and, reciprocally, violators understand the reluctance of most people to confront their breaches.

Working through these stiff protocols often dominates time spent in the elevator, where compression intensifies the social field and makes more acute demands on demeanor and behavior than in spaces that are larger and more accommodating. On the other hand, forced propinquity can also give rise to compensating courtesies and opportunities. I can remember when I decided I would come out of my regulated shell and make conversation with people I encountered—generally à deux—in the elevator. One of my most useful opening lines concerns the "door close" button on the elevator at my new digs on Varick Street. This button produces exquisite satisfaction because—almost uniquely in my experience—pushing it actually causes the elevator doors to close immediately. (In general, the "door close" button is just a pacifier, and the door closes in its own sweet time. If that happens to be shortly after the button is pushed, *post hoc, ergo propter hoc*. If the wait is longer, we curse the button for the delay.) Sharing my delight at having found button nirvana with my fellow travelers often evokes similar delight in them.

The "door close" button, however, must be used with some probity, like the more infrequently used "door open" button. Here, the issue is to what degree a person trying to catch a departing elevator may infringe on the right to depart of those already boarded. I hold to the running—or at least accelerating—standard in cross-lobby use of the "hold" button and do not stop the door for someone who shows no willingness to speed up. At short range, it's up to the person approaching to get a hand in. Of course, if someone yells "Could you hold it (please)?" I feel obliged to go for the button. If I am quick-reflexed, I can generally catch it. Sometimes there are confused theatrical feints toward the button when someone gets a hand in the door after I've failed to hold it. And I think a door held demands thanks, if only a nod.

We all have a general right not to have our time wasted, and there's a reciprocal obligation on us not to waste others' time. While the elevator drama is enacted on a field of altruism, the same economy applies to other acts of time wasting, whether being put on hold, forced into unreasonable queues, pinioned by the indifference of civil servants, and so on. The same principles are reproduced in space, a nexus that includes both time and motion. Coming up behind people strolling three abreast on a narrow sidewalk, for example, often obliges throat clearing and an "excuse me" from more rapid walkers. The conflict between access to a configuration of conviviality and the right to passage along the sidewalk at a chosen speed typifies the ground of communal relations. What's important (again I think of India) is the negotiation and what each party brings to it. Just as one has an obligation to respect the pleasure of a family strolling abreast, so the blockers of the sidewalk should be sensitive to the probabilities of thwarted passage for those behind. Civility in the city is often marked by giving ground, and the territories can be microscopic.

If the elevator at 145 Hudson arouses Freudian thoughts, at 180 Varick they are more Pavlovian. I have learned my elevator skills like a monkey savant and, having unlocked their secrets, am eager to employ them as often as possible. The over-elevator floor indicators in the lobby at 145 took the form of a plate in which the number of every floor was inscribed in backlit punchouts. The horizontal movement of the illuminated number across its face was a pleasing and legible analogue to the vertical movement of the elevator. At 180, the indicators are "digital": they show only the number of the floor at which the elevator sits or is passing at that moment. What the three gauges at 180 offer, however, is the opportunity to play the game of elevator slots. When one enters the lobby, the jackpot is "triple L," meaning all three cabs are on the ground floor, providing the luxury of a leisurely stroll, no waiting, and a private ride. I have learned that the elevators are sequenced to depart from left to right and enjoy the smug satisfaction of being able to place myself in front of the door about to open, a variant on the shell game: three-cab monte.

A related game—elevator roulette—can be played when a crowd awaits the descent of the elevators. The objective, as always, is to travel to one's floor (I am now on nine, out of seventeen) with the fewest stops and the least company. As the elevators descend, the lobby crowd generally shifts in the direction of the elevator that seems likely to arrive first. This is not an unnuanced calculation, as the rate of descent—which depends on the number of people waiting on various floors—is uneven, descending elevators sometimes speeding past those paused ahead to pick up passengers. The trick here is to pick the sequence and timing of the arrival of the second and third elevators. This allows holding back a bit (being too obvious gives up the game by luring other players). The gold standard is to stride directly to an open elevator and ride solo to your floor, especially after witnessing a crowded cab depart moments before. Two is sublime.

There's an additional wrinkle at 180. The building is full of architects, and we are a notoriously competitive, gossipy, backstabbing bunch. This means that the building is filled with people I don't particularly want to meet (although there are plenty of others I wish to witness my virtuously early arrival, or late departure, or with whom it's nice simply to swap greetings). The shared captivity of the elevator forces the issue. Unlike the street, which allows various strategies of avoidance—averted eyes, looks of distraction, crossing to the other side, and so on—the elevator is a Skinner box of induced behavior, testing the limits of indifference.

The neighborhood around my new building—still struggling to brand itself—is also a museum of the architectures of constraint. This begins with the mammoth Federal Building a block north, which houses a number of agency branches, including the Passport Agency, the Veterans Administration, the Environmental Protection Agency, a post office, and other departments, including, according to rumor, a branch of the gulag of secret terrorist detention facilities. Since 9/11, this building has deployed a forest of defensive devices to guard it from attack. These include CCTV cameras pointing in all directions, an airport-style set of magnetometers, X-ray machines and armed guards at the Passport Agency, innumerable cops from previously unknown formations, including a fleet of white cruisers from the Homeland Security Police that are parked all around the neighborhood, and a ringing barricade of high-security bollards and massive concrete "planters" to guard against car bombs (although offering no protection to pedestrians).

These provisions have become ubiquitous. A walk through the neighborhood—which contains a number of office buildings, a huge UPS sorting facility, a smaller FedEx version, institutional buildings, and the entrance and vents for the Holland Tunnel—reveals astonishing numbers of surveillance cameras, their fields of vision encompassing virtually every public space around. These include not just streets and sidewalks but elevators, lobbies, and corridors. It is not possible to determine the degree to which they are networked, but it is certain that they are. (Chicago's comprehensive system has been made public, London is saturated, Shenzhen not only has thousands of cameras but obliges each citizen to carry a GPS-sensitive ID.) This question, at the core of every free citizen's anxiety about the new "homeland security" regime, is exactly how big Big Brother actually is. Every day, I use credit cards, cash machines, phones both fixed and mobile, and the Internet and pass dozens and dozens of cameras (I can see fifteen of them on the one-block walk to Starbucks), not to mention cops and security guards of every description. None of this gives me a feeling of security.

To the east of my building—in the block between Varick (Seventh Avenue changes its name south of Houston Street) and Sixth—there are a substantial number of residences, including fragments of early-nineteenth-century row housing and the in-mixed tenements typical of the western side of SoHo, a block away. A few blocks to the south—on and below Spring Street, where the zoning changes—there has been a flurry of residential construction, including the final, posthumously constructed work of Philip Johnson, a lumpy, undistinguished piece of luxury goods being marketed as the Urban Glass House. This is an attempt to evoke the image and cachet of the famous (suburban) Glass House, the 1949 work that put Johnson on the architectural map.

The big glass box acquired its bulk via the transfer of air rights from the tiny 1817 Federal house next door (home of the beloved Ear Inn). Now millionaires can look out their windows at the Holland Tunnel ventilation tower across the street. While this seems conclusive evidence that the "evolution of modernist luxury" (per the advertising) hasn't exactly led to intelligent design, there is a certain survival-of-the-fittest aspect. The Urban Glass House replaces an earlier Johnson effort to build a cartoonish thirty-six-story "habitable work of art," hooted down despite efforts by the developer to whip up community support for the giant zoning variance required by suggesting that resistance to the project was simply philistine.

The Johnson project is one of a number of similar buildings that have gone up in the last two years, all in an area of only a few blocks. While varying enormously in quality, all boast facades that are almost entirely glass. There's something striking about this (most of the surrounding context is masonry) that has to do with both consumption and paranoia. The original Glass House became iconic not simply for its architecture but as a medium for self-exposure. In a masterstroke of celebrity, the house made the career of its creator by putting not simply *itself* but *himself* on display. Like David Blaine suspended next to London's Tower Bridge (or Eichmann boxed in Jerusalem), the work of architecture was made performative by the visible character of its inhabitation. Indeed, the Glass House combined the transparency of Blaine's box (simply a window on his stunt) with the protective quality of Eichmann's.

We're all running scared now, and the raft of new glass buildings shares this anxious quality. Like the Johnson tower, all (the majority face west) have windows that are either sealed or barely operable. In an era of raised environmental consciousness—in which cross ventilation is the minimum level of architectural common sense—there is something perverse here. However, it is perfectly attuned to the post-9/11 culture of anxiety and the contemporary phenomenology of safety. As the media endlessly alert us to the risks around us and increasingly identify surveillance with protection, this glass architecture apparently satisfies the nominally contradictory demands for isolation and exposure.

This architecture sees the environment as pathogenic and gaskets itself away from it. The glass house next to the tunnel extract fan is metaphorically precise. Windows should not be opened for fear of filling the room with carbon monoxide (or the avian flu, or sarin gas). Yet the activities within remain visible. If safety is identified with panoptic transparency, self-exposure is a medium for reducing risk. More and more of daily life is governed by the management and manipulation of fear. A trip to the airport obliges surrender to close vetting and intrusive examination as the price of protection. (Have you been through one of those air-puff explosives sniffers yet?) The police can now check any bag and pat down any rider in the subway. Public service announcements caution us to be on the lookout for people who dress unusually, which covers just about everyone around here. The result is a shrink-wrapped city, designed for the pleasures of danger.

Such actuarial aesthetics have become pervasive, and they're making me nervous. While it is the duty of architects to protect the public from danger (and the hard-fought history of health and safety codes surely marks our progress in this), a line must be drawn between sensible protection from risk and pandering to the morphology of fear. Although we seem to have largely gotten over the mimetic anxiety of "deconstructionist" architecture, with its vapid celebration of trauma and its claims to channel the spirit of an anxious age, the pervasiveness of "terror" as a driver for architecture and urbanism grows by the day. A 2005 show at the Museum of Modern Art was called *Safe* and dealt with the assimilation of various countermeasures into the discourse of "good" design. The architectural press publicizes the high-tech ha-has now being installed everywhere to protect us from truck bombers. We are swept along in a frenzy of the fear of fear and look for reassurance in the usual wrong places.

A society can be judged by the risks to which it chooses to respond, the dangers it values, the targets it gives high priority. Hurricane Katrina was shocking not simply for its elemental ferocity but because it peeled back the layers of indifference so selectively applied to certain urban areas. The "news" paused in its usual preoccupations to reveal something it habitually obscured: the horrible poverty and inequality that the collapse of the levees made visible. In the numbers game of lives and dollars, we were forced to wonder why our priority was the weekly expenditure of dozens of lives and billions of dollars in Iraq when our own citizens were so miserable and our own infrastructure so lacking. And we could clearly see that the "better" people and parts of town disproportionately enjoyed the tools and resiliency to recover.

I have spent some time on the Mississippi Gulf Coast, working with my students on a reconstruction scheme. Everyone was waiting for FEMA to determine the new legal topography and come up with a cogent strategy for managing hurricane risk. Now that benchmarks have been promulgated, there will certainly be restrictive zoning, new building standards, and a shakeout in the insurance industry, including some revisiting of the federal flood insurance that makes building on such dangerous shores feasible. At a minimum, the federal government must stop subsidizing risky behavior, stop being the fiscal enabler of the wanton development of our fragile coasts.

Unfortunately, the solution may make things worse. One dangerous possibility is that new regulations will lead to dramatic up-scaling, the building of "safe" high-rise buildings to replace more susceptible houses: Class A construction rode the storm out well. In this scenario, risk becomes a privilege, and higher insurance and mortgage rates, coupled with more restrictive building codes, exclude the poor from these areas forever. Declared dangerous, life at the shore will be enjoyed only by those who can afford to defend themselves against nature (although the rest of us will keep on picking up the tab for infrastructure). The Gulf Coast will probably become very much like my corner of Manhattan, defined by a lavish, overscaled architecture of self-protection and marked by unassailable exclusivity, by habitable, hurricane-proof, high-rise works of art.

ALTERNATIVE
ROUTES

The Walk From Annabel Lee to 180 Varick is substantially shorter than my old walk to Hudson Street, involving a new set of routes and with them a reconfiguration of the social and physical space of the journey. Almost invariably, the trip now begins with a right turn on Waverly Place, which seals my daily encounter with the corner newsdealer, materialized in small banter at the moment of transaction or waves when passing at other times of the day. The revised complex of possible routes also takes me by a new set of cafés and shops. A Chinese art shop and a café with unusually delicious pancakes have taken their tolls on both my waistline and my bottom line.

On some days I drop laundry off at the Tatyana Cleaner across the street, a business run by congenial Russians. I'm known to them and no longer need to announce my name for them to print out a receipt on their computer. The owner, Jacob, has an appealingly dry sense of humor. Although they've been on the block for years, I still feel a twinge of betrayal going to Tatyana because we abandoned our beloved old cleaner—Henry—to do so. Henry, also an immigrant (from Taiwan), used to occupy a shop just across Sixth Avenue on the corner of Gay Street, which now houses a nice, if overcrowded, café. Driven out by a rent increase, Henry moved a few blocks farther away, well beyond the distance over which I can comfortably carry giant bags of laundry. We still chat from time to time, and I follow the progress of his smart and studious daughter, whom I used to see doing her homework behind the counter of the shop and who has now gone off to college.

At the end of the block, I make a left turn on Sixth Avenue, passing over the big West Fourth Street subway station, which runs four blocks underground and is four levels deep—as large an enclosed architectural space as any in the Village. The New York City subway is a consolidation of three networks (two of which were—until 1940—privately owned), and this station is a major confluence and transfer station of the former Independent Subway (the first, nomenclature notwithstanding, built by the city). The current Sixth Avenue line replaces an elevated predecessor that dominated the street until 1938. Many people continue to refer to subway lines by these former names. One relic of the separate origins of the different lines is that the dimensions of the cars vary, and they cannot run on the tracks originally built for other systems. The IRT, one block away on Seventh Avenue, for example, uses smaller cars. The West Fourth Street station has not yet been visited by the ongoing rehabilitation of the system and is a remarkably grotty and miserably ventilated environment, although, at this point, the trains themselves are pretty uniformly air-conditioned. Still, there is something remarkable about this particular lamination, the way in which a gigantic piece of urban infrastructure exists more or less invisibly in the midst of a ground-level fabric scaled very differently.

This coexistence is part of the genius of the developing city and its ability to create new and unanticipated juxtapositions and configurations over time. It also begs all sorts of questions about the differential gravity of preserving and enhancing specific elements of the cityscape. The Village waterfront provides a clarifying example. Once a classic "working waterfront," lined with piers—including one that awaited the *Titanic* on its fateful maiden voyage—our stretch of the Hudson has not seen a ship dock in over forty years. Gone, too, are the inland influences of the waterfront: the tangle of trucks, trains, and other transport; the warehousing activity; the stevedores and their bars and lunchrooms and union halls; and the community of their families, many of whom lived in the blocks nearest the water. Although there is a small residue of Hispanic shops and restaurants on Fourteenth Street—once the center of shipping from Latin America—a whole maritime ecology has simply disappeared, leaving behind only an infrastructure of remnants.

Many of these are being replaced or reused according to the current municipal paradigms for the waterfront, which has undergone a dramatic transformation over the years. In most American cities, waterfronts were long primarily industrial, used for shipping, logistics, warehousing, railways, and trucking. In the period after World War II, however, passenger shipping was virtually eliminated by air travel, and the urban docks and piers used for freight were abandoned for the enormous tarmacs of containerization. Dereliction was widespread, but these vast, unencumbered sites were particularly suited for another form of transportation: freeways. Numerous cities chose to cut themselves off from their finest natural assets by lining their coasts with impassable miles of concrete. More recently, many have recognized their error, and some—including San Francisco and Boston—have demolished these barriers, reopening their waterfronts to nonautomotive use.

Westway, a Big Dig–scaled underground highway budgeted at more than a billion dollars a mile (in 1980s dollars), was the last act of New York's own urban interstate drama. Its authors claimed that their idea was to see just how much they could leverage from that 90 percent federal subsidy. Accordingly, they proposed filling in the Hudson to the pier line (eight hundred feet), from Fifty-ninth Street all the way to the Battery. On this fill was to be considerable park space and very considerable space for real estate development, thus ensuring it enjoyed the backing of the real estate industry, the construction industry, and the city government. In all probability, it represents a last effort to expand the actual surface area of Manhattan horizontally, although its vertical multiplication still has years to run, and there are a number of proposals afoot to build up waterside sites in the other boroughs.

The Westway scheme was idiotic—a hyper-expensive trucking highway running through Manhattan and a real estate giveaway of the first water, both characteristics it shared with the failed Lower Manhattan Expressway. Opposition was fierce and,

ultimately, successful. Many realized that such massive investment in the city should be directed at its crumbling public transit
system instead, and behind the leadership of the legendarily feisty
congressperson Bella Abzug legislation was passed to allow a trade-
in of federal highway dollars for public transit subsidy. But the real
deathblow to Westway proved to be a lawsuit filed on behalf of the
striped-bass population—shepherded through the courts by the
activist Marcy Benstock—that sought to protect their breeding
grounds in the pilings beneath the piers that the fill would have
eliminated. After this was decided in the federal courts, Mayor Ed
Koch, a Westway supporter, reportedly uttered, in frustration, the
most memorable line of the affair: "If those striped bass need a
place to fuck, I will build them a motel in Poughkeepsie." After
many years of construction, there is now a thin but useful and
beautifully maintained park (that includes several rebuilt piers) on
the opposite side of a very broad surface road, as wide as Westway
would have been but called a "boulevard," rather than a highway.

The Westway plan—and the construction of Battery Park
City—were crucial in defining what is now the municipal default
for developing the 650-mile New York City waterfront. At the moment, there seem to be only two paradigms, and they recur in plan
after plan. The first is the idea of an Olmstedian park—like Riverside Park—a band of well-landscaped green space but with a limited range of "parklike" activities. The second is a relatively narrow
green space and promenade fronting new high-rise development.
The problem isn't that either of these prototypes is exactly meretri-
cious: both have local histories and can be produced congenially.
The issue is with the severity of the limits, with the distaste for
maritime and industrial possibilities, and with the vast predominance of upper-income construction on these superb sites (and
rich folks' special privileges over the waterfront parks in front of
them).

I've already mentioned the effects on the Village of the spate of
luxury high-rises going up along our new gold coast. I don't question the inevitability of change or delude myself that shipping

and manufacture will return in their former form to Manhattan. What is less clear—as a matter of principle—is what to do with their physical remains, how to deal with the shifting demographics produced by the transformations of local economies and their populations, and how to enlarge, rather than contract, the variety of waterfront forms and activities. The waterfront is of particular importance now because the city's morphological endgame is increasingly being carried out on smaller fields of play: the grid is just about full, the development-versus-conservation argument has been well articulated on both sides, and the era of wholesale urban-renewal-style demolition seems largely over. Our big plans are mainly taking place on residual sites (many of them very big, to be sure)—over rail yards and highway cuts, in undeveloped territories of abandonment, on remaining industrial areas, and along the waterfront. We are doing absolutely nothing to deal with the risk posed to large areas of the waterfront by an impending rise in sea level.

The final struggle will be over what to value in undertaking these transformations and how to do them. One easy principle is to deal with what's actually there. Although there is much conjuring of the Village waterfront as it existed in the eighteenth and nineteenth centuries, the current remnants are much later, almost entirely twentieth century. Their histories include not simply their role in a vanished maritime ecology but, more recently, an intense use by a mainly gay population as covert sexual playgrounds. A group of piers has already been converted by Roland Betts, a Bush crony and a power in lower Manhattan development politics, into the vast Chelsea Piers, a private, upmarket athletic and recreational complex. Gone is any manifestation of a once tough waterfront culture, beginning with the old seamen's and stevedores' bars and followed by "rough" leather bars, themselves victims of unstoppable gentrification.

Symptomatic is the reconstruction of a piece of infrastructure called the High Line, an elevated railway viaduct, long abandoned, that runs down the West Side from the Penn Station yards, often passing directly through buildings and plunging deep into the West Village and beyond. It has been the object of preservationist attention for years and has finally been not simply saved but converted to a linear park, which allows people to walk through gardens, above the hurly-burly of the street, for a distance of more than thirty blocks, a great idea. As is inevitable with such public infrastructure, it will transform its surroundings, adding—like Central, Prospect, and Riverside Parks—tremendous value to them. The formal start of the project has resulted in a flurry of development along its route, stimulated in part by a re-zoning of the area to encourage adjacent construction. Like the High Line itself, many of these are being designed by leading architects. Not surprisingly, all of them are aimed at the top end of the market and will only further accelerate the departure of the remaining middle-class and poor populations.

This kind of dramatic transformation has already made over the meat market area at the west end of Fourteenth Street, the northern boundary of the Village. With the departure of the Fulton Fish Market, the meat market was the last remnant of the wholesale food trade in Manhattan. Until little more than a decade ago, it was a warren of low buildings and irregular streets, home to dozens of meat merchants and butchers, as well as to the symbiotic, still-existing Old Homestead restaurant, a historic object of carnivore pilgrimage. The streets were bloody and carcasses were slung from meat hooks on metal tracks that conveyed them from trucks, along the sidewalk, into various flanking establishments. Near the abandoned piers, the meat market acquired a double meaning and a double use, as an after-hours scene of coupling and prostitution. But in the city, geography is destiny. This area, tight against the West Village and Chelsea and opposite the renewing waterfront, was transformed in the blink of an eye to a raging epicenter of trendy restaurants, boutiques, and new hotels as well as other new buildings—including a big one for Diane von Furstenberg. The well-heeled have now almost totally displaced the well-hoofed.

Joan and I are not infrequent visitors to the place. Many of the restaurants are good, and many feature large sidewalk cafés that, in aggregate, create a scene of alfresco conviviality that is unique in the city. Traffic is relatively light: the old buildings and cobbled streets provide a nicely patinated envelope for the fun, the strolling is relaxed, and home is fifteen minutes away on a route that runs through some of the tastiest blocks in the Village. The symbolism, however, is stark. Once again, a neighborhood dedicated to production has been transformed into one for consumption. As someone who believes that an internal balance between these activities is vital to the health, character, and autonomy of the city, I find that the sight of yet another zone of high-priced good times gives me the willies, even as I tuck into my perfect branzino in the lovely back garden of the delightful Italian restaurant.

Sixth Avenue, a thoroughfare once distinguished by the particulars of its locality and now a strangely contested mix of multinational franchises and local businesses, is another battleground. To be sure, Sixth Avenue is not a strictly local street but a highly trafficked (above- and belowground) north-south axis. As such, it enjoys the great style of serial reincarnation of many Manhattan avenues, remade every dozen blocks or so to reflect the neighborhoods through which it passes, including the residual quaintness of the Village, the great late-nineteenth-century department stores of the Ladies' Mile, and the towers of Rockefeller Center. Our busy stretch reflects the fact that the Village remains an entertainment destination for a very wide variety of people and houses a huge number of students, a population of temporarily limited means but with an unlimited desire to party.

The blocks of Sixth Avenue near Annabel Lee are an extremely fluid intersection between a very wide variety of interests, ranging from the most distinct to the most generic, and a vivid seam between a spreading suburban homogeneity and urban resistance. On the one hand, the street is lined with a large number of banks, chain drugstores, national fast-food, clothing, and sneaker franchises, and other multinational commercial activity. On the other, a few local shops manage to hold on despite the spiraling rents, although many of these do high-volume business, including an extremely popular Chinese restaurant from which a stream of deliverymen issues forth round the clock. Also hanging on are a few high-end grocery stores, of special importance in this food-obsessed city, and their own transformations are important markers in the unfolding history of the neighborhood.

When we first moved in, there were two legendary food stores on Sixth Avenue. The first was Jefferson Market, located in a very old building on the west side of the avenue. A throwback to former times, the place was staffed by men in long white aprons and straw boaters who, stationed behind a central counter, would retrieve groceries from high shelves with a special apparatus and then use mechanical adding machines, rather than registers, to ring up the bill. There were no lines; rather, you simply awaited the attention of one of these men who then took care of you in an intimate and personal style of transaction. In the next room was Jefferson Market's excellent butcher shop with its own cast of characters. The store also sold everyday, mass-market items like cereal and detergent, a comprehensiveness that, in eschewing the erotics of exclusivity, made the market all the more desirable.

Across the street was Balducci's, long presided over with a strong Italian inflection by "Mama" Balducci and her husband. Located on the ground floor of a postwar apartment building, it lacked the small-town, sawdust-on-the-floor character of Jefferson Market but made up for it with a cornucopian delicatessen, superior produce, and an excellent *salumeria* at the center of the store, where a variety of delicious dishes was prepared from Mama's ancestral recipes and under her scrupulous supervision. This ready-made food was a godsend for both the cooking- and the time-challenged (us on both counts), and surely one of the cultural ornaments of the neighborhood. Although the store interior consisted of modern shelving, lighting, and appliances, it was a brilliant environment, a bit crowded—but not so much that it couldn't be managed with either a handbasket or a miniature shopping cart—and slightly labyrinthine, which induced a conviviality not unlike that of the street. It was miles away from the freeway-scaled aisles, long parallel slabs of shelving, and digestive taxonomy—produce on the far right and frozen food a mile down on the left—typical of supermarket chains. Balducci's had the right goods and the right organization: the categories perfectly mapped the priorities and sequence of our desires.

Both stores are now gone from their original locations and configurations. Jefferson Market has moved across the street to more spacious—but much more ordinary—quarters, and the men in aprons are gone, replaced by a more conventional checkout arrangement. It's possible that the tradition was simply unsustainable, that the production of such elderly grocers came to an end, and that any attempt to reproduce it would simply be too Disneyesque. The atmosphere is still cordial, and there has been a welcome enlargement of the prepared-food department, more perfectly reflecting contemporary habits of consumption. Balducci's has disappeared from Sixth Avenue entirely. Its matriarch and patriarch died, and the business was sold to an out-of-town entrepreneur who had hoped to take the brand national. A reincarnated version opened on Fourteenth Street, a mere shadow of its former self, but it, too, recently closed. In place of the former Balducci's, there is now another "quality" grocer—Citarella—the full-service expansion (there are several branches around the city) of a distinguished fish store on the Upper West Side. The quality is quite good—the fish remarkable—but the organization has become too rational, the aisles a bit too wide, the sense of personality gone, the flavoring aura missing.

Still, the avenue manages to hold out against lethal tidiness. The remnant raffishness of our stretch of Sixth is secured by several very particular presences that act as effective guardians against its being overwhelmed by too much niceness or too much global sameness. The first is a two-block row of sidewalk booksellers, mainly homeless black men, who offer used magazines and books for sale from folding tables that line the sidewalk. Their right to do this without a commercial license is the result of Local Law 33,

passed by the city council in 1982. This law makes a special exception for street vendors of written matter on free-speech grounds,
but with those famous "reasonable time, place, and manner"
restrictions.

However, in 1993, Local Law 45 was signed into effect. This
came after intense lobbying from several BIDs and under the influence of an increasing focus by the police on "quality of life" crimes,
minor infractions (drinking or pissing in the street, loud radios,
graffiti writing, and so on). These were, following the famous 1982
"broken windows" theory of James Q. Wilson and George Kelling,
held to be "gateway" crimes that, left unaddressed, invited more
serious forms of lawlessness. To create the desired sense of order,
Local Law 45 regulated the placement and number of book vendors,
setting up mandatory distances from building and subway entrances,
street corners, and bus stops, eliminating them entirely from streets
from which other forms of vending—like food, souvenirs, and
clothing—had been banned. The legislation also required that the
vendors set themselves up in such a way as to allow a minimum
twelve-foot-wide pedestrian path along the sidewalk, and they were
forbidden to touch any part of a building with their tables or merchandise. In the Village, the law had the immediate effect of cutting
in half the space available to the book and magazine sellers, the
struggle that's currently being played out in SoHo with street artists.

In his excellent 1999 book, *Sidewalk*—an ethnographic study
of these same Sixth Avenue vendors—Mitchell Duneier reports
that the effect of Local Law 45 was to produce conflict among the
vendors for the reduced number of spots allowed (and the most
favorable locations). The previous, informal system of self-regulated
distribution of space, with its longtime standards of tenure, broke
down. In its place sprang up a system of "holders," people who
would occupy spots through the night and then extract payment
from vendors to turn them over in the morning. The police were
increasingly called in to adjudicate disputes that often grew angry.
For their part the police set up strict boundaries, sometimes with

spray paint on the sidewalk, and often seized the goods of vendors whose stock overstrayed their lines. Although the local BID, set up after the passage of Local Law 45, has also done its bit to discourage vending with its cleaning crews and space-consuming tree planting and street furnishing, the situation has largely stabilized, and the area is now dominated by a regular core of merchants.

The second guardian against McWorld is the regular presence of several political activists, panhandlers, and homeless advocates who distribute literature and raise funds from fixed spots along the street. The western end of Eighth Street had been the territory of antipornography and antivivisection campaigners, both brandishing ghastly images of brutalized victims, human and animal. These particular tables have been gone for a while, although one corner continues to be held down by advocates for the homeless, a big plastic office watercooler jug awaiting donations. Like the panhandlers farther along the block, they are attuned to the possibility of rendering queasy the consciences of the delicacy-laden shoppers emerging from the nearby Jefferson Market and Citarella. For us, the interior monologue runs through the gamut of gave-at-the-office, only-official-charities-legitimate, can't-really-put-down-these-heavy-bags, gave-yesterday, and the rest of the repertoire of disquieting but affirming excuses. Joan does have one panhandler in particular to whom she is generous, and I help Dale with regular twenties.

The third of these colluding activities is a garish row of sex shops and tattoo parlors clustered on the west side of the avenue a couple of blocks down. These are cause for chagrin among many locals (and fascination and patronage by others), and they, too, are subject to regulation. For example, sex shops are forbidden to open in the vicinity of schools. While I am personally mystified by the incredible popularity of tattooing nowadays, I do appreciate that it is a medium of artistic and self-expression. Likewise, although I buy many of the arguments against the degrading, violent, and dehumanizing aspects of contemporary pornography, I didn't live through the 1960s to object to other people's chosen forms of pleasure, nor do I wish to see the historic character of the Village as a space of sexual freedom and experiment threatened. I am ambivalent over why this particular range of shops should be designed to look like a tiny version of the old Times Square, with their blinding fluorescent interiors and screaming signage. Yet given that Times Square has largely purged itself of such emporiums (a major reason that so many have relocated here), it is possible that this distributed arrangement in which every neighborhood supports a tiny neon version of the Deuce is the best alternative.

The triple configuration of chains, local shops, and "exceptional" activities operates in effective concert. The combination certainly serves to curb the gentility that abounds on many surrounding outlets. Despite the plethora of fast-food shops, cellphone outlets, and chain drugstores, this is not the mall, with its rigorous exclusion of undesirables, its prohibitions on the exercise of free speech, and its G-rated content. The interaction of this space with these marginalized activities can be seen as an urban coping mechanism, in which an array of powerful urban antigens are drawn to the site of multinational malignancy. Once again, the unyielding spatial character of a neighborhood with strong preservation protections ensures that the upward spiral of scale that characterizes so much suburban retail is frustrated. The inconvenience of the historic city becomes a bulwark for the protection of diversity and the local.

One day not long ago, returning home, I noticed a crowd gathered around the subway entrance on the corner of Sixth and Waverly. Because this entrance is cut into the front of the corner building, there is a big area overhung by a ceiling. This creates a gathering space used by transit workers hanging out between shifts, by police sheltering to update their notes or chat, by people waiting on rendezvous, and—until the official attitude turned implacably hostile—by homeless people bedding down for the night. It's an

unplanned but very important gathering space, created by the spe-
cifics of its inadvertent architecture.

From behind the wall of backs belonging to this particular
crowd, I heard Mozart being played on string instruments, and
played well. Pressing in, I could see that the performers (on violin,
viola, and cello) were kids, two boys and a girl, the oldest of whom—
the violin-playing boy—looked about twelve years old. The crowd
was enormous and very diverse, less a Village crowd than a West
Fourth Street subway crowd. In front of the musicians was an open
instrument case, and it was filled with money, most of it the folding
variety. As they continued to play, the kids were virtually showered
with dollar bills, the accolade coming both from the well-heeled
and from those very much less so, including—I noticed—several of
the guys who run the printed-matter tables on Sixth Avenue. Unless
the market for last year's *Vanity Fair*, *Nugget*, or *National Geographic*
is greater than I imagine, these are not people making a very generous living, and their giving is thus all the more so.

Perhaps the reason that the three kids (whose father hovered
nearby keeping a watchful eye on his talented brood and papering
the crowd with flyers announcing the trio's availability for private
events) were the object of such studious, even reverential attention
is that they were black. Of course, they were very talented, but
outside the music they seemed oddly emotionless, their eyes blank,
even when the crowd cheered and applauded. I wondered whether
they were victims of a stage father who drove them too hard, forcing them to perform when they'd sooner go out and play something
other than their instruments. Maybe they were just little kids and
shy in a crowd. Setting this aside, though, they did represent the kind
of self-affirming fantasy—African-American kids playing Mozart—
that somehow describes a part of the liberalism of "our" Village.

Unfortunately, the desire for tolerance and diversity is not
quite the same as the thing itself. Although the crowds on Sixth
Avenue are truly mixed—our entertainments are very varied and
our accessibility superb—they do not describe our resident population, which has only a small minority of African-Americans (the

percentage was also low in Jane Jacobs's day), trending downward as prices trend up. Here's the Disneyland problem again. Obviously, it's better to have that jostling, variegated street than not, to have the book vendors, to have that asphalt basketball court on West Fourth Street that attracts crowds to the teams that play there, almost all of them 100 percent African-American and almost all of them from other parts of the city (and almost all of them playing at a very high level). The NBA is also dominated by black Americans, and nobody cavils at the location of Madison Square Garden: professional sports aren't neighborhood-scaled activities. And it's a plus for the Village to have this mini-Garden in our midst.

Village tolerance is both authentic and superficial, increasingly unsupported by residential and economic diversity. We play our roles in this via a combination of choice and constraint, just like the people in Chinatown not so far away. Again, there's that nexus of opportunity, choice, and something close to imprisonment, the same battles over the terms of authenticity and over the care and conservation of the tangle of ecosystems that converge to make any community. Ethnic enclaves have been around for a long time in American cities, and there's almost no town of good size that lacks its Chinatown. Our own, which now has an even larger twin in Flushing, Queens, continues to be fertilized by ongoing immigration, point of entry to American life, and is home to tens of thousands of new arrivals, many of them illegal. To these, it offers protection, acculturation, opportunity. Large numbers ship out immediately to the archipelago of Chinese restaurants and other businesses around the country, and there are many employment offices that specialize in just this.

But these illegals are often badly exploited, housed in lightless, overcrowded warrens as terrible as any photographed by Jacob Riis and forced to work in sweatshops to rival the Triangle Shirtwaist Factory. Many, too, have been plundered by smugglers to whom they've consigned their life savings to be shipped to the land of opportunity in containers. And yet does anyone want Chinatown to disappear? Do we want the person pushing the cart at the Dim

Sum Palace to be a struggling actor from Utah or Tennessee? Do we want to do without this rich and energetic fragment of another place plunged into the midst of the city?

These are easy questions. More difficult are those that ask whether—with everyone looking for digs in Manhattan—we support Chinese real estate brokers who rent only to other Chinese or, at the opposite end of the spectrum, whether we wish to see neighborhoods, like the ersatz "quarters" of Disneyland—Tomorrowland, Frontierland, Main Street, U.S.A.—maintained as phony representations of ecologies that they do not actually support, food courts with pretensions to depth. Clearly, it would be tragic if, in cities around the world in which diversity is growing, the idea of local homogeneities was supplanted by a recombinant super-homogeneity in which the demographic and cultural character of all places is simply the same. This scintillating dialectic of equality and difference is at the core of the struggle to find the form of the good city.

ESPRIT
D'ESCALIER

Writing this little book has taken forever, a conspiracy of fits and starts. Begun well over a dozen years ago, it describes a walk that has changed in cycles and epicycles, over years, days, and hours. This long march has allowed the insinuation of great events into what was to have been a low-key memoir of the everyday. While I cannot exactly pretend that 9/11 didn't happen, that it didn't transform the course of my life and my sense of the quotidian, it registers on my walk only obliquely. The towers no longer figure in the skyline downtown. The burgeoning apparatus of homeland security is deployed everywhere. But the streets are long back to normal, and planning and building continue with their business as usual. Private internalizations notwithstanding, the world of rents and croissants and homelessness still functions in its familiar way. This is both reassuring and depressing.

At Annabel Lee, too, changes have taken place. Carl is gone and his apartment is being renovated, as is the facade of the building. Both of these are being pursued in typically sporadic fashion: work on the facade has been suspended until "warm weather," and work next door is unpredictable. However, even as I write this, the hall is filled with aluminum replacement windows for all the apartments in the building. How long have I dreamed of this day! Well-sealed sash! An end to the creeping carpet of dust on the windowsills. Will these windows be the tip-in type that will actually allow us to wash them? Most of us old tenants in the building are too fatigued to wonder at this flurry of activity, which seems to be the result of a long list of building code infractions and, of course, the legal rent increases that the landlord will be able to pass along to us.

As the real estate market crested, the block itself became virtually scaffold lined, and one property after another is being fixed up. Several row houses formerly subdivided into apartments are being converted back to single homes. There are indoor lap pools and beautiful details. The renovation of Washington Square is also moving along, with the western half now fenced off and construction crews at work. The idiotic plan to move the fountain on line with the axis of the arch is under way, congruent with a general increase in preference for old-fashioned styles of order: symmetry and spycams are markers of the imperial city of the twenty-first century.

The move to Varick Street has given me a new set of streets to micromanage and a new neighborhood to assimilate. Indeed, I've just received a "stakeholders survey" from an incipient BID, asking for my comments about changes I feel might be necessary or desirable. Unfortunately, the questionnaire limits the choices. While it inquires after my preference between the urgency of restaurants open for breakfast, lunch, and dinner, there is no category where I can indicate a desire for affordable housing (or office space). I do not feel a strong need for joint marketing of businesses or a buffing up of local "identity." As the industry seeks to slot "Hudson Square" into the repertoire of urban product, clear handwriting appears on the wall as the neighborhood drifts in interregnum between what it has been and what it will be. Despite blowing smoke about making us into the city's "first economically diverse and environmentally sustainable neighborhood," the BID seems mainly interested in the usual street discipline and the attraction of "higher-quality retailers."

A particularly egregious example of the kind of mixed-income, sustainable development that the list of real estate types forming the BID may have in mind is currently under construction two blocks to the south, although at the moment building is halted following an accident in which a construction worker was killed and a long list of previous violations by the concrete contractor was uncovered. The structure is the Trump SoHo, a forty-five-story "condominium hotel" containing four hundred apartments, ranging in size from 425 to 10,000 square feet, priced at three thousand dollars per, and said to be selling briskly. The building, now topped out, is, by far, the tallest in an area characterized by structures of six to fifteen stories. Like most Trump projects, the architecture is completely bland, another glass box. Because of its size, however, it whimsically rescales the entire neighborhood, permanently marring the low roofscape that stretches downtown and culminates in the lower Manhattan skyline. On the sky, it's an awful scar. As urbanism, it's vandalism.

The controversy that surrounds the building, however, is focused on questions that exceed size. Use is the real issue: the hotel-condominium bifurcation is Trump's strategy for building a residential structure in a neighborhood zoned for manufacturing, one of the last such districts in lower Manhattan. Although this zoning category does not permit residential structures, it does allow conventional hotels, which the code describes as facilities where units "are rented on a daily basis" and used "primarily for transient occupancy." The condo hotel is a relatively new real estate product, introduced to New York in recent years and, to date, only in areas with residential zoning. It's clear, though, that the zoning code was written well before any of its framers could possibly have imagined this particular bending of the idea of a "transient hotel."

Because of this lack of specificity and obvious precedent, it has been necessary to finesse the nature of the project's occupancy in order to create a standard of transience. According to the deal struck between Trump and the city (via a "restrictive declaration" now described as "voluntary"), though the tower is clearly an apartment building—that is, a building filled with units that in every way resemble apartments, with kitchens, baths, bedrooms, and the rest—individual owners will be permitted to occupy their apartments for a maximum of only 120 days a year, and no more than

29 out of any consecutive 36 days. There appears, however, to be no legal obligation to rent when vacant, although there will certainly be strong financial inducements to do so.

Despite gales of criticism from activist groups (who recently staged a demonstration at the construction site)—and despite the discovery, during excavation, of a cemetery from a pioneering abolitionist church that once occupied the block—the project moved ahead at breakneck speed. Recently, if tardily, a consortium of community organizations has announced a lawsuit against the city for permitting the project, and the city has promised to defend it, arousing further outcry about the use of taxpayer money to pull Trump's chestnuts out of the legal fire.

The suit's claim will undoubtedly focus both on the appropriateness of the building—which will be a tough call against arguments that it is, thanks to the loophole, technically "as of right"—and, perhaps more promisingly, on Trump's claim that it is actually going to be a hotel. Here the issue devolves on whether what walks, flies, and quacks like a (residential) duck is actually another species. Trump has advertised the units as "residences" (there has been much heat about advertising that crosses this line, is subsequently discovered by the opposition, and then pulled from various media), and the legal confrontation will surely fix on the semantic technicalities of the meaning of "transience." To be sure, the jet-set masters of the universe who buy into the property are an extremely transient class, but this certainly can't have been what the framers of the code had in mind when they distinguished "residential" hotels (not permitted) from "transient" ones (allowed).

One obvious question is why Trump and his partners aren't simply building an actual hotel on the site. According to Julius Schwarz, executive vice president of the Bayrock Group (which initially secured the site with the Sapir Organization before bringing in Trump for his inimitable brand) and the managing partner for the project, "It's a financing mechanism" designed as a hedge against a potential glut of hotels. "You can model it out ten years. Right now, there's a shortage of hotels. So people are going to be building hotels, and the rates will eventually come down. Hotel rooms will always be in high demand, but you can't rely on the twelve-hundred-dollar-a-night rates. Even with a very high-end luxury hotel like this, you have to convince a lender. That's the most important thing; otherwise the deal doesn't get done."

What this is likely to mean is that the lawsuit will focus on Trump's intentions, on the enforceability of his "voluntary" agreement to limit the days his high rollers are actually in the building. Will he really send the concierge to remove the owner of a ten-million-dollar unit about to stay for a thirtieth straight night? It likewise seems highly unlikely that the Buildings Department—on which responsibility for enforcement rests—will have either the resources or the inclination to monitor four hundred apartments on a daily basis to see exactly who's behind the closed doors. The scope for scams and greased palms is virtually limitless, and the only real question is whether the city actually believes in the enforceability of the arrangement or is simply acquiescing in a situation it knows to be absurd.

The fate of the lawsuit is not clear and seems a long shot for this particular project. Part of the intent of litigating, however, is to force the city to close the loophole in the zoning code that has permitted the tower. The lawsuit seeks to head off similar "Trojan horse" projects that might rise in other manufacturing zones around Manhattan, including chunks of Chelsea, the Village, Tribeca, SoHo, and the Garment District. Unfortunately, the Department of City Planning has not indicated that it sees any urgency to revise the code. Big buildings for big money are at the top of the municipal development agenda, and the site—although it is in a manufacturing district—adjoins some of the most expensive residential areas in the city.

The building's real affront is broader than the fact that another developer has found another way of manipulating the zoning laws to his advantage. It has to do with ideas about both the city's mix of uses and its mix of people. Certainly, the outcry would have been much less had the site, which was vacant, been developed with a twelve-story building for moderate-income families or a child-care center. Many of us still idealize a vision of urban vitality that includes manufacturing and other industrial uses, although both the national economy and the local real estate market remain inhospitable. But the category of manufacture (like the widespread resistance to the city's tide of luxurious residences and Class A offices) also encodes the idea of a working class and reflects alarm at the increasingly monochrome, if glossy, character of the town.

Like the nation as a whole, New York lacks an adequate industrial policy, and the Trump SoHo—like its eponymous neighborhood next door—represents the transformation of an "obsolete" industrial neighborhood into something more congenial to the current market. This transformation reproduces, at the scale of the city, something that is going on globally, a kind of spatial segregation—or zoning—of continental reach: New York's industrial neighborhoods are now in China or Mexico. What is sacrificed locally is not simply blue-collar employment but a vital idea of what constitutes a city, an idea that includes notions of self-sufficiency and diversity. One of the things that can make a city great is the spectacle of equity, a sense of a "right to the city" that combines access to both its places and its possibilities. We rely on public space and public policy to lay out a framework for this freedom.

The motto emblazoning the construction marquee surrounding the new Trump project is succinct: "Possess Your Own SoHo." In the vulgarity of their sumptuary obsessions, Trump and his hotel are fine symbols of an urbanism of pure extraction that has little interest beyond the bottom line. The city becomes the territory of mere acquisitiveness, of the sort of civic disengagement suggested by the lifestyles of those who can afford to own multimillion-dollar apartments they will occupy for only a month at a stretch. For them, possession displaces participation as the reason to be in the city, and their privilege is a growing affront. They come to spend, and it's no wonder that municipal authorities so often find the froth of growth irresistible for their own bottom line.

The gathering storm of development—ratified by the Trump
hotel, the emergence of our own BID, and a rash of construction—
will surely have a number of consequences. One of them is that
Dale, my homeless friend, will be forced out of the neighborhood.
Because of the relatively large number of empty buildings, parking
lots, sidewalk bridges, and other marginal sites, Dale—who mi-
grated up from Tribeca at about the same time I did—has been
able to establish places to sleep and places to store and sell his
books around the area. The "higher-quality" retailers and uni-
formed street patrols the BID will bring are certain to spell the end
of Dale's, and other street people's, comfort zone here, although he
could desperately use a room in a decent transient hotel, something he resists as a compromise to his independence.

That Dale finds this area congenial speaks to a set of possibilities that I also value (beyond the truly deracinated idea of equity
that sees some justice in a street at once secure and underused
enough to provide a keep for homeless people). This is a neighborhood that has quiet, shadowy places, places where it is possible—
however evanescently—to be alone. Part of this has to do with
empty buildings, part with certain uses—such as the huge UPS
warehouse/garage that operates largely in spasms at the beginning
and end of the day. The fact of homelessness is a crime committed
by society, and Dale and his cohort simultaneously identify a space
both of oppression and of freedom. Just as civil libertarians defend
hate speech, however odious, as part of an expansive view of rights,
living on the streets (or fucking on the piers or riding bikes slowly
in traffic) guards the possibility for myriad activities and behaviors,
known and unanticipated. Both psychically and physically, the good
city abounds with useful margins, the slack of indifference.

Meanwhile, back at Annabel Lee the landlord has just completed the installation of those replacement windows in our apartment. Joan was there when the job was done, and Lou appeared to
kvell over the work and to let Joan know how much had been spent
(eleven hundred dollars a window, he claimed). They are typical

New York windows, green aluminum frames, insulated glass, easily opened. And transparently clean. The removal of the ancient sash (the inaccessible exterior of which might well have been unwashed for a century) has rendered our views spectacularly vivid, and this transparency has left us both delighted and thinking anxiously that it might be time for shades (certainly bathrobes).

This morning, after taping a note to FedEx, which had missed two deliveries because the doorbells, as usual, are broken, I went down to the basement to thank the landlord for the new windows. I first met his assistant Jim, who, when I thanked him, asked whether I'd come downstairs just for that. I said I had, and he thanked me for it. Next I went up to find Lou, who was, as usual, on the phone. In typical fashion he ignored me and kept talking. When he finally hung up, I thanked him, praised the workers, admired the windows. He assured me that the cost would be passed along to me, including that of the fifty-dollar-a-tube matching grout. Rather than extend the conversation, I said goodbye and departed.

Outside the door I met Rose, arriving. I repeated my fulsome pleasure regarding the new windows.

"You'll pay, you'll pay," she said.

And then I walked downtown.

ACKNOWLEDGMENTS

Parts of this book appeared in *The Village Voice* and *Architectural Record*, and I am grateful to them for letting me have my say for so long. Special thanks to three wonderful friends who read and commented on this manuscript: Christine Boyer, Nevin Schreiner, and Mike Wallace. Despite the last-minute request from me, they cleared their decks and offered incisive and generous comments. Of course, any errors and infelicities that remain are entirely my own. Finally, thanks to Vivian Constantinopoulos at Reaktion, who offered good suggestions and endured more than any editor should have to for so small a volume.

Some names in this book have been changed to protect the author.